AF592996

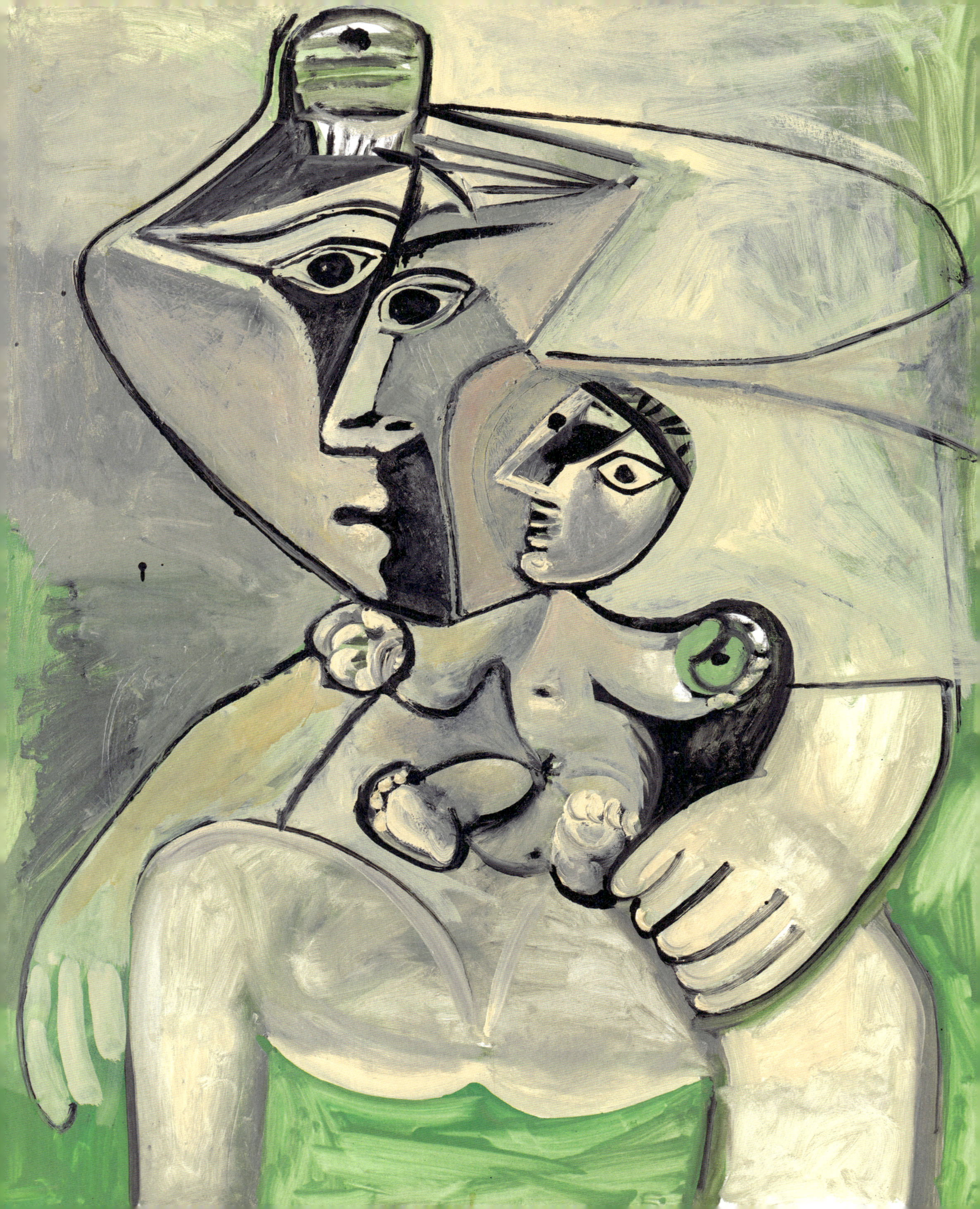

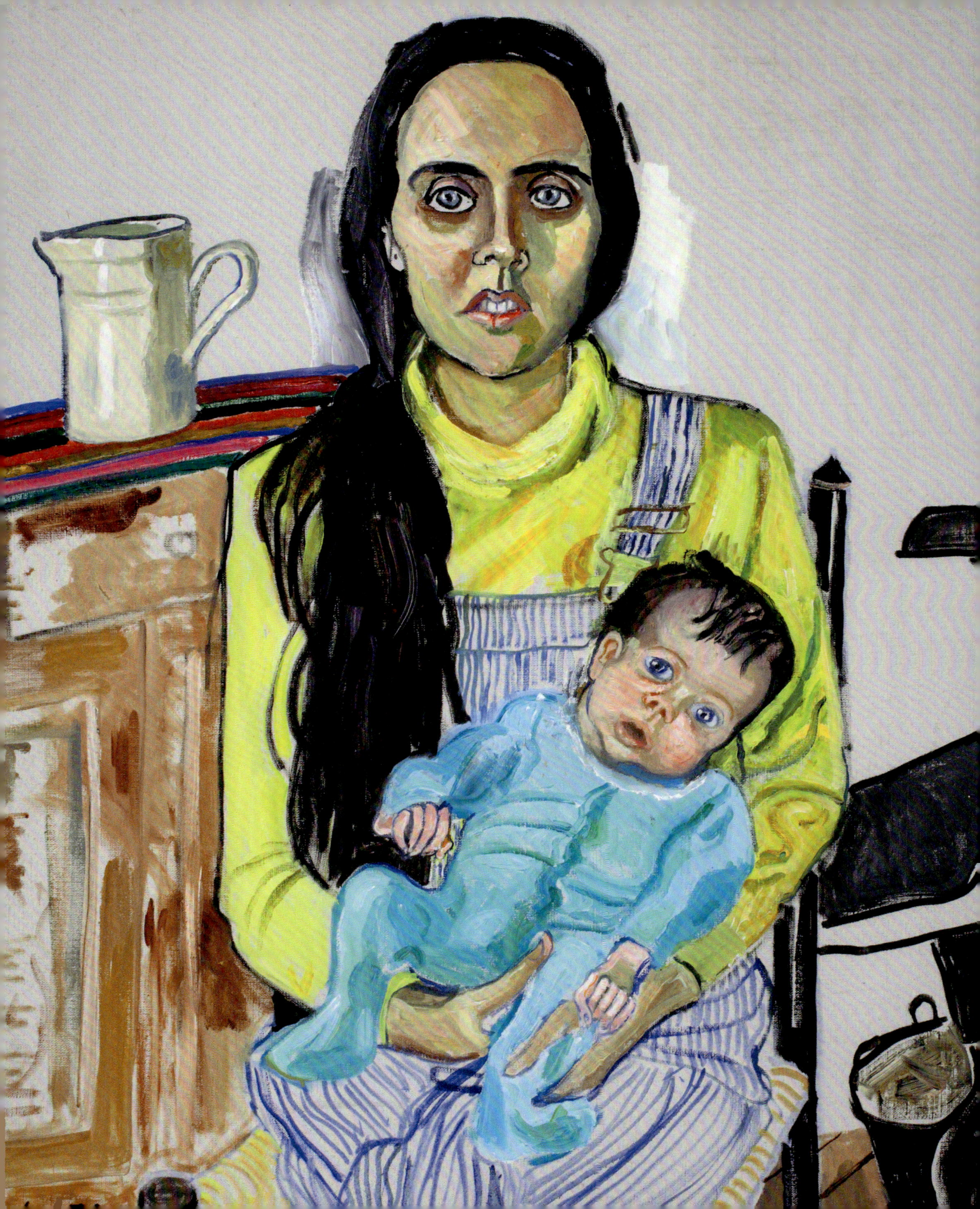

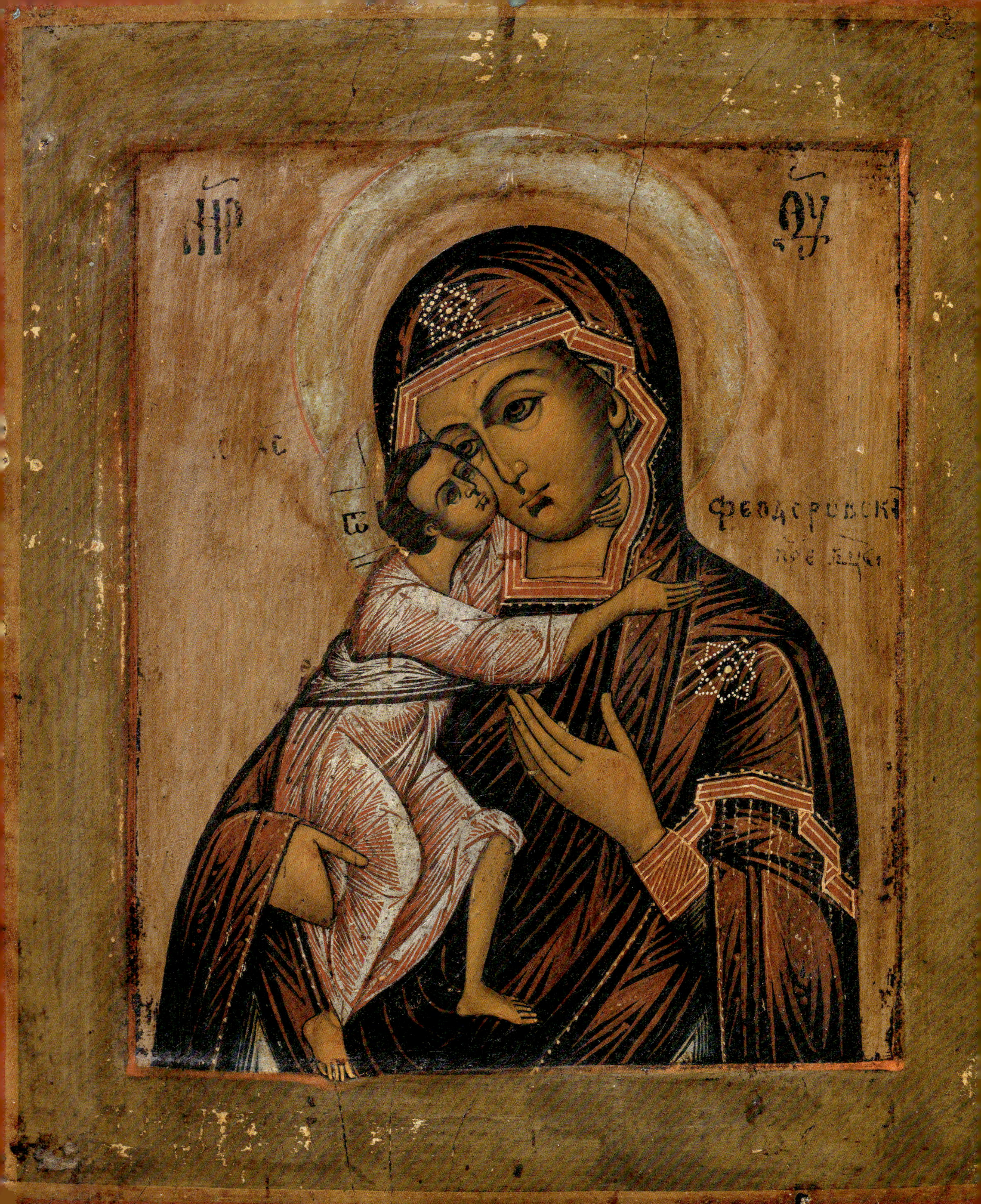
МР
ѲУ
ѲЕОДОРОВСК

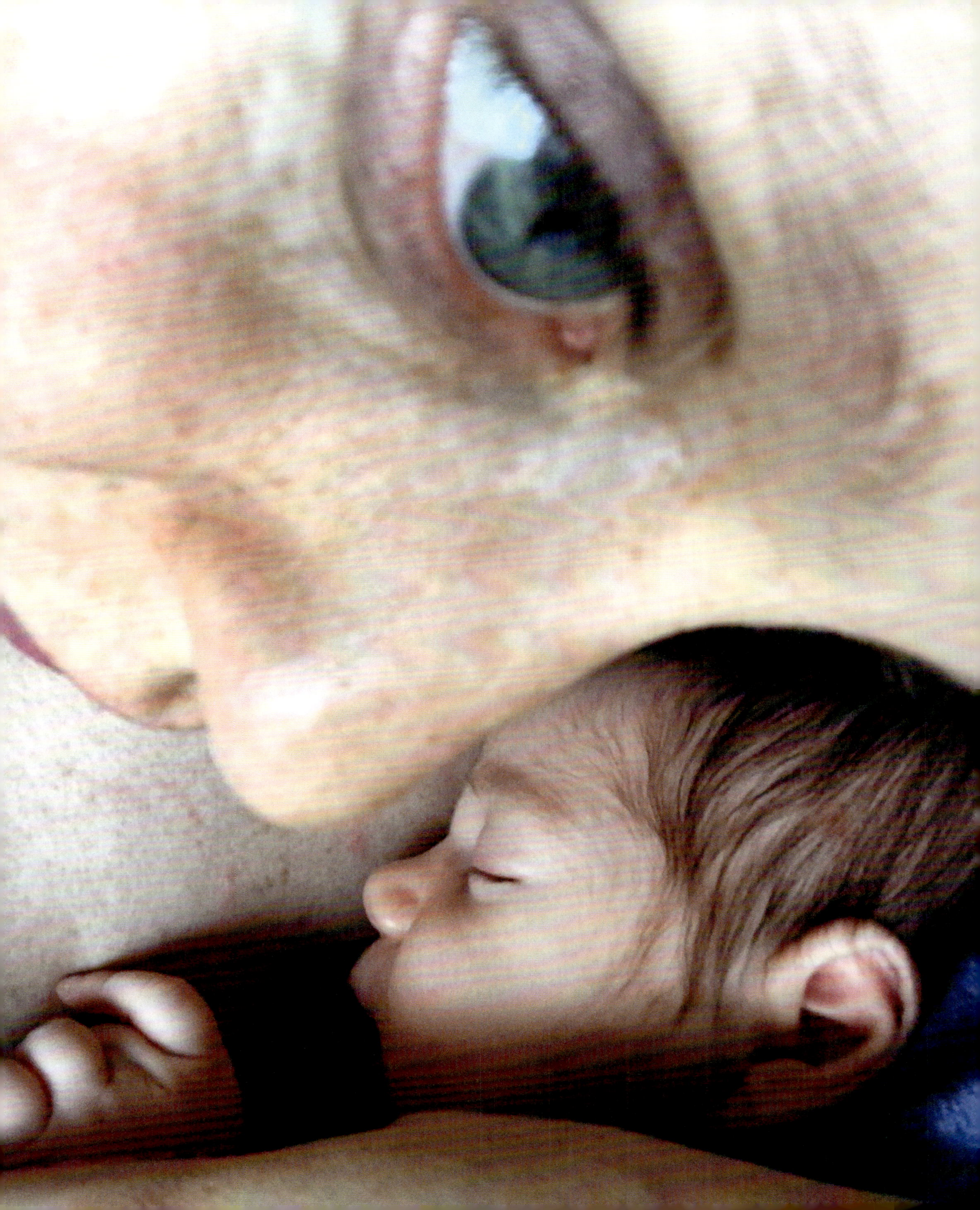

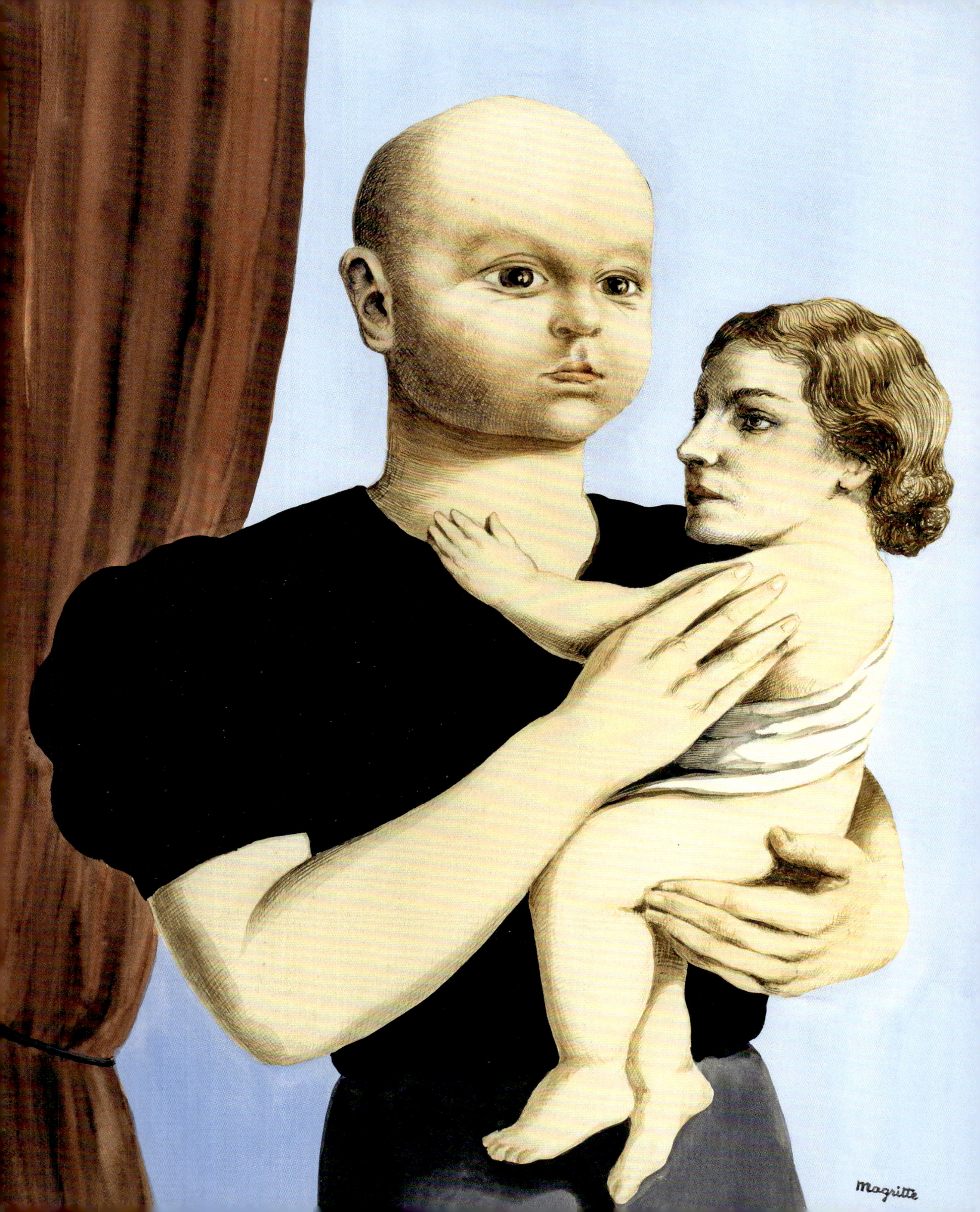
Magritte

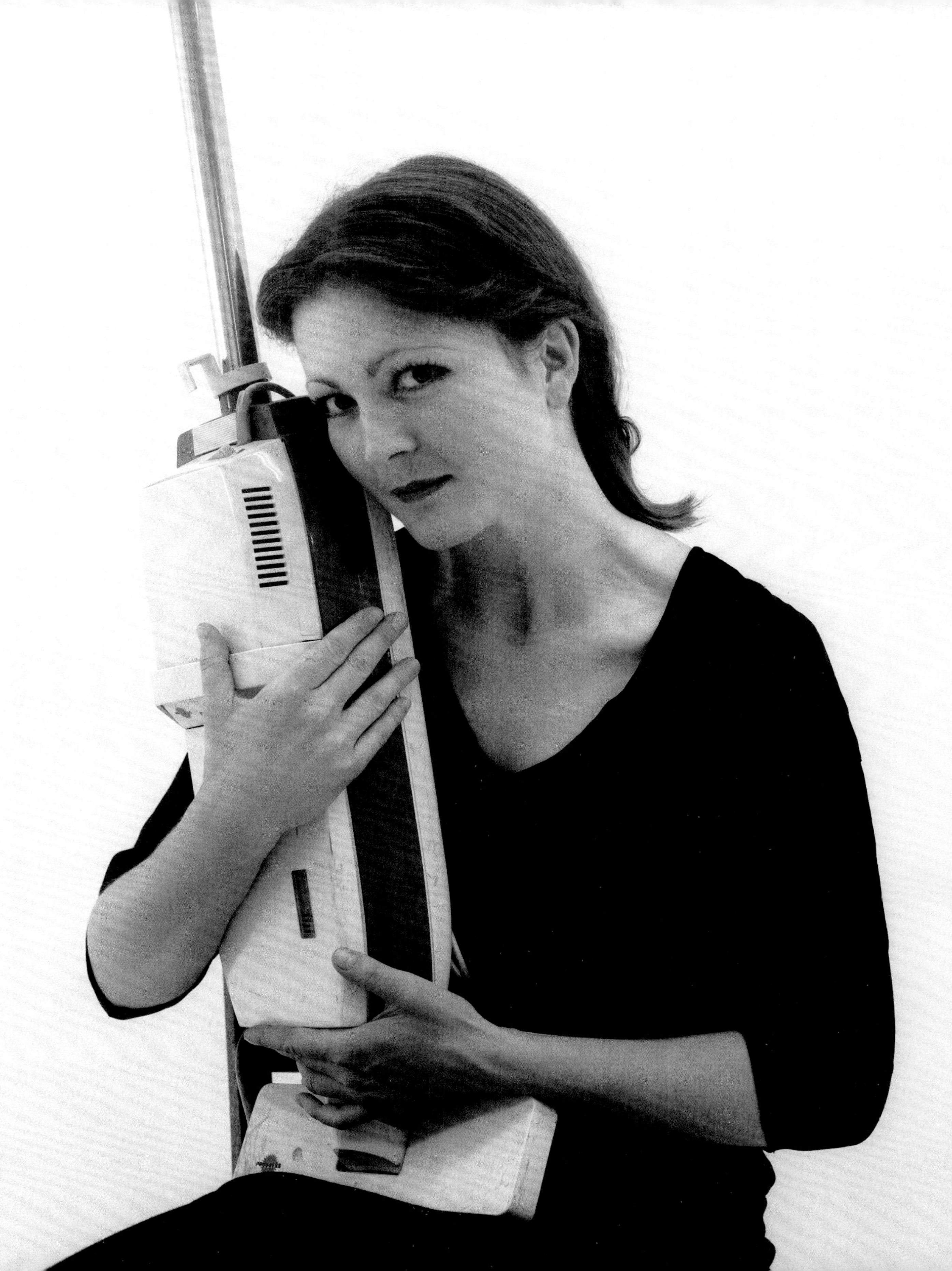

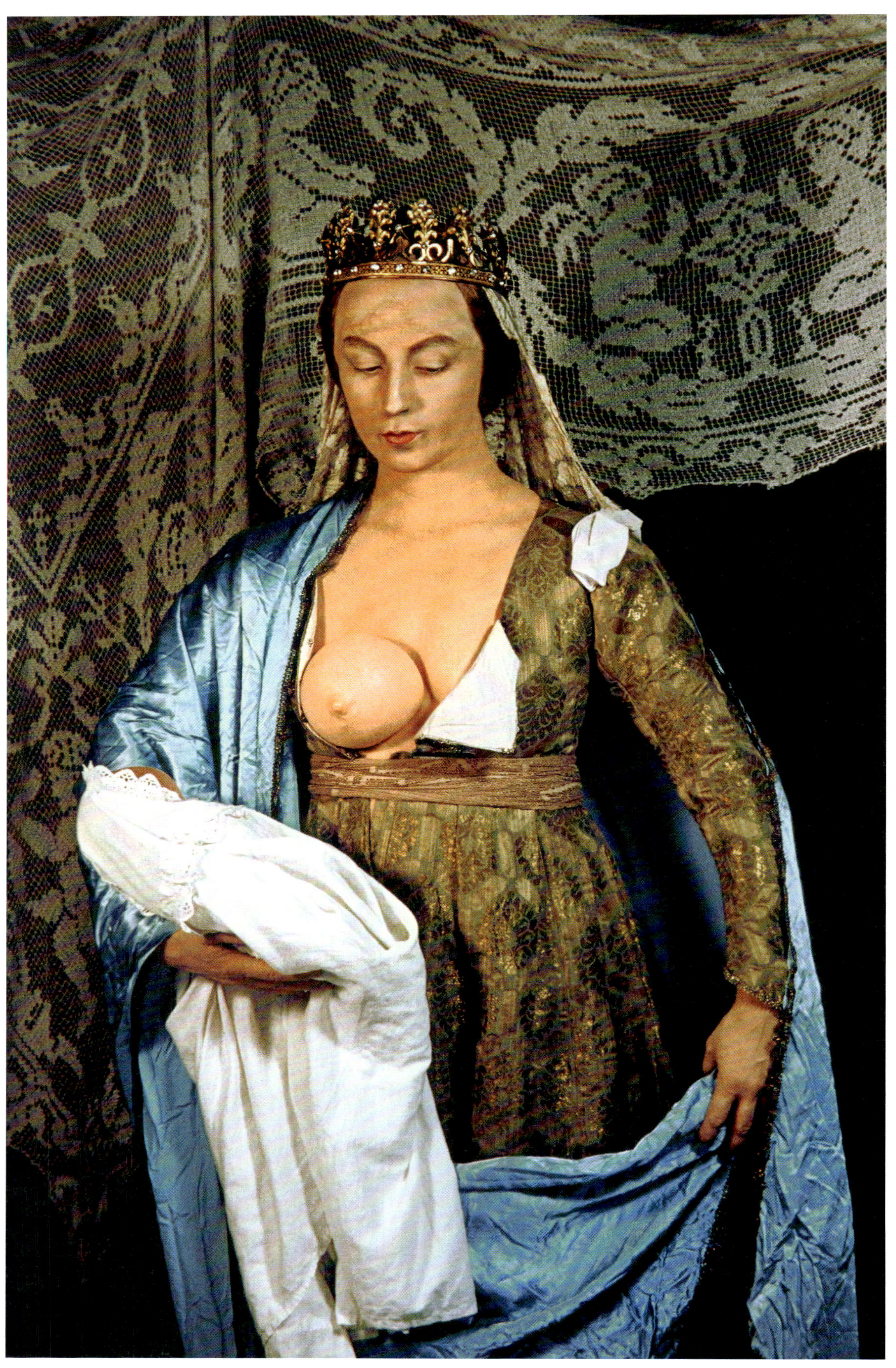

Mother!

Origin of Life

Page 1: cat. 85
Alice Neel: *Ginny and Elizabeth*, 1975 (detail)

Page 2: cat. 147
Mother of God Feodorovskaya, Russia, 1800-1850

Page 3: cat. 109
Manjari Sharma & Irina Rozovsky: *To See Your Face*, 2016-2017
(detail)

Page 4: cat. 60
René Magritte: *The Spirit of Geometry*, c. 1936

Page 5: cat. 21
VALIE EXPORT: *Ohne Titel*, 1976
Untitled (detail)

Left page: cat. 110
Cindy Sherman: *Untitled #216*, 1989

Foreword

Mother! Origin of Life takes up a vast and inexhaustible theme: motherhood as interpreted in Western art and culture in the 20th and 21st centuries. Unfolded in more than 150 works and objects, the exhibition paints a complex portrait of mother figures in the culture. The Holy Mother, memories of mother, the mother's voice, mothering, fertility and the fate of motherhood in society are thematic approaches to the expansive motherland charted in the exhibition.

Motherhood is a fundamental human theme. Everyone has a mother. Mother ushers us into the world. She is bound up with our social and cultural heritage. Whether she is present of absent, we all carry our mother with us through life. The existential and psychological ties between the mother and the adult child are at the heart of many great works of modern art, literature and cinema. But the mother is also the maternal body, the biological wellspring of all human life, fertility. Mother figures and symbols are found as far back as prehistoric times. As an ideal or a figure portrayed from outside, mothers have appeared in art throughout the ages. However, the experience of becoming a mother, motherhood portrayed from the point of view of the mother herself, only finds a significant place in art through the feminist art of the 1960s and '70s. Our view of motherhood changes over time, as motherhood evolves along with the rest of the culture.

Mother! Origin of Life explores the mother figure from the perspective of art, cultural history, philosophy and psychology. The selected works range from prehistoric mother goddesses and Renaissance Madonnas to the uncanny mothers of horror films and new interpretations of motherhood by contemporary artists. Revolving around the mother figure, the works examine basic existential themes like ancestry and attachment, changing ideas of femininity, death and the act of giving life. A line of cultural history charts the social developments that, in the last century or so, have changed cultural norms and expectations of motherhood – from women's suffrage to current discussions of the rights of rainbow families and queer parenting.

Crossover exhibitions like this have become a tradition at the Louisiana. They make it possible to explore the connections between art and larger cultural movements. Art is not an isolated entity inhabiting its own aesthetic island. It engages with other areas of culture, taking inspiration from them and influencing them in turn.

The Louisiana is a house of pictures that, despite its designation as a "museum of modern art", is home to stories extending beyond a narrowly defined field of objects. The museum's programme embraces art, music, literature, architecture, design and film. It was conceived that way from the beginning; virtually unlimited scope is baked into the museum. In addition to outstanding works of modern art, the museum also holds a collection of Greek antiquities belonging to the Louisiana's founder Knud W. Jensen and a large collection of pre-Columbian art donated by the Niels Wessel Bagge Art Foundation. Artefacts like these, originating from a magical-religious perception of images, captivated modern artists interested in the visual languages of other cultures. *Mother!* gives these objects relevance and new life, showing the existence of fertility goddesses and symbols in cultures across the globe. The objects are brought together with a work in the museum's collection that most Louisiana visitors will know well from its usual spot in the museum's North Wing: Alberto Giacometti's *Spoon Woman* (1926/1927), here displayed alongside fertility figures of the kind that inspired the artist. That's what it's like to be a museum: culture is in constant motion and, in turn, the artworks and artefacts that have been preserved can change places and meaning.

As the acknowledgments on the following page show, there are many lenders to this exhibition. We are exceedingly grateful for the support and trust the museum has been shown in a time of upheaval, and in the face of shutdowns and restrictions brought on by the corona crisis.

Likewise, we thank the many artists who have contributed to this exhibition. Special thanks to Laure Prouvost and Frida Orupabo who made new works specifically for the exhibition.

We thank all our colleagues and friends – no one mentioned, no one forgotten – with whom we were in touch along the way, and who have lent their professional advice and assistance in mounting this exhibition. Without their help, the exhibition would not have found its final form.

Warm thanks to the writers for their insightful and illuminating contributions to this publication – Neville Rowley, Pia Fris Laneth and Adam Bencard. Furthermore, we thank the Louisiana's dedicated

cat. 18
Nathalie Djurberg & Hans Berg: *Once Removed on My Mother's Side*, 2008

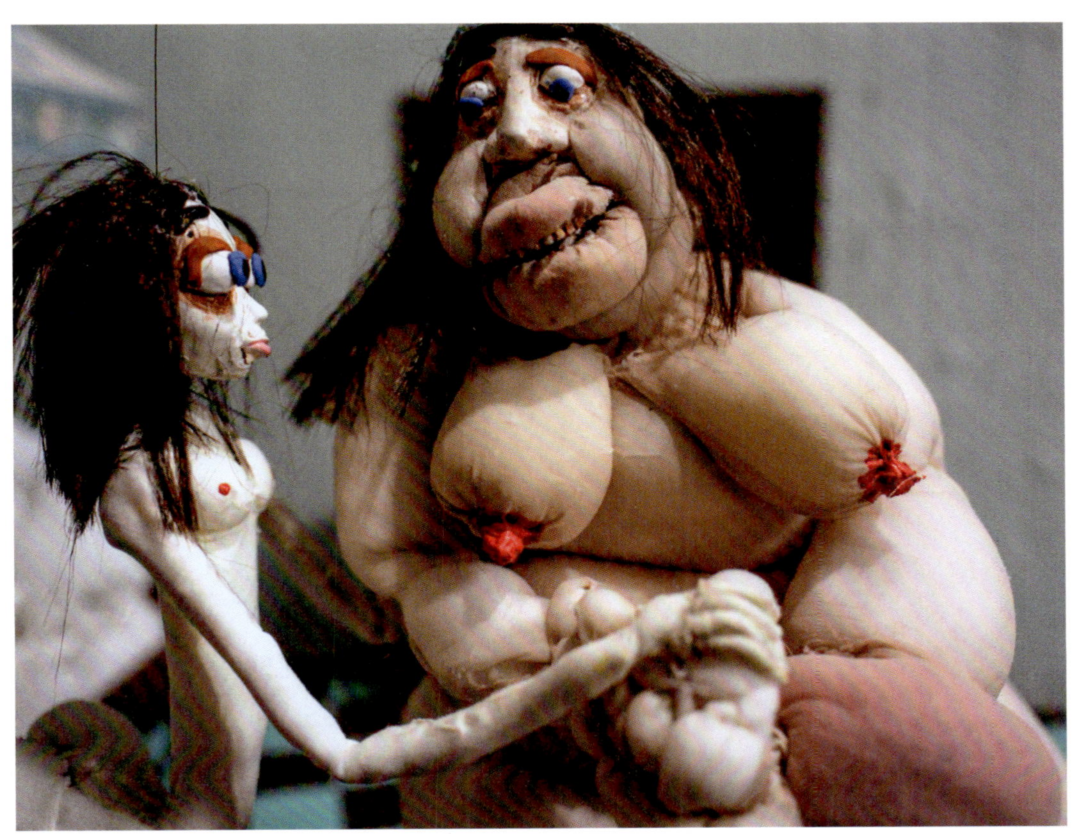

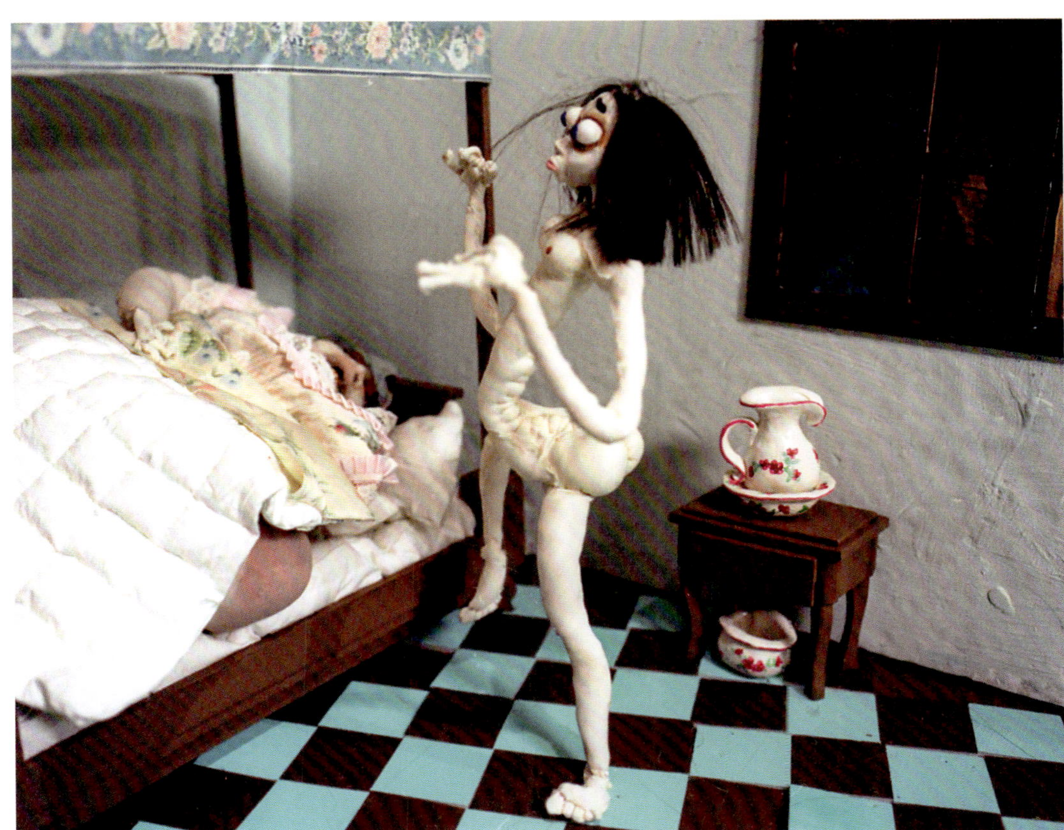

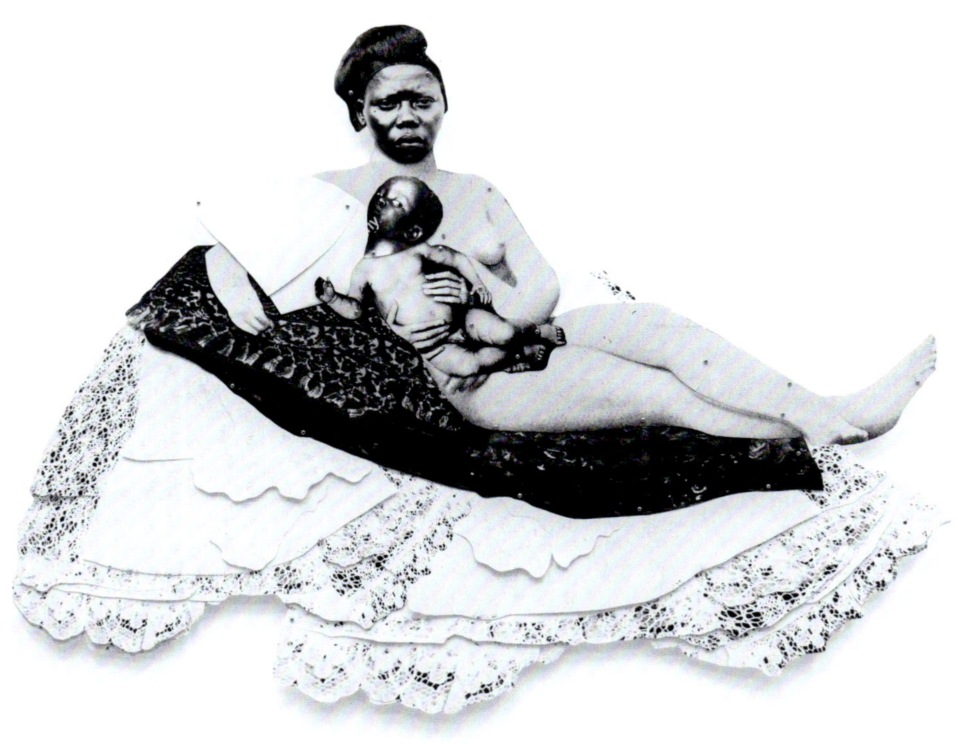

cat. 98
Frida Orupabo: *Love at First Site*, 2020

Mother! team, including exhibition coordinator Eva Lund, exhibition producer Ulrik Staal Dinesen, graphic designer Marie Lübecker and editor Lærke Rydal Jørgensen, who have been following the project with great engagement. Special thanks to curatorial assistant Nanna Stjernholm Jepsen, who contributed curatorial research and helped shape the content of the exhibition. Thanks as well to architect Anne Schnettler for her monumental effort in creating the exhibition's architecture and design.

This exhibition would not have been possible without the financial support of the Aage and Johanne Louis-Hansen Foundation, the Obel Family Foundation and the Augustinus Foundation – thank you for your generosity.

Finally, we thank the Kunsthalle Mannheim, Germany, which will host the exhibition after its initial run at the Louisiana, for their gracious and professional partnership.

Poul Erik Tøjner
Director

Marie Laurberg
Curator

Kirsten Degel
Curator

Thanks

We thank the following lenders and galleries

Alice Neel Estate, New York
Art Gallery of New South Wales, Sydney
Astrup Fearnley Museet, Oslo
Atelier VALIE EXPORT, Vienna
Bauhaus Dessau Foundation, Germany
The Danish Film Institute, Copenhagen
The Danish National Archives, Copenhagen
DENTSU / Ginger Design Studio / Apex, Tokyo
The Design Museum, Munich
Deutsches Medizinhistorisches Museum, Ingolstadt
Fergus McCaffrey Gallery, New York
Galerie Nordenhake, Stockholm
Galerie Perrotin, Paris
Hamburger Kunsthalle, Hamburg
Hammer Museum, Los Angeles
Hasselblad Foundation, Göteborg
Hauser & Wirth, Zurich
Irish Museum of Modern Art, Dublin
Jean Paul Goude Studio, Paris
Jenny Livingston, New York
Kunsten – Museum of Modern Art Aalborg
Kunsthalle Mannheim
Kunsthaus Zürich
Kaari Upson Collection, Los Angeles
Leeds Art Gallery, Leeds
Leopold Museum, Vienna
Lindenau-Museum, Altenburg
Lisson Gallery, London
Manjari Sharma & Irina Rozovsky Studio, New York
MASI – Museo d'arte della Svizzera italiana, Lugano
Medical Museion, University of Copenhagen
Metro Goldwyn Mayer Studios, Beverly Hills
Mitchell-Innes & Nash, New York
Moderna Museet, Stockholm
Musée national Picasso, Paris
Museum Sønderjylland, Haderslev
National Museum of Women in the Arts, Washington
The National Museum, Copenhagen
Natural Cycles Nordic AB, Stockholm
Ny Carlsberg Glyptotek, Copenhagen
Obricht Collection, Essen
Parkwood Entertainment, New York
Peter Hujar Archive, New York
Pilar Corrias, London
Regen Projects, Los Angeles
Richard Saltoun Gallery, London
Rigshospitalet, Copenhagen
Rineke Dijkstra Collection, Amsterdam
SONY, Nashville
Stadtmuseum Berlin
SMK, National Gallery of Denmark, Copenhagen
Stiftung Museum Kunstpalast, Düsseldorf
Studio Prouvost, Antwerp
Tate, London
Terra Foundation for American Art, Chicago
The Easton Foundation, New York
The Henry Moore Foundation, Perry Green, Hertforsdshire
Universal Studios, Universal City, CA
University of Copenhagen
Victoria Miro, London
Von der Heydt-Museum Wuppertal
Walt Disney Studios, Burbank, CA
Worcester Art Museum, Worcester, MA
Yoko Ono Studio, New York

And private collectors who wish to remain anonymous

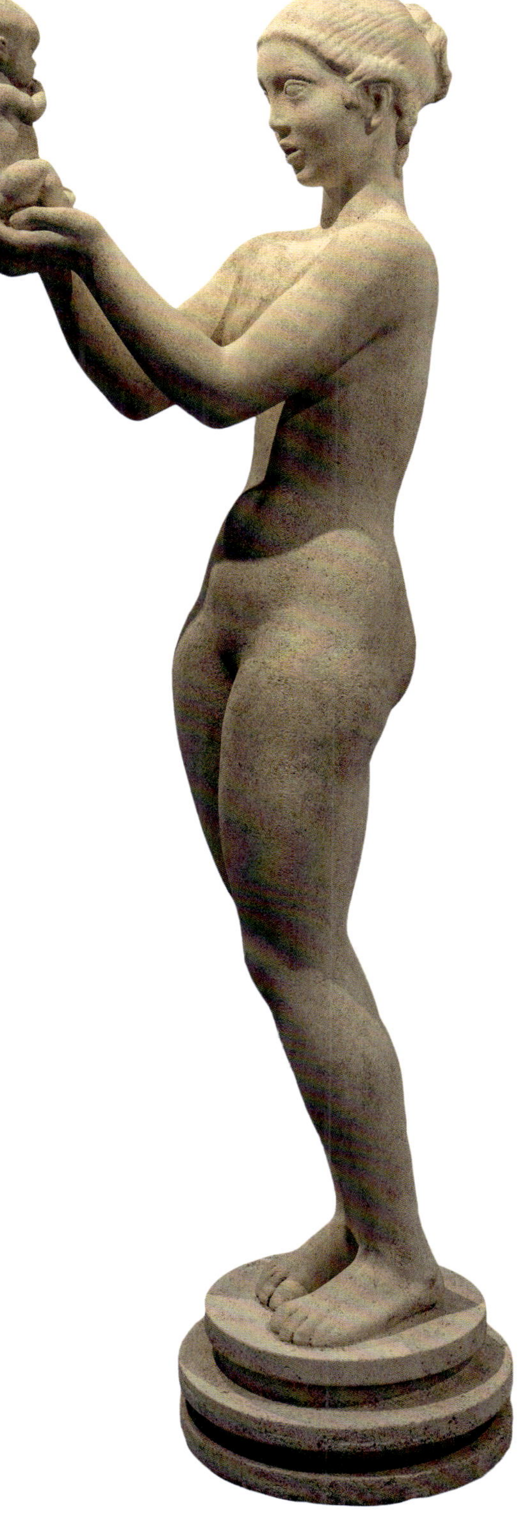

cat. 87
Kai Nielsen: *Venus with the Apple*, 1918-20

MOTHER!

By Marie Laurberg

Marie Laurberg is a Louisiana curator and curated the exhibition *Mother!* together with Kirsten Degel. Laurberg's past exhibitions include *The Moon: From Inner Worlds to Outer Space*, *Homeless Souls* and *Yayoi Kusama: In Infinity*.

Cold or warm, present or absent, everyone has a mother. The archetypal mother, the female figure as a symbol of life and fertility, exists across all times and cultures. Our physical and cultural origin, she ushers us into the world. Even if she is lost or absent, we are all sons and daughters. *Mother!* takes up a vast, inexhaustible theme, unpacked in more than 150 works of art and other objects. An aim of the exhibition is to include the experiences and life choices associated with motherhood among the great existential themes of art.

In recent years, a new generation of artists and writers have been making motherhood the centrepiece of their work. This trend can be viewed within a broader context of autobiography and intimate relationships: the artist or writer's mother is explored in works of literature or visual art merging the gaze of the child and the adult. The theme is also linked to discussions about queer identities and changing gender roles in the culture at large. A new generation of artists are becoming mothers and letting the subject flow back into their work. The daughters of 1970s feminists are adding new chapters to the women's history their mothers were concerned with telling. While motherhood in art is typically associated with 1970s feminism and its focus on politics and the female body, the theme is expansive. The mother of art is the Madonna of Christian iconography. She is the Medea of tragedy who, abandoned by Jason, kills her own children. She is the Oedipal heart of horror films. She is fertility and caregiver, or a clingy and hurtful administrator of her child's mental life. She is an intimate family relation, who harbours her own secrets. Mother is legs for children to cling to or a woman who gives her child away. She is the wicked stepmother of the Brothers Grimm fairytales. She is disappointed, dead, seductive or loving. She is the motherland and the body that bore us. She is the transgendered mother of the ballroom scene. She is an animal with breasts or a pregnant pop star who performs even with a big belly. The mother of art and culture has many faces.

The exhibition mixes art with cultural history, religion, literature, music, film, design and the history of medicine in a thematic exploration of motherhood and the mother figure as expressed in 20th- and 21st-century art and culture. The interdisciplinary focus underscores that art is not separate from the rest of the culture but deals with more fundamental conceptions at work in the culture at large. In a few instances, the exhibition goes back in time to show how images of modern art often tap into a long pictorial tradition, including religious contexts like prehistoric fertility goddesses and the Christian Virgin and Child. Such images have seeped into modern art as sources of an aesthetic vocabulary or as icons whose meaning can be turned in new directions.

The exhibition's thematic focus makes it possible to narrate a different kind of art history independent of isms and style categories, focusing on art's role as an interpreter of existential questions, life events – big issues like birth, attachment and death. The narrative of the exhibition is not chronological but thematic and interdisciplinary, clustering around such themes as The Holy Mother, Memory, The Mother's Voice, Mothering, and Fertility. The themes have grown out of the curatorial research and in dialogue with the artists. The artworks, several having a documentary or autobiographical premise, let us view life through the lens of the individual artist. In art we can mirror ourselves or gain insight into unfamiliar worlds and life events.

Madonna

Art history is full of images of mothers. In Western culture, the great ur-image, against which all others are measured, is the Virgin Mary, the Madonna and Child. In 1454, Dieric Bouts, with the painstaking detail characteristic of the Dutch Renaissance, paints a moving portrait of the Madonna and Child dressed in iconographic blue and purple garments linking her to a long Christian pictorial tradition. Bouts's empathetic realism renders acutely present, even five centuries later, the mother's tender gaze at the child she is delicately cradling. The vast majority of mother images in modern Western art before the 20th century originate from the Madonna and Child, writes art historian Rachel Epp Buller in her comprehensive study of art and motherhood. The bulk of images are by male artists and are bound up with a singular concept of motherhood as a cultural institution: "the myth of the all-loving, all-forgiving and all-sacrificing mother".[1] The mother is portrayed from outside, as an ideal image with no room for the more complex aspects

cat. 5
Dieric Bouts: *Virgin and Child*, after 1454

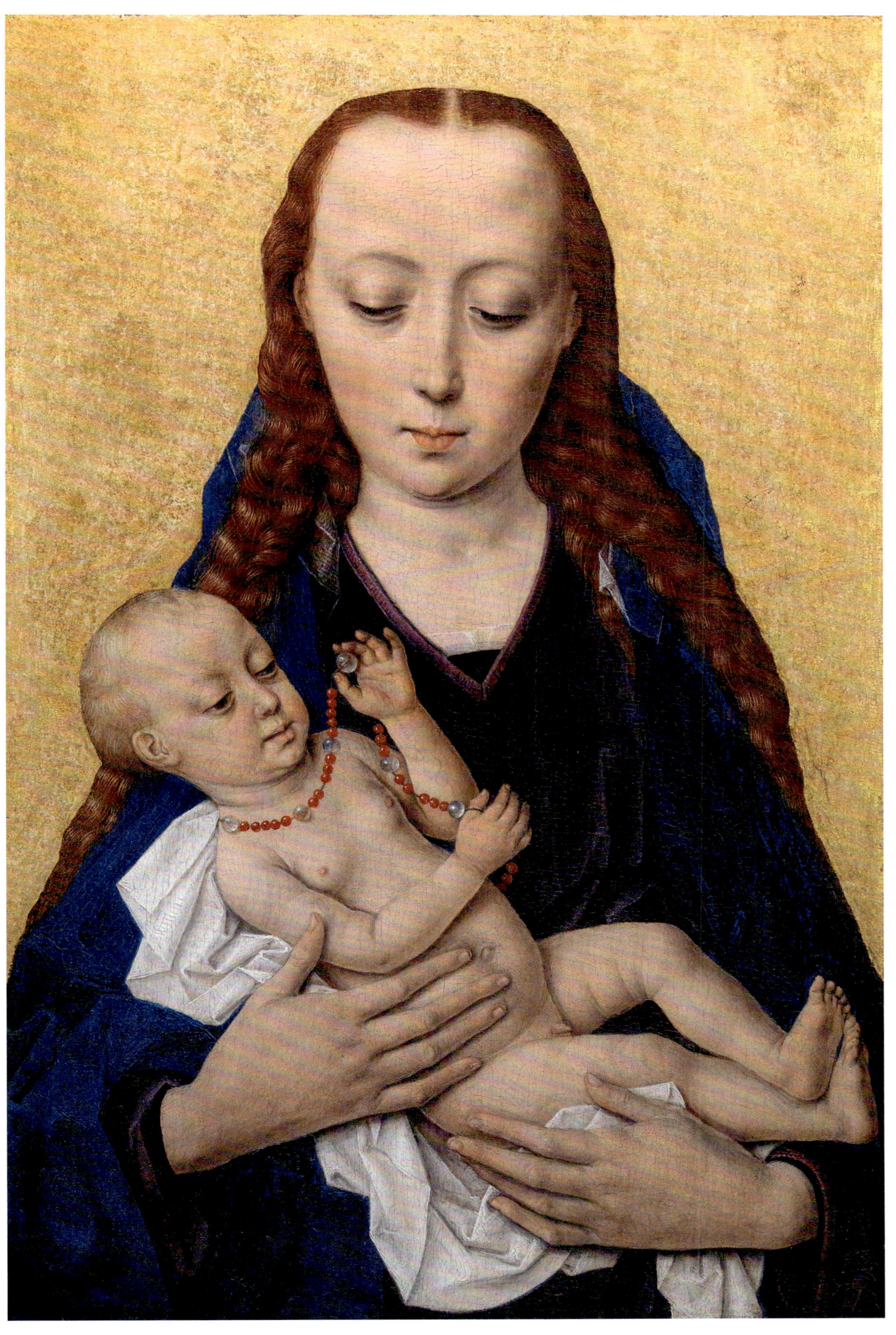

of motherhood as an experience and a lived reality. This powerful, still-active myth has its cultural roots in Medieval and Renaissance Europe, where worship of the Holy Virgin sets the stage for the elevated, virtuous, self-sacrificing mother role that proliferated in the following centuries. In art, most images of mother and child adhere to this tradition as late as the 20th century.[2] Elsewhere in this catalogue (p. 50), Neville Rowley dives into the evolution of the Madonna and Child motif. Residing in our consciousness as the ideal mother, the Madonna and Child is a powerful image that can be annexed and interpreted in many directions.

To illustrate how the idealized Madonna and Child still exists as a myth in our culture, we need look no further than Beyoncé. In 2017, the American pop star announced the names of her newborn twins on Instagram. A portrait photograph by the artist Mason Poole shows her posing with her babies in her arms, dressed as the Holy Virgin in blue and purple under a resplendent flower arch (back cover). Her half-nude body evokes fertility goddesses, while the setting recalls Baroque gardens. All in all, she fashions a sumptuous icon of herself as the Great Mother, a contemporary version of the Madonna and not only Child, but Children, an image redolent of power and abundance. This image is interesting because Beyoncé actively uses motherhood as a position of strength to support and expand her power base as a female icon. By the logic of the image, motherhood makes her more powerful and attractive, marking a cultural shift away from past female icons, whose artistic career required them to tone down, or actively opt out of, the role of mother. Not all of Beyoncé's followers agreed with this rosy depiction of (twin) motherhood, however, and the internet subsequently ran over with pictures of mothers showing more realistic everyday life with twins.

Modern Madonna

Beyoncé uses the Madonna figure to build her image as a powerful pop goddess. Her interest in the motif is part of a broader cultural trend, which finds eloquent expression in contemporary art, where references to the classical Madonna and Child underlie a great number of artworks that twist the motif to give it new meaning. For this exhibition, the Norwegian-Nigerian artist Frida Orupabo made her own Madonna and Child, *Love at First Site* (2020, p. 10), a collage combining a wealth of visual sources – a Renaissance Madonna, photos of a Japanese geisha, a historical photo of a Nigerian mother with her baby strapped to her back, a doll's dress, Kristian Zahrtmann's portrait of the death of Leonora Christina (for which the Danish artist's mother posed) and much more. In a modern variation on the theme, a contemporary hack of a classical subject, Orupabo creates a celebration of her own child.

The American artist Alice Neel painted a number of gorgeous, personal portraits of her relatives. In one, *Ginny and Elizabeth* (1975, p. 1 and 17), the artist's daughter-in-law and granddaughter are cast as the mother and child. Their individual features – the distinctive eyes, the mouth and teeth, the baby slumping in her mother's lap – highlight their personal, everyday presence. The sacred, the painting seems to say, is in the imperfect, the here and now. Related, though more physically intrusive, is Rineke Dijkstra's photograph of a new mother standing with her child in her arms (p. 45). The hospital underwear and her strong, dark gaze imply that she just gave birth. Dijkstra likes to photograph young people after a big event. There is a striking kinship between this new mother and Dijkstra's portraits of young men immediately after a bullfight. The body is enshrined in the image, and birth becomes a rite of passage. In general, contemporary variations of the Madonna and Child are distinguished by the addition of new meaning to the basic motif. Photographing herself bare-chested suckling her son, the word "Pervert" emblazoned like a scar across her collarbones, Catherine Opie incorporates a different female image into the subject matter, one linked to queer identity and sexuality (p. 17). A self-portrait by Elina Brotherus, pained and angry after a failed fertility treatment, with a dachshund in her arms and an aggressive gesture at the viewer, is entitled *My Dog Is Cuter Than Your Ugly Baby*.

Unfolding the Madonna in new directions, contemporary artists add layers of complexity to the subject of mother and child. This sets their art apart from the attractive, more classical variations on the theme that carried over from the 19th century into modernism, as in the work of Pablo Picasso (inside cover), whose many stylistic variations of mother and child are centred on the overriding theme of nurture. In that regard, Picasso extends a long modernist tradition of depicting motherhood through an idealizing lens maintaining, even under various aesthetic guises, the purity of the Madonna.

A fascinating exception to this paradigm is the French artist Suzanne Valadon, an acquaintance of Picasso. Her biography charts an extraordinary life

cat. 7
Elina Brotherus: *My Dog Is Cuter Than Your Ugly Baby*, 2013

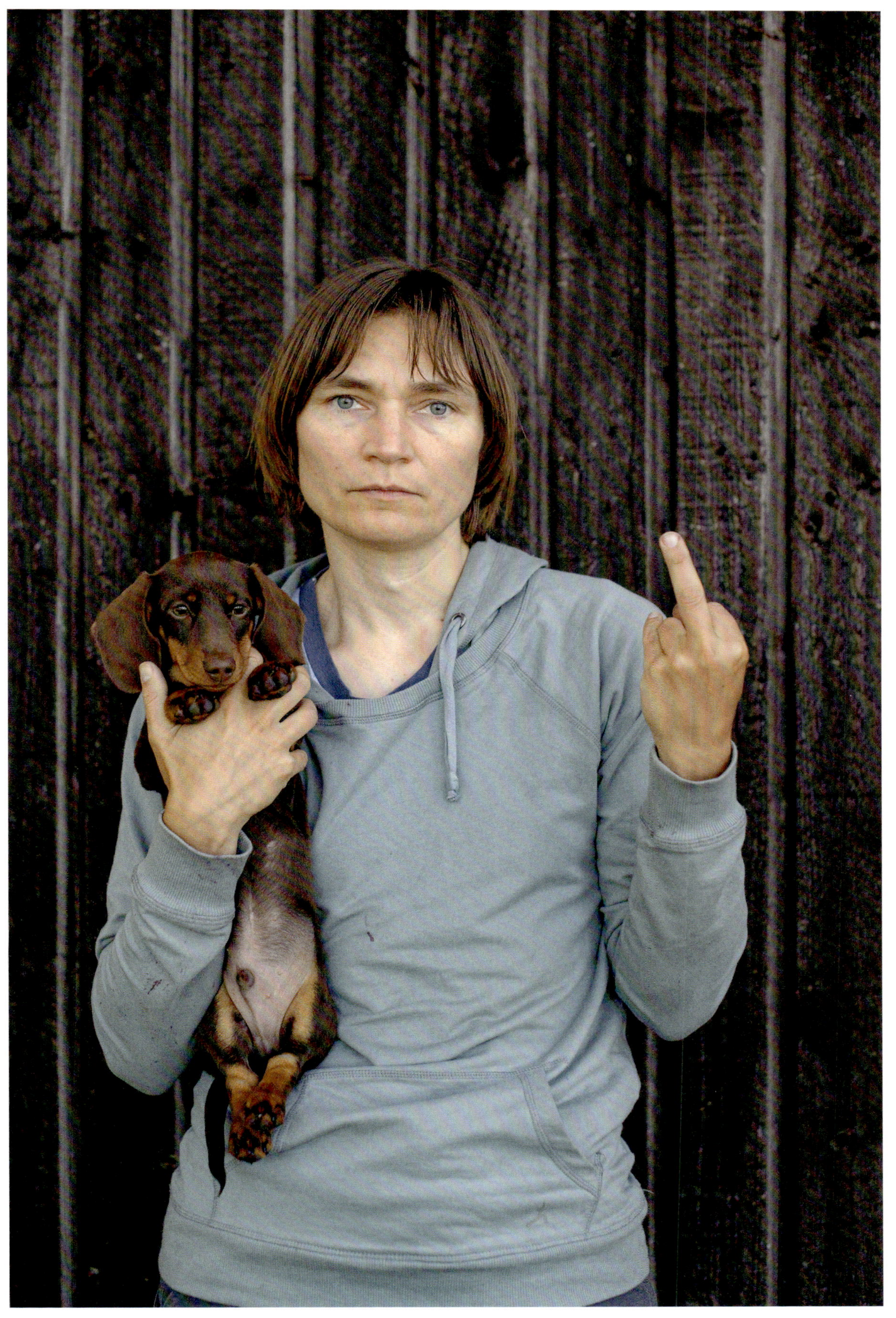

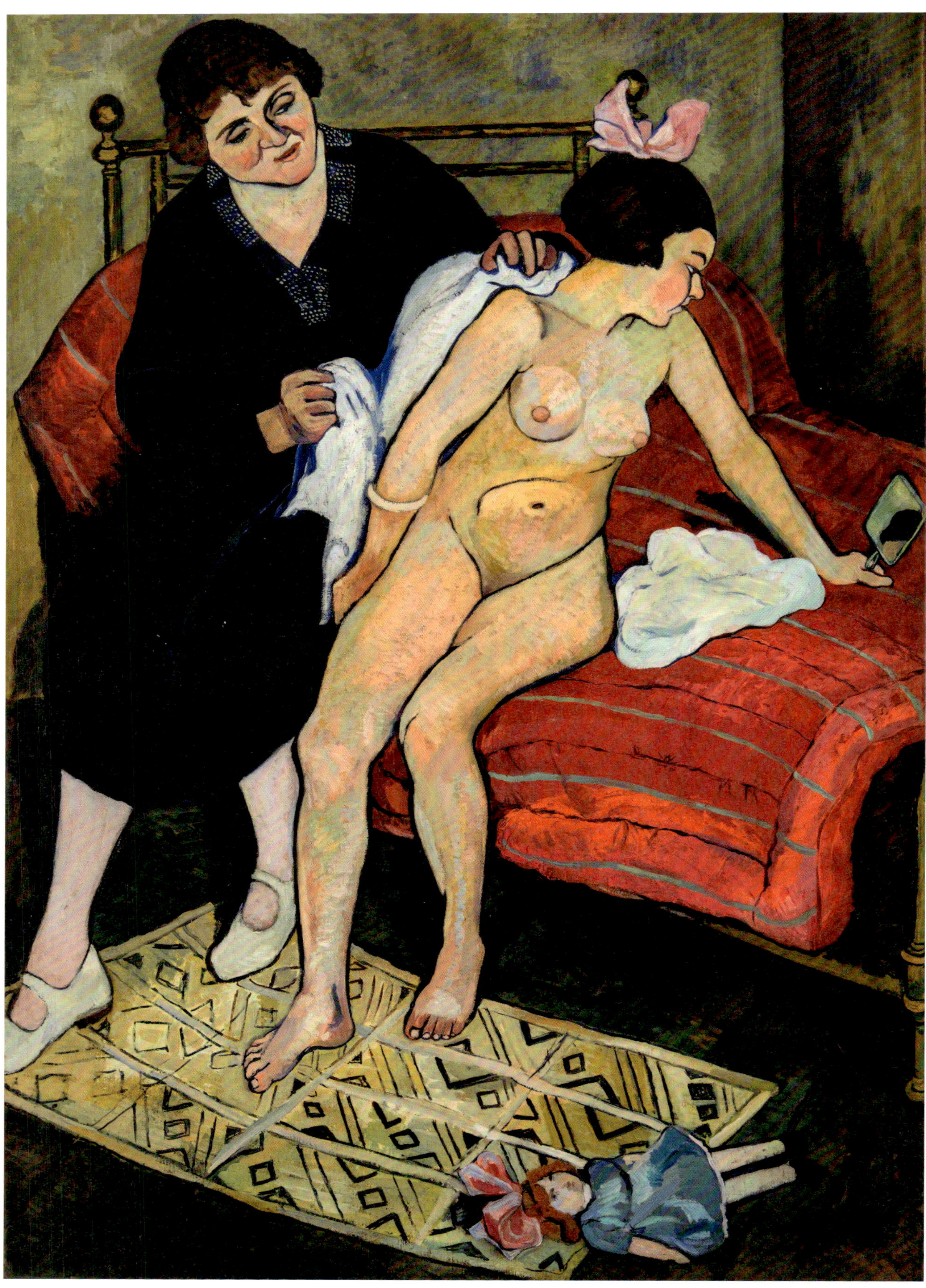

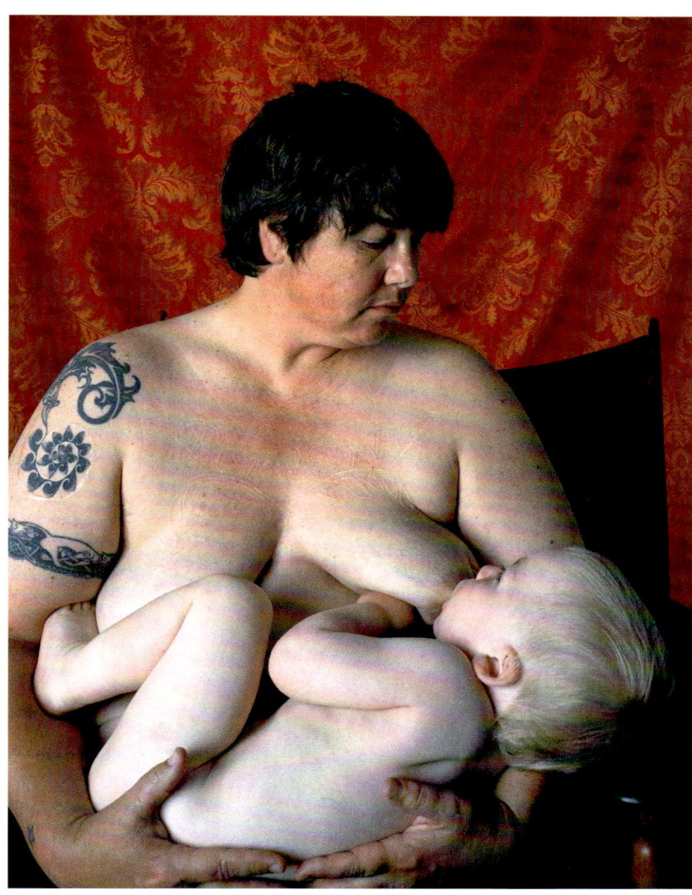

cat. 96
Catherine Opie: *Selfportrait / Nursing*, 2004

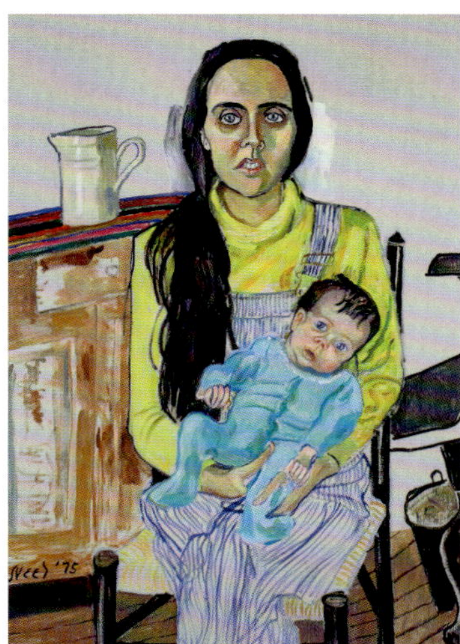

cat. 85
Alice Neel: *Ginny and Elizabeth*, 1975

Left page: cat. 117
Suzanne Valadon: *The Abandoned Doll*, 1921

as a woman and mother. The daughter of an unmarried washerwoman in Montmartre, Valadon as a child worked as a vegetable seller and circus performer. She later modelled for prominent painters of the day and was the first female artist to be admitted to the Société Nationale des Beaux Arts, in 1894. Valadon was the mother of one child, and her paintings of mother and child hold complex psychological narratives that are rare in period depictions of the subject. *The Abandoned Doll* (1921) shows a mother, dressed in black, drying her naked daughter with a towel. A bow in the hair of a doll on the floor matches the daughter's – a remnant of the childhood her body is evidently outgrowing. The painting is a snapshot of the transition from childhood to adulthood, but also of the transition in the relationship between mother and child. From today's perspective, her nurturing looks odd and inappropriate, an act that should have been directed at a much younger child, not a young woman with breasts. Is this an aging woman's jealousy of youth, a variation on the story of Snow White with the daughter admiring herself in the mirror? Among the layers of meaning is the story of separation. The painting portrays a black-clad mother about to let go of her child with all the sorrow that entails. It is also an image of three ages of life, unfolded through the composition: childhood, young womanhood and old age. The three figures – doll, daughter and mother – are seen as stages in the life of one and the same person. As in several other works in this exhibition, the mother figure is associated with reflection on the cycle of life.

Valadon is an example of how women artists, in particular, over the course of the 20th century gradually started thematizing motherhood and the mother figure from new angles. Motherhood was separated from the tradition of idealized representation, and space opened up for more complex examination of the relationship between mother and child. A prime example is the Norwegian playwright Henrik Ibsen's 1879 *A Doll's House*, which has Nora leave her home and husband and their children, when she realizes that her obligations as a wife and mother have made her a doll for her husband to play with as he pleases. The play stands as a portent of women's rebellion against the normativity of the 19th-century bourgeois mother role. Leaving her home, Nora marches into the 20th century, a period marked by one march after another. A notable one was held to mark the amendment to the Danish constitution that gave women the right to vote in 1915. A film by Julie Laurberg and Franziska Gad documents white-gowned women marching to the courtyard of Amalienborg Castle. Laurberg herself is an

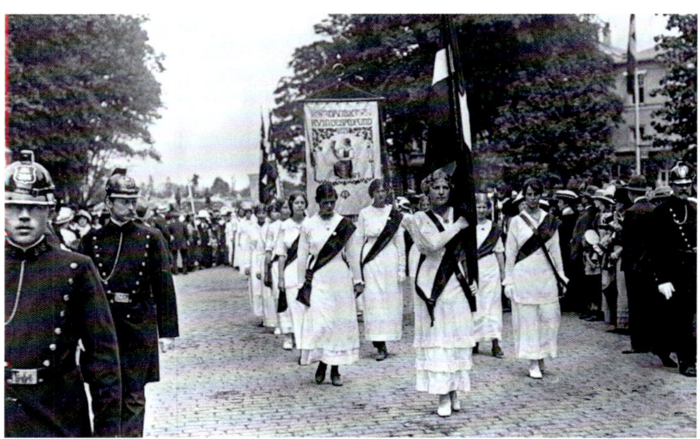

VI CHRISTIAN DEN TIENDE
AF GUDS NAADE KONGE TIL DANMARK/ DE VENDERS OG GOTHERS/HERTUG TIL SLESVIG/HOLSTEN/STORMARN/DITMARSKEN/LAUENBORG OG OLDENBORG/
Gøre vitterligt: Rigsdagen har paa den i den gennemsete Grundlov af 5. Juni 1849 § 95 foreskrevne Maade to Gange vedtaget og Vi stadfæste nu ved Vort allerhøjeste Samtykke

DANMARKS RIGES GRUNDLOV

I

§ 1 Regeringsformen er indskrænket-monarkisk. Kongemagten er arvelig. Arvefølgen er den i Tronfølgeloven af 31. Juli 1853 Art. I. og II. fastsatte.

§ 2 Den lovgivende Magt er hos Kongen og Rigsdagen i Forening. Den udøvende Magt er hos Kongen. Den dømmende Magt er hos Domstolene.

§ 3 Den evangelisk-lutherske Kirke er den danske Folkekirke og understøttes som saadan af Staten.

II

§ 4 Kongen kan ikke uden Rigsdagens Samtykke være Regent i andre Lande.

§ 5 Kongen skal høre til den evangelisk-lutherske Kirke.

§ 6 Kongen er myndig/ naar han har fyldt sit 18de Aar. Det samme gælder om de kongelige Prinser.

§ 7 Forinden Kongen tiltræder Regeringen/ afgiver han skriftlig i Statsraadet den edelige Forsikring ubrødelig at holde Grundloven. Af Forsikringsakten udstedes tvende ligelydende Originaler/ af hvilke den ene overgives Rigsdagen for at opbevares i sammes Arkiv/ den anden nedlægges i Rigsarkivet. Kan Kongen formedelst Fraværelse eller af andre Grunde ikke umiddelbart ved Tronskiftet aflægge denne Ed/ føres Regeringen/ indtil dette sker/ af Statsraadet/ medmindre anderledes ved Lov bestemmes. Har Kongen allerede som Tronfølger aflagt denne Ed/ tiltræder han umiddelbart ved Tronskifte Regeringen.

§ 8 Bestemmelser angaaende Regeringens Førelse i Tilfælde af Kongens Umyndighed/ Sygdom eller Fraværelse fastsættes ved Lov. Er der ved Tronledighed ingen Tronfølger/ vælger den forenede Rigsdag (§ 65) en

cat. 57
Julie Laurberg and Franziska Gad:
Women's March on the occasion of the Constitution of 1915

cat. 155
The Danish Constitution of 1915

Right page: cat 108
Egon Schiele: *Tote Mutter I*, 1910
Death Mother I

example of a woman who opted out of the institution of marriage and motherhood. Opening her own photography studio in the Magasin du Nord department store at the end of the 19th century, Laurberg was deeply involved in the feminist cause, and remained unmarried and childless. As described by Pia Fris Laneth in her essay in this catalogue (p. 84), a series of laws enacted in Denmark and much of the rest of the Western world over the course of the 20th century changed the social position of women. This development was obviously hugely important to motherhood and the role of mother. From their primary place in the home, women enter the public sphere and gradually gain legal rights, including the rights to vote, dispose of their own property and have custody of their children.[3] While motherhood is associated with the ultimately universal – fundamental human experiences that have existed at all times – it is always embedded in historical and social contexts. Consequently, the concept of motherhood changes over time. This balance between the universal and the historically and culturally specific characterizes artistic explorations of motherhood.

Origin

"All human life on the planet is born of woman. The one unifying, incontrovertible experience shared by all women and men is that months-long period we spent unfolding inside a woman's body. Because young humans remain dependent upon nurture for a much longer period than other mammals, and because of the division of labor long established in human groups, where women not only bear and suckle but are assigned almost total responsibility for children, most of us first know both love and disappointment, power and tenderness, in the person of a woman. We carry the imprint of this experience for life, even into our dying,"[4] writes Adrienne Rich in her 1976 book *Of Woman Born*. Her words are from a time when childcare was largely the mother's domain. Rich's observation speaks to a long tradition of autobiographical art revolving around the mother. A host of artists have portrayed their – often aging – mothers, and the history of literature is full of memoirs dedicated to the writer's mother. For many artists, the figure of the mother becomes a way back to childhood, a figure of memory that enables the adult self to trace their development by returning to their point of origin.

The French writer Marcel Proust's 13-volume autobiographical novel, *In Search of Lost Time* (1913-27, p. 65), which defined the modern memoir, is a key work

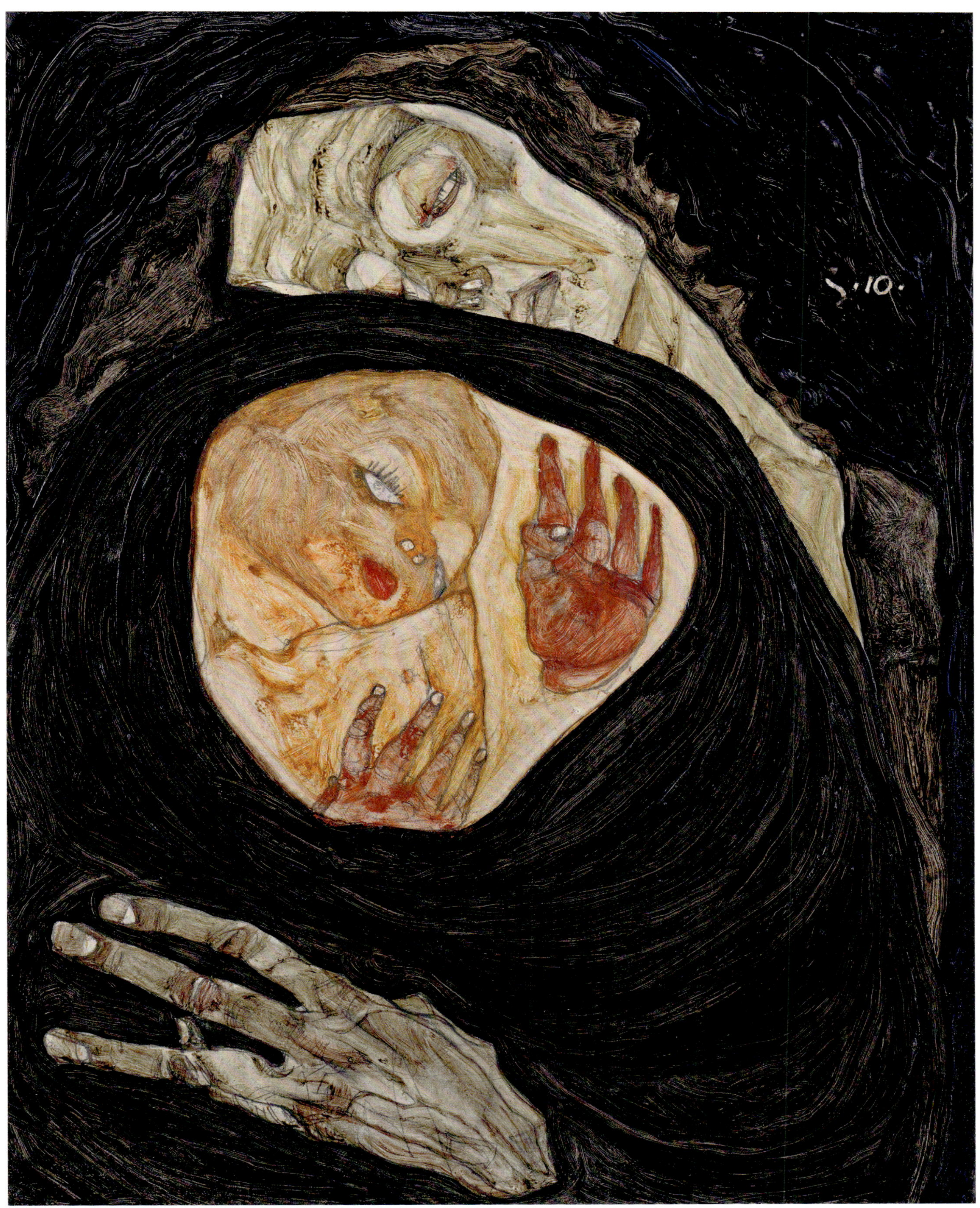
S.10.

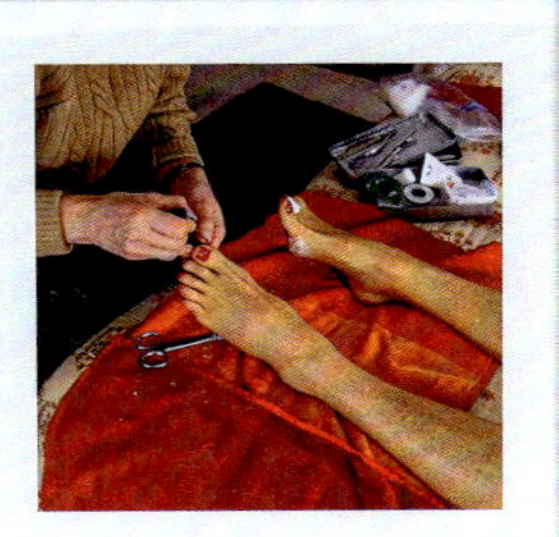

Monique wanted to see the sea one last time.
On Tuesday, January 31, we went to Cabourg.
The last journey.
The next day, "so my feet look nice when I go":
the last pedicure.
She read *Ravel* by Jean Echenoz.
The last book.
A man she had long admired but never met came to her bedside.
Making a friend for the last time.
She organized the funeral ceremony:
her last party.
Final preparations: she chose her funeral dress,
- navy blue with a white pattern -;
a photograph showing her making a face for the tombstone,
and her epitaph: *I'm getting bored already!*
She wrote a last poem, for her burial.
She chose Montparnasse cemetery as her final address.
She didn't want to die. She said this was
the first time in her life she didn't mind waiting.
She shed her last tears.
The days before her death, she kept repeating:
"It's odd. It's so stupid."
She listened to the Clarinet Concerto in A major, K. 622.
For the last time.
Her last wish: to leave with the music of Mozart in her ears.
Her last request: for us not to worry.
"Ne vous faites pas de souci."
Souci was her last word.
On March 15, 2006, at 3 P.M.,
the last smile.
The last breath, somewhere between 3:02 and 3:13.
Impossible to capture.

in this artistic tradition. The mother plays a prominent role throughout as a figure associated with the intimacy and nurture that the grown man seeks to rediscover in his love life. The germ of this motif is found in the first part of the novel, set in earliest childhood. A great drama is played out around his mother's goodnight kiss. It reaches a crescendo one evening when the family has guests over and the child in his bed tries to call his mother back by sending a note down to the living room by messenger. In the child's eyes, his mother is transformed before the guests into an actress on stage. He only wishes she would cast off this role and become what she is to him, a mother. The kiss is the moment that connects them. "I never took my eyes off my mother. I knew that when they were at table I should not be permitted to stay there for the whole of dinner-time, and that Mamma, for fear of annoying my father, would not allow me to kiss her several times in public, as I would have done in my room. And so I promised myself that in the dining-room, as they began to eat and drink and as I felt the hour approach, I would put beforehand into this kiss, which was bound to be so brief and furtive, everything that my own efforts could muster, would carefully choose in advance the exact spot on her cheek where I would imprint it, and would so prepare my thoughts as to be able, thanks to these mental preliminaries, to consecrate the whole of the minute Mamma would grant me to the sensation of her cheek against my lips, as a painter who can have his subject for short sittings only prepares his palette, and from what he remembers and from rough notes does in advance everything which he possibly can do in the sitter's absence."[5] The young boy is already an artist trying to capture the memory of his mother's image.

A host of writers stand on the shoulders of Proust. Among the most powerful works is the French philosopher Roland Barthes' *Camera Lucida* (1980). Written shortly after his mother's death, this slim volume examines photography's relationship to memory. His attempt to recall her personality is a hinge for reflecting on photography's strengths and weaknesses. Alone in the apartment where his mother recently died, Barthes reviews photos of his mother one by one, travelling back through time and his mother's life. But photography's wealth of detail is an impediment to memory. He remembers a person more poorly before a photograph of them than by merely thinking about them, he says. "I had acknowledged that fatality, one of the most agonizing features of mourning, which decreed that however often I might consult such images, I could never recall her features (summon them up as a totality)."[6] Curiously, the photograph that brings him closest to his mother was taken long before he was born and shows her as a child. Recognizing his mother in a childhood picture is bound up with the actual experience of saying goodbye to the mother he cared for and fed in the period up to her death. In a reversal, the nurture was now directed from child to mother. "She had become my little girl, uniting for me with that essential child she was in her first photograph."[7]

cat. 9
Sophie Calle: *Obituary*, 2012

Works of Farewell

Like literature, visual art is full of farewell works dedicated to the artist's mother. The aging mother, often captured in intimate or introspective situations, appears in a wealth of artworks using autobiographical experiences to address more general, existential issues. In such works, the aging – or even dying – mother becomes an image of the full course of life from birth to death. Visualizing this connection between the mother's death and the greater cycle of life, Egon Schiele's *Death Mother I* (1910, p. 19) shows a rosy infant encircled by a greyish-black mother figure. The painting was made during a period when death in childbirth was a real and prevalent danger. Schiele's picture suggests social realism, but rises above it by virtue of the simplified, expressive painting style. The woman's face and hands are thin and skeletal. Shrouded in black, she is an image of death itself. Amid the darkness glow the child's pink hands, new life, encapsulated in a rounded, uterine form. The two figures are more than mother and child. They are life and death, captured in a painting whose specific tragedy points to the tragedy – and reality – of life itself: we are born and we die.

Where Schiele links the figure of the mother to a more general artistic exploration of the cycle of life, artists today tend to examine the death of the mother as an actual, autobiographical experience. This device can be compared to the literary genre of "autofiction",[8] where writers base their work on their own lives. Real places, people and recollected events are mixed with made-up and poetic elements, elevating specific experiences and adding new nuances to universal themes, not unlike Barthes sifting through his mother's old photographs to make a more general statement about motherhood, mourning and memory.

"Her life did not appear in my work, and that annoyed her" is Sophie Calle's introduction to her big 2013 series dedicated to her mother. The artist's works are permeated with autobiographical material,

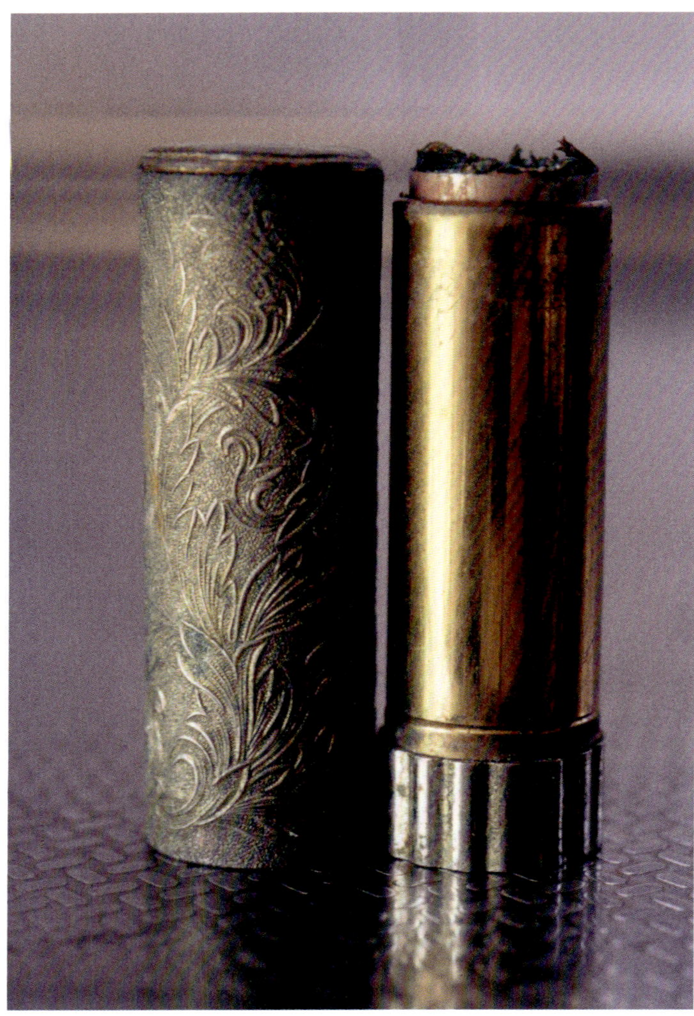

cat. 42
Miyako Ishiuchi: *Mother's #54*, 2002

Right page: cat. 116
Kaari Upson: *Mother's Legs*, 2018-19
Installation view Louisiana Museum of Modern Art

intimate details of her own and others' lives; transgressing the boundary between public and all-too private has been her artistic inspiration for decades. Even so, her mother does not appear in Calle's art until she is on her deathbed. A few days before losing consciousness, she gives her daughter a box of photo albums and notebooks, aware that she is providing material for an artwork. From this material, Calle makes a series of sculptures, books, photographs and texts on the subject of mourning, seeking to pinpoint her mother's nature (p. 20). To a photograph of a sculpture of a woman reclining in the grass are added the words: "On December 27, 1986, my mother wrote in her diary: 'My mother died today'. On March 15, 2006, in turn, I wrote in mine: 'My mother died today'. No one will say this about me. The end." The death of her mother severs Calle from the family line she is not herself continuing. The artist is training on her mother the searching gaze of a child. Richly detailed, Calle's portrait of her mother renders an individual in all her complexity. Her mother, Monique, is not captured merely in her capacity as a mother but as a person of desires, frustrations, impulses and ideas; it is the indivisibility of the personality her work seeks to represent.

A more melancholy note pervades the Japanese artist Miyako Ishiuchi's *Mother's* (2000-2005, this page and p. 56), a series of photographs made immediately before and after her mother's death. One section of the series shows her mother's intimate belongings in close-up – lace underwear, worn-out shoes, a brush with tangled strands of hair in its spokes, used lipsticks of different shades – objects that her mother carried close to her body or that bear marks of her mother's body, the person who has been disintegrated, burnt to ashes, according to Japanese custom.[9] The other section of the series consists of black and white, highly detailed extreme close-ups of her mother's body – feet, breasts, belly, armpit. Wrinkles and fine lines cover her entire body. Her skin looks paper thin and transparent in places,- like the chrysalis of a butterfly. In other places, it is thickened by scar tissue or dotted with moles.Marks of a life lived. Despite their extreme intimacy, the predominant theme of the images is absence. The work is suffused by the melancholy negation of presence: no matter how close up we get, the mother remains a distant figure, unknowable, unapproachable. These are all her secrets, but who was she, actually? All we are left with are the traces of a person. We get up so close that the totality disappears. We never get to see her face.

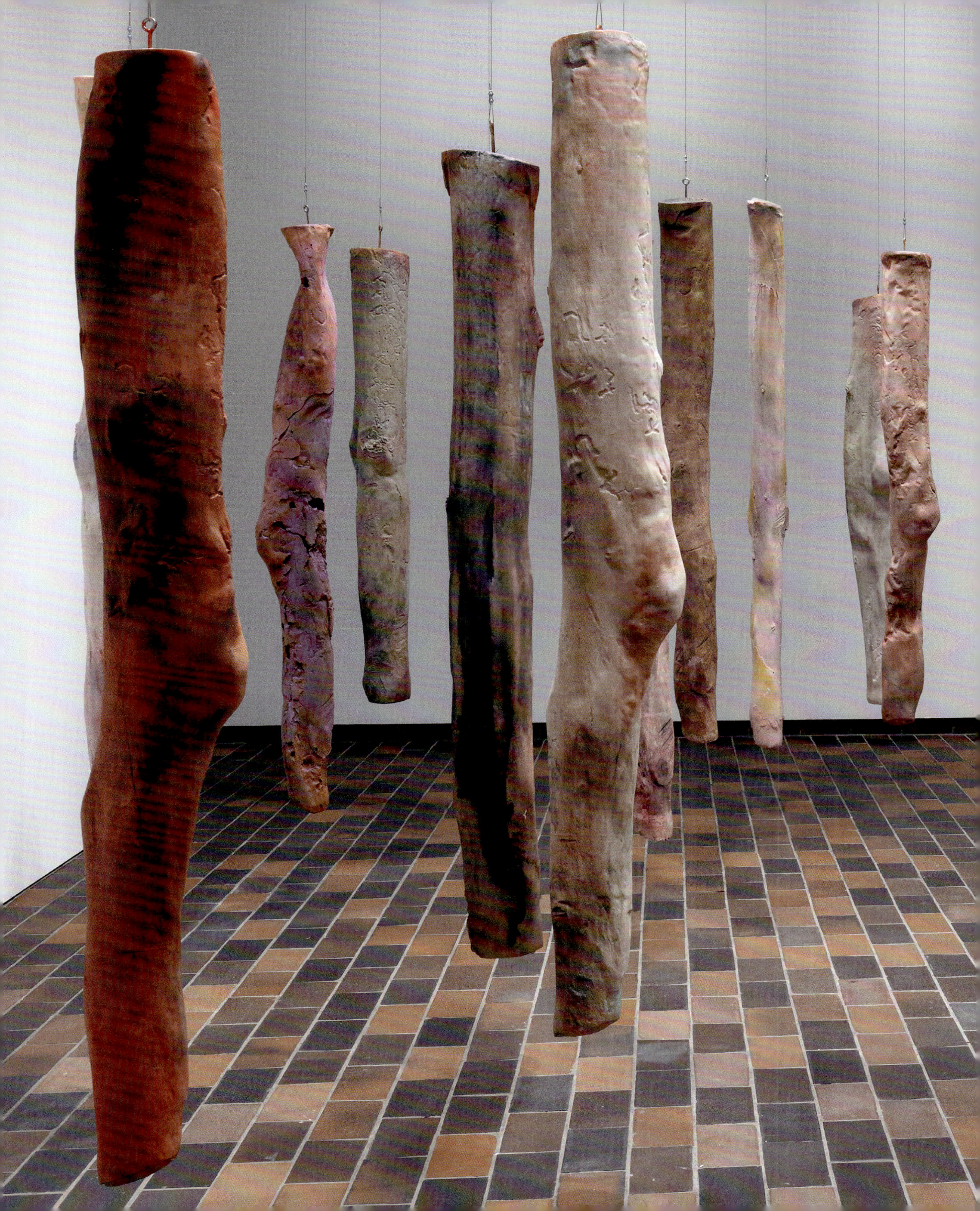

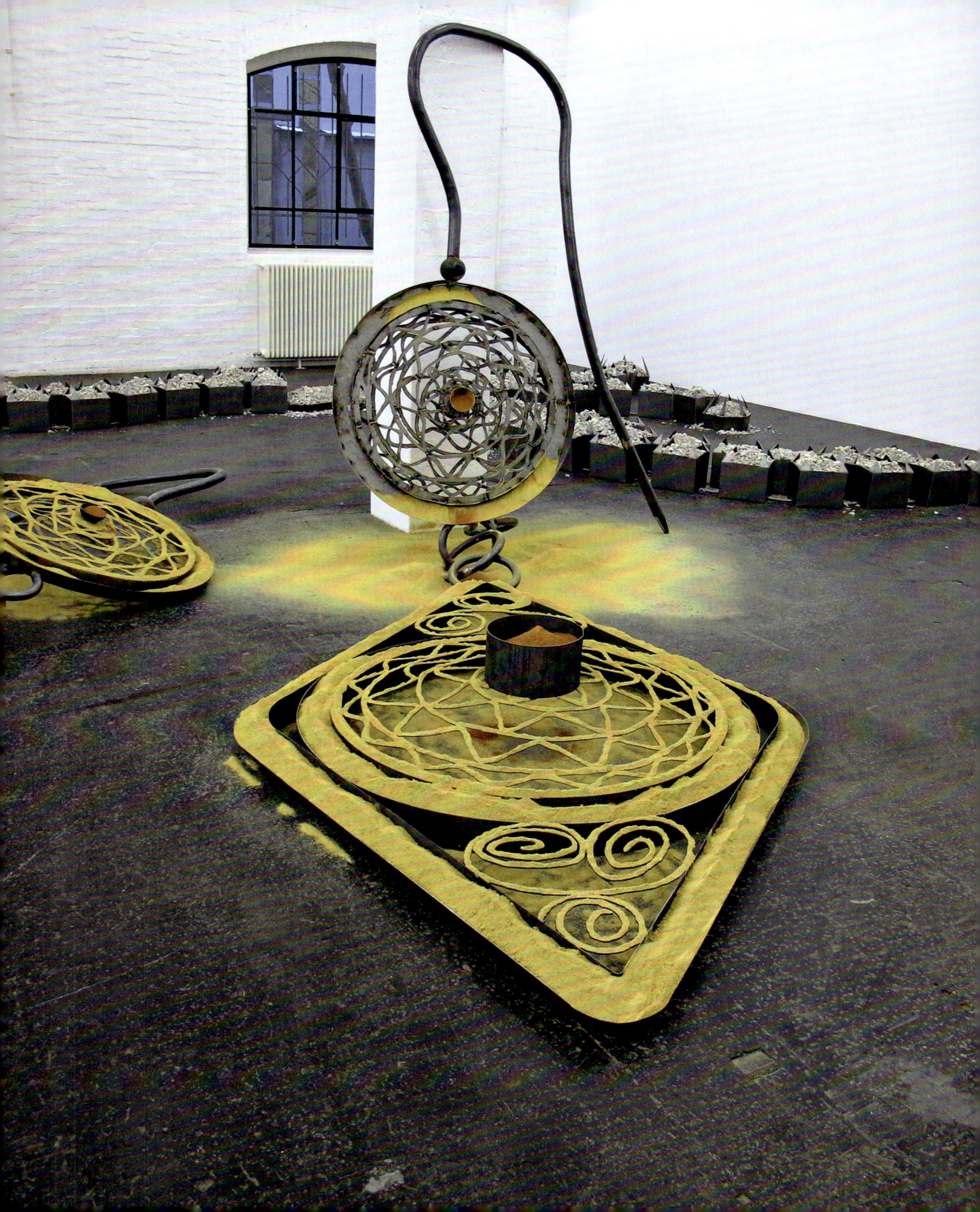

The Motherland

In contemporary portraits of mothers, the body of the mother is closely tied to the artist-self's social and psychological place in the world. As mother tongue, the word for our first language, implies, the mother, both as a biographical fact and a cultural figure, is our pathway into the social and cultural arena. Memorial works in contemporary art use secret documents, sudden sensory impressions and other effects to lead us along winding psychological roads back to the maternal origin. The search for the mother is closely related to a search for an own identity.

It is the first time dear that you have a human shape (2012), a sculpture by the Kosovo-born artist Petrit Halilaj, travels through the artist's mother in search of a lost cultural identity. When he was a child, Halilaj and his family fled war-torn Kosovo. Before leaving, his mother buried some of her jewellery and a collection of her son's drawings in the family's garden to ensure that physical memories of the family's history would survive in case they lost everything during their escape. Halilaj has enlarged two of his mother's earrings, sprinkling into their ornamented metal ducts the yellowish powder of their demolished family home. By a few simple devices, Halilaj creates an at once both intimate and fragile monument to a land of childhood that no longer exists because the civil war has wiped it off the map. The mother is the motherland.

The American artist Kaari Upson primarily works in sculpture and video, and her mother is a recurring figure in her work. In her installation *Mother's Legs* (2018-2019, p. 23), we move through a strange forest of bald, man-high logs hanging on thin wires from the ceiling. Painted in shades of rose and equipped with astonishingly naturalistic knees, the logs are transmuted into fleshy, lifelike legs, the wormholes on the surface of the wood convincingly translated into varicose veins on thighs. These are all the mother's legs. Placed in the perspective of a small child, our eyes at knee level, we are ready to clutch the legs at any moment. A safe harbour, were it not for the deathlike violet shades and the occasional remains of blood-red paint on the dangling legs lending a whiff of the abattoir. The underlying creepiness is fully unfolded in Upson's videos that double and blend the daughter's and the mother's personalities. The artist appears with her mother's face painted on top of her own in bright colours. The mask is obviously painted-on and fake, but all the more eerie because it moves so convincingly along with her facial expressions. Mother and daughter become one, the boundaries blurring. Upson is employing a classic horror trope – the too-close relationship between mother and adult child. The Oedipal undertones foster uncanniness by destabilizing the autonomy of the self and implying that subconscious, uncontrollable urges are driving the person to commit unpredictable and destructive acts. This effect is familiar from Alfred Hitchcock's *Psycho* (1960, p. 26), where the woman killer Norman Bates, in a key scene, leaps at his victim armed with a knife, dressed in his dead mother's gown. In one of the last scenes in the movie, it is revealed that the deranged Bates, who lives a secluded life in a house on a hill, has been storing his dead mother's body. The son's attachment to his mother is so strong that he cannot let go of her even after she is dead; his serial killings of women can be traced back to a lost son's destructive communication with a powerful mother figure. Hitchcock's classic obviously draws on the psychoanalytic theories of Sigmund Freud. Indeed, Freud's thinking had tremendous impact on the perception of the mother role in the 20th century. According to Freud, the mother's nurture directly affects the child's development and well-being, making the mother responsible for the slightest psychological disturbance in the adult child. In his theory of the Oedipus complex, Freud articulated a sexualized attachment to the mother that crucially influenced the perception of the mother-and-child relationship in culture as well as in art. This is the origin of the horror-movie trope of the terrifying, domineering mother.

cat. 26
Petrit Halilaj: *It is the first time dear that you have a human shape (diptych 1 – earring)*, 2012

The Mother's Voice

Art history abounds with portraits of the artist's mother – from Rembrandt van Rijn and Lucian Freud, who made a moving portrait of his aging mother (*The Painter's Mother Resting, I*, 1976, p. 57), to contemporary artists taking an investigative look at the mother. But what about the artist herself as a mother? What about the experience of being a mother? The theme is interesting because motherhood as a lived experience has historically been a problematic source of artistic inspiration. Mother or artist, either/or, was the choice faced by women, as prominent living artists like Tracey Emin and Marina Abramović discuss in interviews even today.

Emin has made a number of distinctive works on this theme. "I do not expect to be a mother, but I do expect to die alone," she writes on one of her quilts (p. 27). Paradoxically, these works employ a number

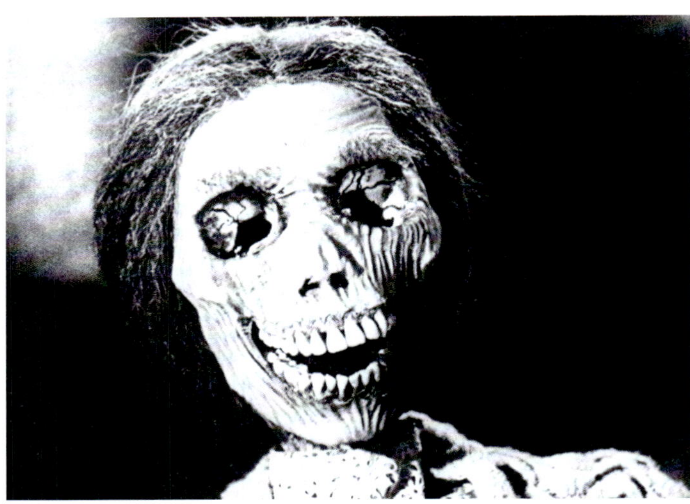

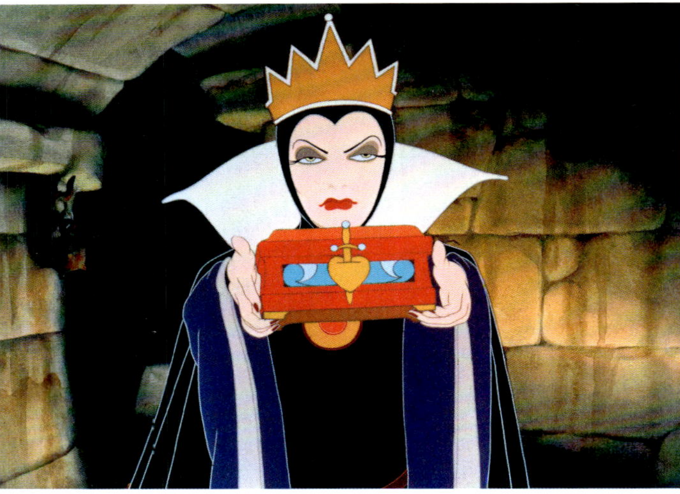

cat. 29
Alfred Hitchcock: *Psycho*, 1960

cat. 15
Walt Disney: *Snow White and the Seven Dwarfs*, 1937

Right page: cat. 20
Tracey Emin: *I do not Expect*, 2002

of techniques and objects that are closely associated with the role of mother – a warming blanket or, as in *Feeling Pregnant II* (1999-2002, p. 64), one of the clearest images of a mother's nostalgia: saved baby shoes. The tiny shoes are lined up next to an autobiographical text-piece laying out, in a sensitive and wildly associative style, the anxiety Emin feels every month about a possible unplanned pregnancy.[10]

Apart from the specific socio-cultural circumstances, such as the time being a mother takes away from artistic activity, Emin's works refer to a deeper cultural perception that one form of creation rules out another, that "procreativity" rules out creativity. Among the most violent artistic testimonies to this is *Votive Picture (Strangling Angel)* (1931, p. 28), a watercolour by Meret Oppenheim that shows her brutally strangling a baby – an artistic antithesis to the Madonna. Oppenheim made the work at 18 when she enrolled at the Académie de la Grande Chaumière in Paris to remind herself of her wish not to have children but to dedicate her life to art, a promise she kept. This fine, brutal work testifies to the conditions of many female artists of her generation. Artist or mother, that was the choice. Even when female artists did have children, they did not include the subject of motherhood in their art.

With the arrival of feminist art in the 1970s, it might be assumed that motherhood would win broad acceptance. However, because a core feminist issue was the emancipation of women from the home and from financial dependence on a male provider, liberation from motherhood, at least in the context of art, became part of the movement. "As white feminists threw off the burdens of motherhood, many also dismissed the experiences of motherhood as a basis for serious art making."[11] Although the body and its representation in art were central to art in the 1970s, pregnancy and birth are all but absent. In a 1976 essay on the period's art, the American art critic Lucy Lippard proposed, "Perhaps procreativity is the next taboo to be tackled."[12]

A notable exception is the American artist Mary Kelly and her two series *Antepartum* (1973, p. 58) and *Post-Partum Document* (1973-1979, p. 58-59). Executed in the sober aesthetics of conceptual art, the series consist of a video of Kelly's own pregnant belly in close-up – the movements of the baby under the skin are visible as lumps moving around – alongside text-based works investigating the act of nurture, Kelly's thoughts about her interaction with her newborn baby, and the baby's appropriation of the culture and the language she is born into. Typewritten text is brought together with plaster casts of a newborn's tiny hands in a work that stands as a classic in the art of motherhood. "I wanted

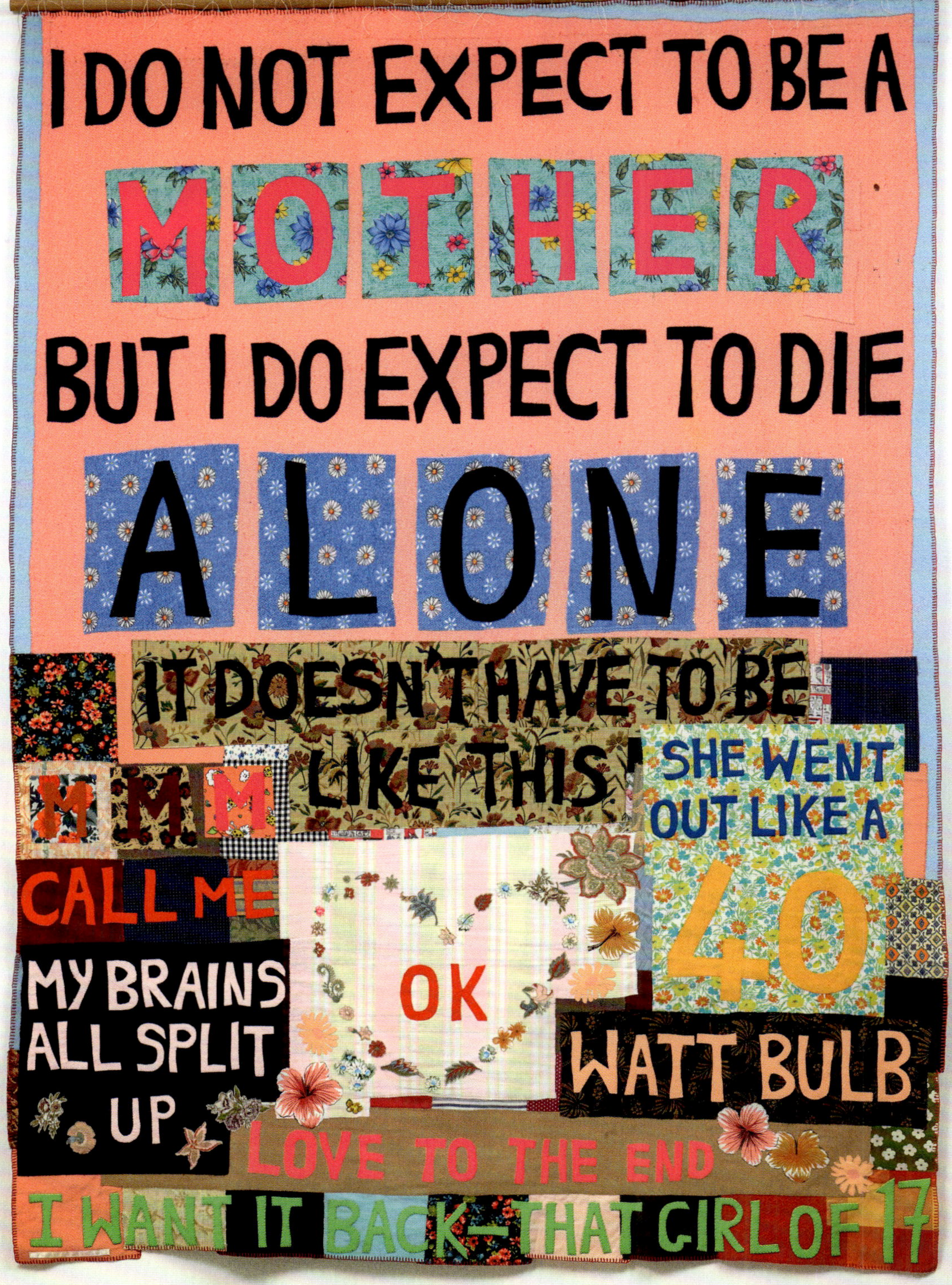
I DO NOT EXPECT TO BE A
MOTHER
BUT I DO EXPECT TO DIE
ALONE
IT DOESN'T HAVE TO BE
LIKE THIS!
SHE WENT
OUT LIKE A
40
WATT BULB
MMM
CALL ME
MY BRAINS
ALL SPLIT
UP
OK
LOVE TO THE END
I WANT IT BACK—THAT GIRL OF 17

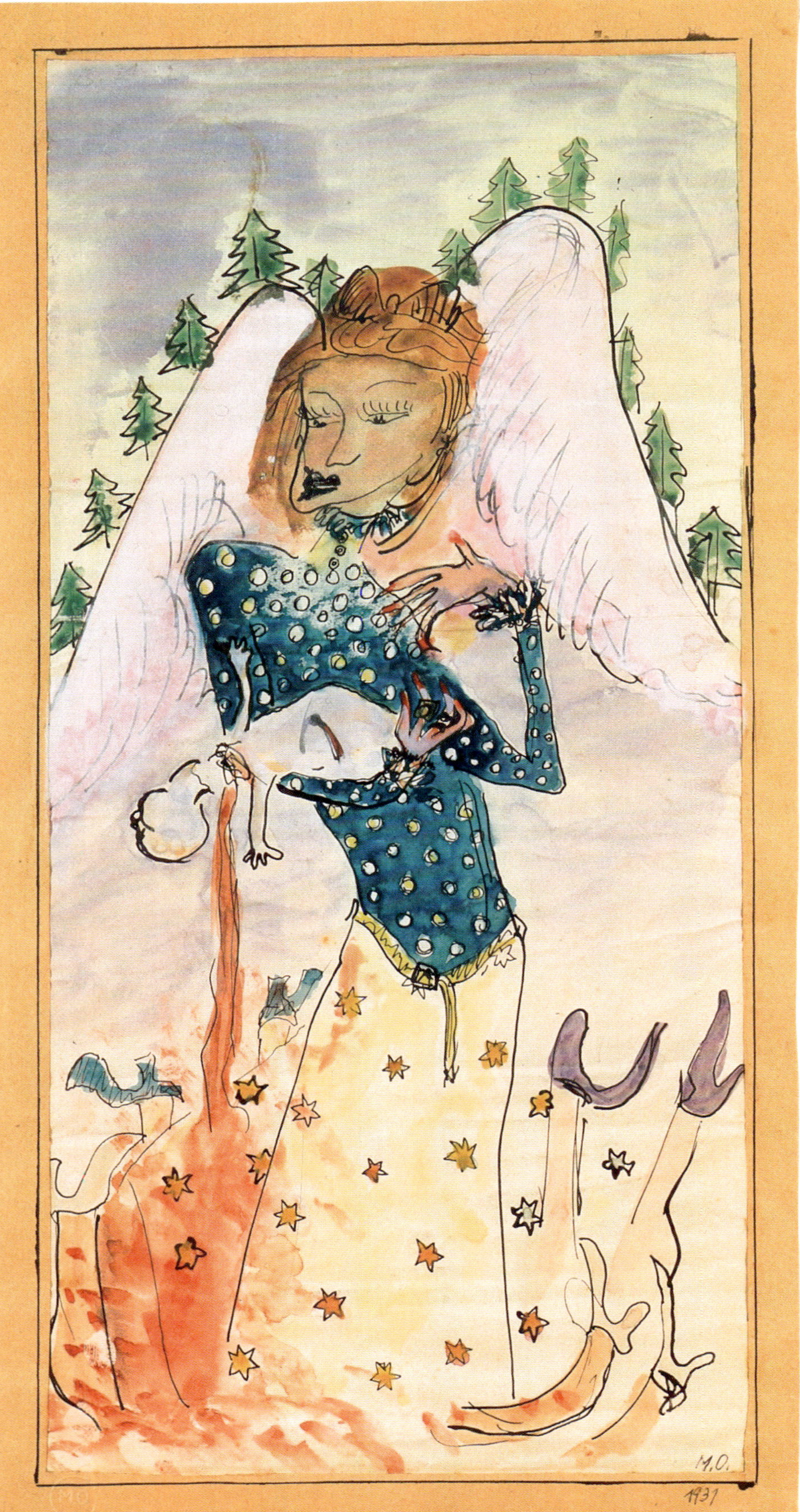

cat. 97
Meret Oppenheim:
Votivbild (Würgeengel), 1931
Votive Picture (Strangling Angel)

cat. 49
Kirsten Justesen:
Omstændigheder, 1969
Circumstances

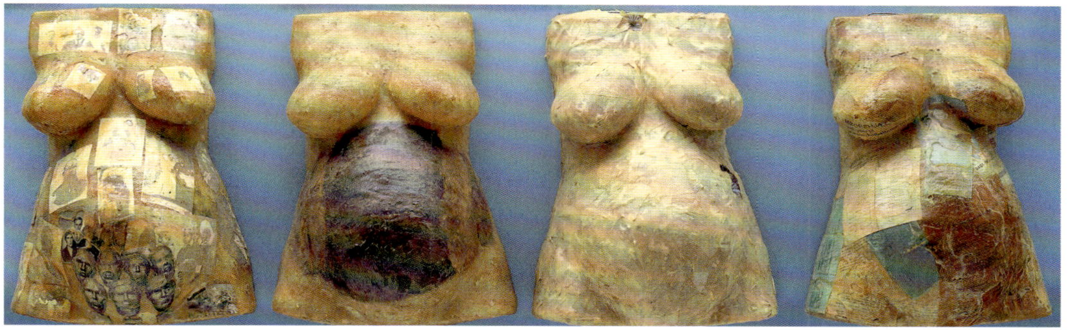

to give way to the mother's voice," the artists says, "I wanted to let the person speak, who otherwise is only spoken about."[13]

The Danish artist Kirsten Justesen also allowed motherhood to inhabit her art. In *Circumstamces* (1969), four casts of the artist's pregnant torso are equipped with objects and pictures that, as in Kelly's work, merge the bodily with the social and political. Two of the casts display material from Mødrehjælpen (Denmark's Planned Parenthood) and photographs of the artist's relatives – the personal history and the cultural context into which the child is born – while the others are covered with natural materials like fur and flowers.

These works by two prominent artists of the women's liberation movement of the 1960s and 1970s testify to a new self-awareness among women artists, who with different aesthetics sought to include motherhood in their work as an experiential horizon and reality. One of the most painful works in this chapter of the exhibition is the singer-songwriter Joni Mitchell's 1966 song "Little Green", written shortly after she signed the papers giving her newborn baby girl up for adoption. The song is a farewell letter to the child she is not able to provide for on her own. The name she gives her child, Green, expresses Mitchell's hope for the child's future: "Little Green, have a happy ending."

The Queer Mother

Contemporary art and literature are seeing a new flourishing of works exploring motherhood from the mother's point of view, and the physical changes and complex emotions it entails. These works, too, offer concrete testimony to the premise of the exhibition: while motherhood is universal, the meanings that culture attaches to it are not static but change over time. Of the literary voices in this conversation, Maggie Nelson's hybrid text *The Argonauts* (2015, p. 80) stands out as an investigation of motherhood beyond conventional gender roles. Chronicling the writer's relationship with the transgender artist Harry Dodge, and her pregnancy and the birth of their child, the book reflects on the multitude of stereotypes and perceptions with which culture imbues motherhood. The question of what is "normal" and what is queer is a throughline in the book. Having viewed motherhood as being bound up with female conformity, the protagonist over the course of her pregnancy sees categories dissolve. "Is there something inherently queer about pregnancy itself, insofar as it profoundly alters one's 'normal' state, and occasions a radical intimacy with – and radical alienation from – one's body? How can an experience so profoundly strange and wild and transformative also symbolize or enact the ultimate conformity? Or is this just another disqualification of anything tied too closely to the female animal from the privileged term (in this case, nonconformity, or radicality)?"[14] Nelson's book is a literary testimonial to a culture where the mother figure is capable of transcending gender identities. New family structures, new fertility technologies, solo moms, queer parenting and rainbow families are diversifying the role of mother and interrogating the nature of motherhood.

What today is a broad social trend has existed as a subcultural phenomenon for decades. The concept of the queer mother is not new. Jennie Livingston's documentary film *Paris is Burning* (1990, p. 101) portrays New York drag queens and their "house culture", shared living arrangements providing a home and community for flamboyant and often socially outcast queer people. Each of these houses is led by an older drag queen, ubiquitously known as the "house mother" – provider, mentor and nurturer to her younger housemates who have been cast out by their families. As one of these mothers puts it: "When someone has rejection from their mother and father, their family, when they get out in the world they search for someone to fill their void ... I'm gay, and they're gay, and that is where a lot of that mother business comes in. Because their real parents give them such a hard way to go, they look up to me to fill their void."[15] Ballroom culture's reinvention of the mother figure as a role you can assume and dress up as severs motherhood from biological kinship and the female gender in the conventional sense. The mother in this case is a set of actions bound up with nurture and guidance, the answer to the emotional and existential void left when someone has been cast out of their family. This perception of motherhood can be traced back to a cardinal virtue of Christianity: charity, love of our neighbour, often represented in the figure of a mother with small children. In this tradition, the mother is associated with idealized nurture, which is given a singular new expression in the flamboyant and queer mothers of ballroom culture.

The French artist Laure Prouvost has made a new installation for the exhibition: a room with an octopus-like mother animal extending her arms to all sides. Under the arms hang masses of breasts in glass jars standing in for suction cups. The figure is framed in a star-shaped cabinet of mirrors, kaleidoscopically fragmenting our reflections as we move around it. This is the exhibition's proposal for a mother figure. The life-giving, nourishing mother animal is a strange creature whose image is constantly changing.

Birth

Putting a focus on the mother also involves examining the origin of life, a theme that is surprisingly underexamined by the great existential thinkers. In philosophers like Heidegger and Sartre, the certainty of death is essential to human existence.[16] Just as common as death, however, is the fact that we are all born. One philosopher who switched the focus from death to birth is the German-born Hannah Arendt. In her magnum opus, *The Human Condition* (1958), Arendt introduces the concept of "natality", the condition of having been born. For Arendt, natality is a path away from cynicism and fatalism. Being born emphasizes that every new human is a new beginning who could, essentially, change everything.[17] Birth points to renewal, a change of generations, but also to humans as social creatures, since natality requires other people to receive the newborn child. For Arendt, life is not just a cycle ending in death but a new beginning with hope of action and change. In that respect, her humanist thinking builds on the Christianity tradition of celebrating birth as a miracle. "[The miracle] is, in other words, the birth of new men and the new beginning, the action they are capable of by virtue of being born. [...] It is this faith in and hope for the world that found perhaps its most glorious and most succinct expression in the few words with which the Gospels announced their 'glad tidings': 'A child has been born unto us'."[18]

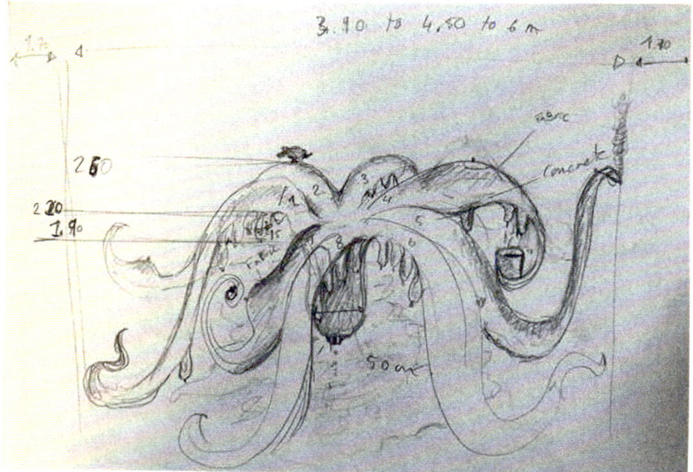

cat. 103
Laure Prouvost: *MOOOTHERR*, 2021 (sketch above)
Installation view Louisiana Museum of Modern Art

Compared to the other extreme of existence, death, our way into the world, birth, is a remarkably untold chapter in the history of Western culture. Before feminist art of the 1970s, there are vanishingly few images of childbirth in Western art. So few, in fact, that it appears to be a visual taboo. With feminism, however, women's experiences become enshrined in art history. The Danish artist Dea Trier Mørch depicts childbirth straight on and unblinkingly in a series of linocuts for her 1976 novel *Winter's Child* (p. 32).[19] Despite the graphic elegance of her delicately carved lines, Trier Mørch's work approximates social realism in its sober portrayal of birth as a physical and social event. A more whimsical and politicized version of the theme is found in the work of the French-American artist Niki de Saint-Phalle. The female figure in *The Pink Delivery* (1964, p. 121), a modern rendition of a prehistoric fertility goddess made from toy animals, fake flowers and a bomber plane, stares at us with empty eyes, while squeezing out a baby in the form of a plastic doll between her legs. Here, we see a more irreverent and critical version of childbirth: a plastic-infected nature goddess whose fertility is wrapped in artificial references to nature.

Arendt's natality is bound up with the child as a new beginning but also with the society around it. More recently, the relationship between birth and society is exquisitely and engagingly portrayed in a photographic work unfolding as a visual dialogue between the artists Manjari Sharma and Irina Rozovsky (2016-2017, p. 33-35). Over a five-month period, the two artists exchanged photos on their smartphones. While this was going on, they both discovered they were pregnant. Much of the series is about light, as reflected in glass, water and

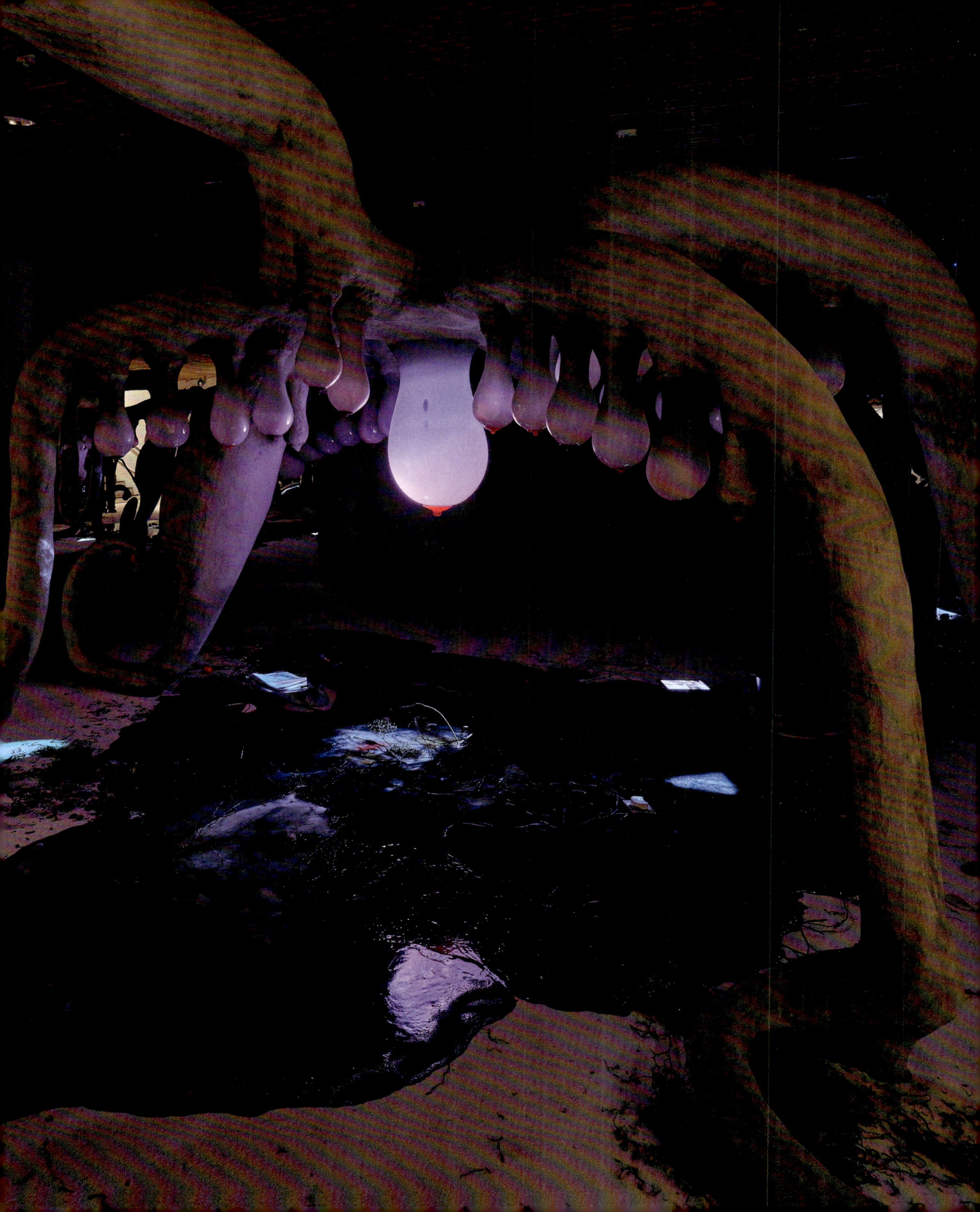

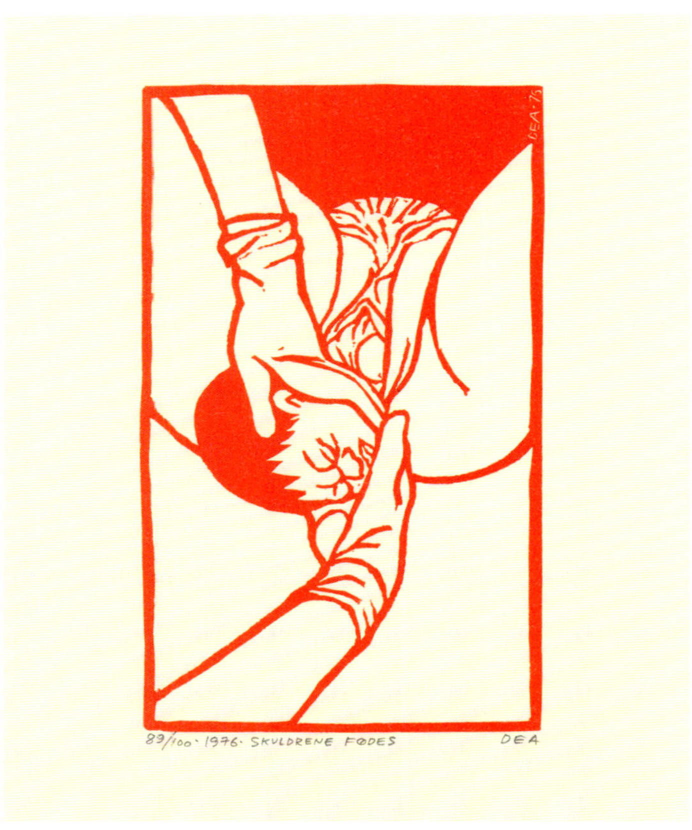

cat. 84
Dea Trier Mørch: *Skuldrene fødes*, 1976
The Shoulders Are Born

Right page and next spread:
cat. 109
Manjari Sharma & Irina Rozovsky:
To See Your Face, 2016-2017 (detail)

clouds. The world is full of beauty, and even the most commonplace details become aesthetically appealing in the artists' close-ups. Intimate pictures of pregnant bellies, peeled vegetables that look like internal organs, and ultrasound images draw us into the expectant space of pregnancy. After the 2016 US presidential election, however, political images are gradually added to the mix. The Women's March in Washington appears like a flash of world politics among these personal pictures. The series concludes with images of the two births, represented by bloody rags of placentas, and touching and tender portraits of the mother and her freshly born baby: the mother in the hospital bed holding the baby in her arms while they both are screaming. Mother and child lying close together, forehead to forehead. The small child sound asleep, enveloped by the giant face of her mother, an odd, protective creature with wide open, blue eyes – you only get this close to the face of someone you love.

Motherhood is eternally relevant and tied to the great existential themes: the beginning and end of life, nurture and abandonment, memory and longing. Cold or warm, present or absent, everyone has a mother.

1 Rachel Epp Buller, *Reconciling Art and Mothering*, Routledge, 2021, p. 1.
2 Buller is referring to the scholar Shari Thurer's cultural-history studies in this field.
3 For an analysis of the relationship between the public and private spheres, and their relationship to democracy as a societal model, see Jürgen Habermas, *The Structural Transformation of the Public Sphere*, Cambridge, 1989 (1962).
4 Adrienne Rich, *Of Woman Born, Motherhood as Experience and Institution* Norton & Company, 1976, p. 11.
5 Marcel Proust, *In Search of Lost Time. Swann's Way*, Volume 1, Modern Library, 1992 (1913), p. 35.
6 Roland Barthes, *Camera Lucida – Reflections on Photography*, Hill and Wang, 1982 (1979), p. 63.
7 Ibid., p. 72.
8 The term "autofiction" was coined in 1977 by Serge Doubrouvsky, but the term only became widespread in Scandinavia after the publication of Norwegian writer Karl Ove Knausgård's six-volume *My Struggle* (2009-2011).
9 Kasahara Michiko, "Traces of the Future" in Miyako Ishiuchi, *Mother's* 2000-2005, The Japan Foundation, 2005, p. 123.
10 Tracey Emin, *Love Is What You Want*, Hayward Gallery, 2011.
11 Buller, p. 2.
12 Lucy Lippard, "The Pains and Pleasures of Rebirth: European and American Women's Body Art" in *From the Center: Feminist Essays on Women's Art*, Dutton, 1976, p. 138.
13 Conversation with the artist in Copenhagen, October 2019.
14 Maggie Nelson, *The Argonauts*, Graywolf Press, 2015, p. 13.
15 Jennie Livingston, *Paris is Burning*, 1990.
16 Heidegger uses the term "being-towards-death".
17 Jørgen Lauritzen, *Hannah Arendt: Tænkning, opdragelse og dannelse*, Forlaget Kohl, 2010.
18 Hannah Arendt, *The Human Condition*, University of Chicago Press, 2013 (1958), p. 247.
19 See also Marie Laurberg, *Dea Trier Mørch – Det grafiske værk*, Louisiana, 2019.

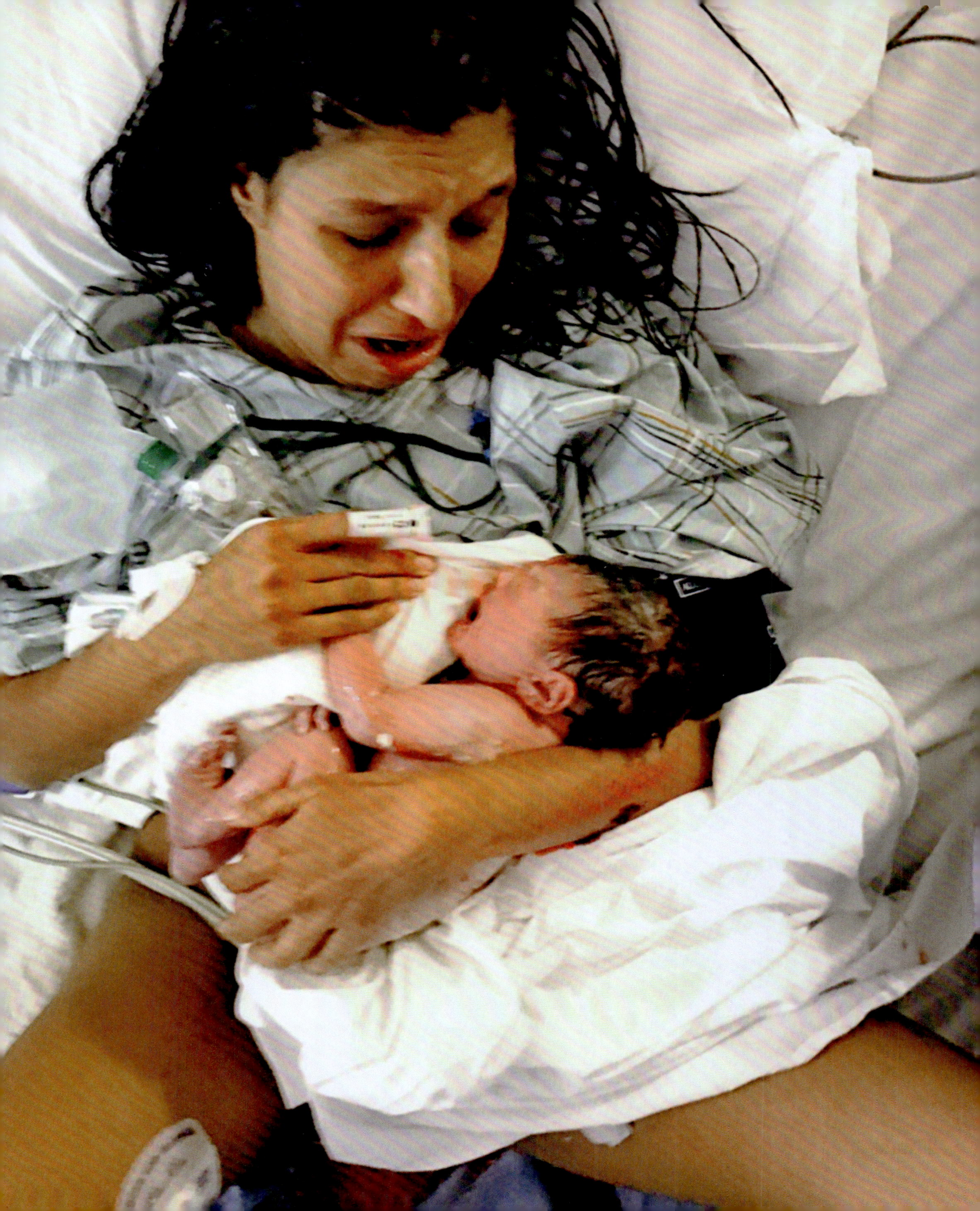

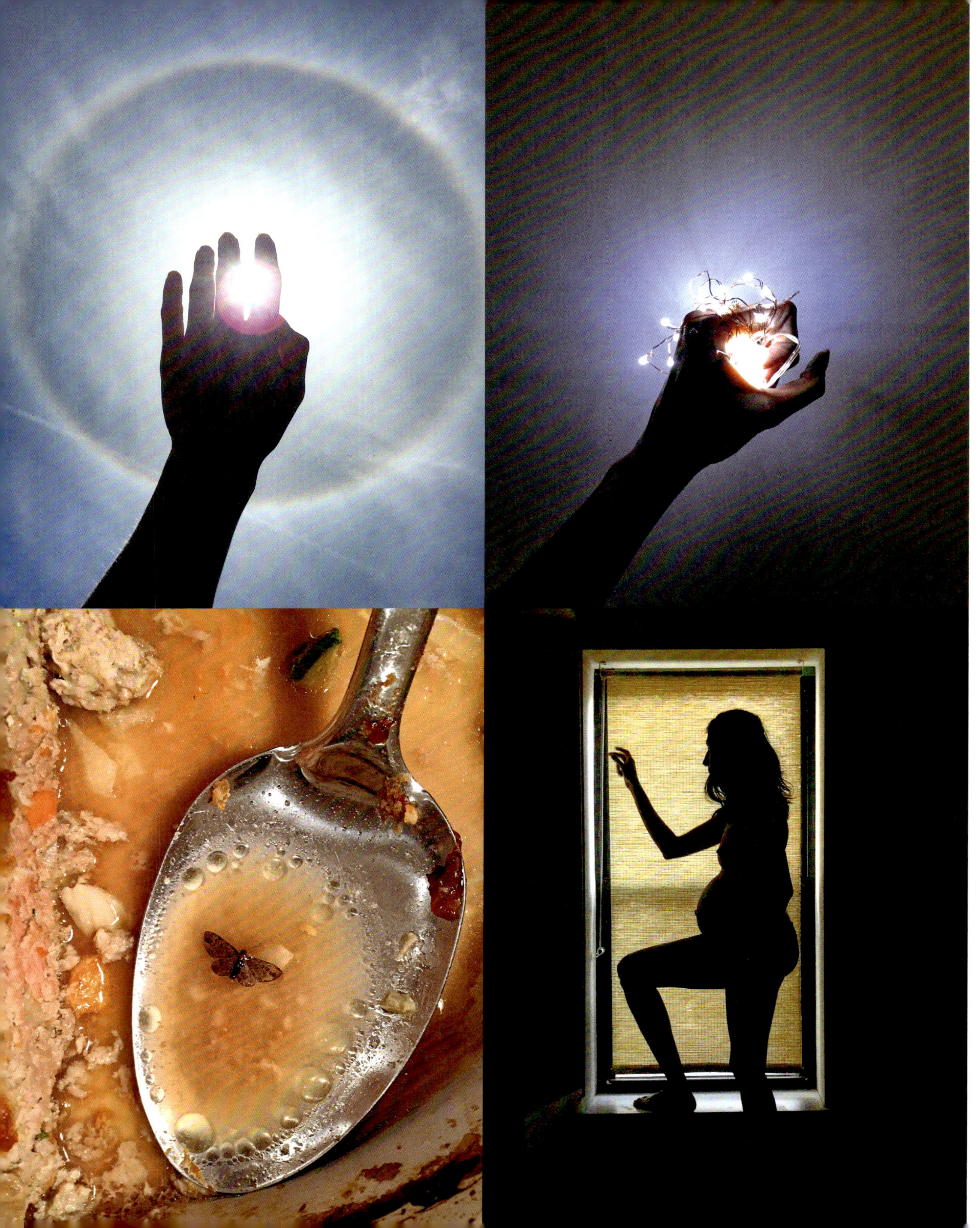

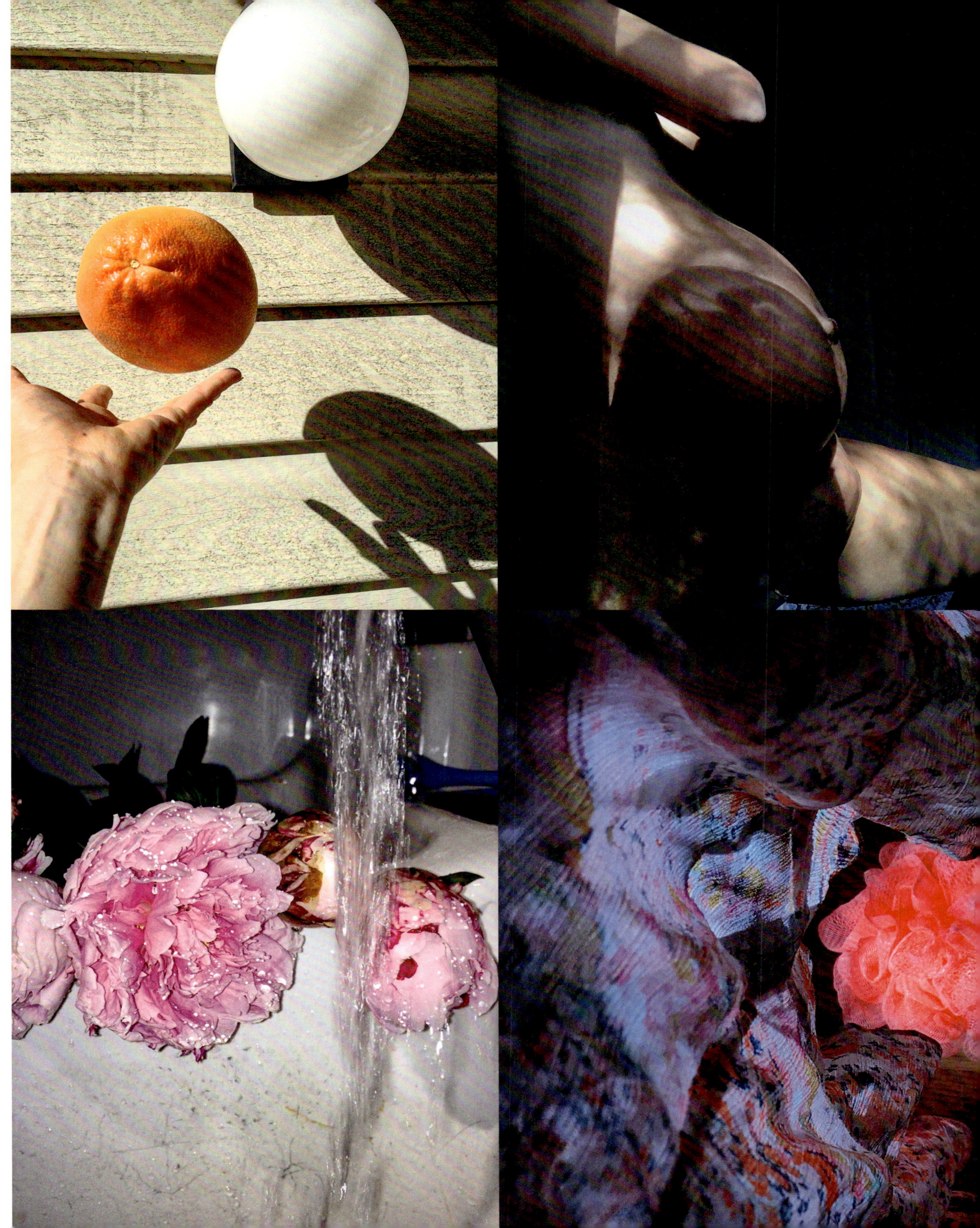

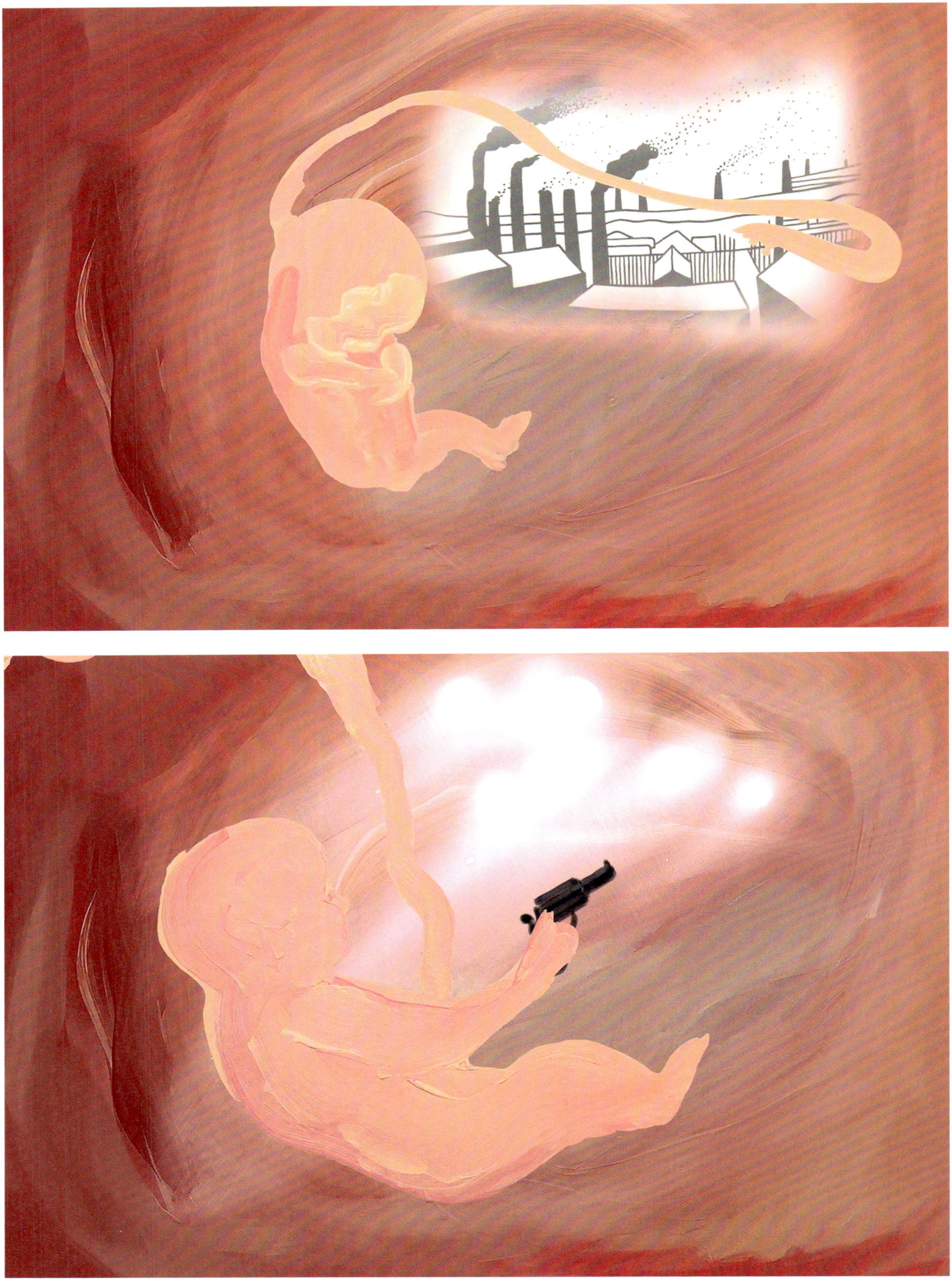

cat. 59
Tala Madani: *The Womb*, 2019

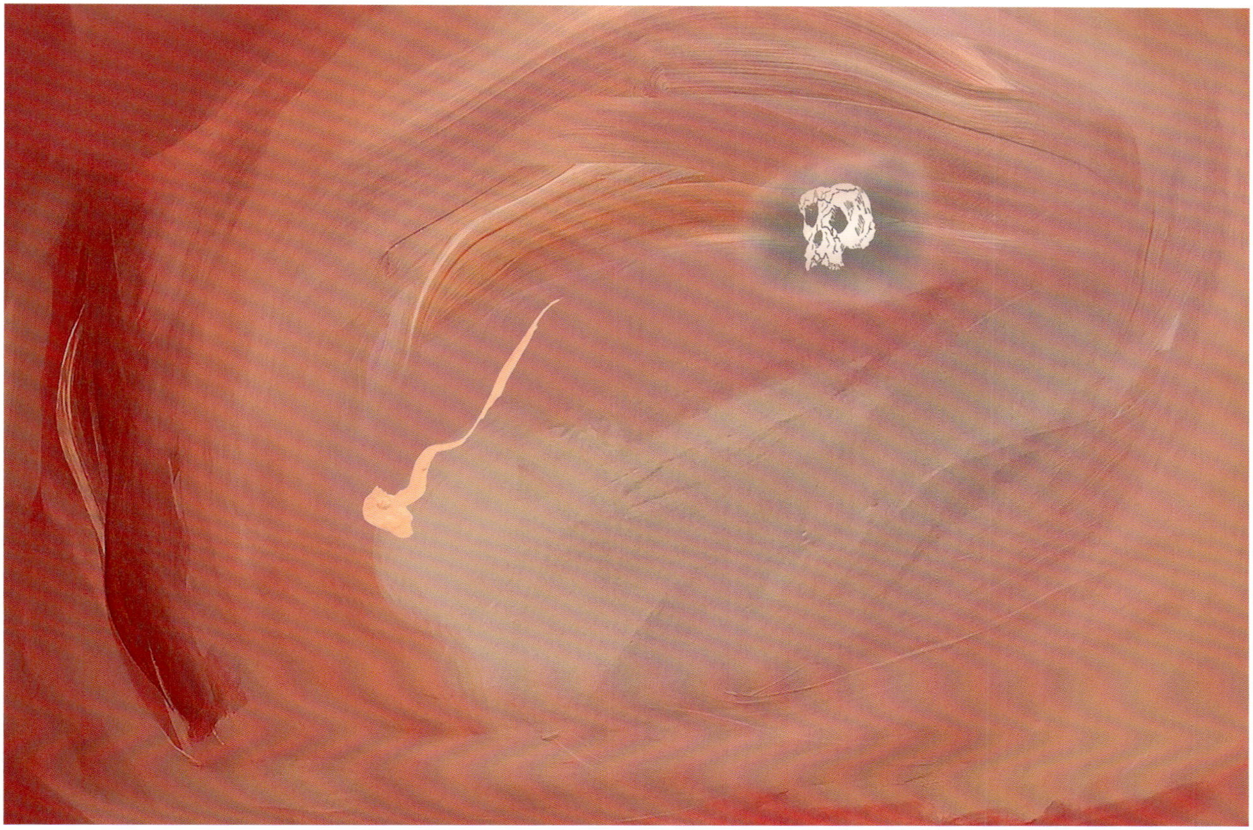

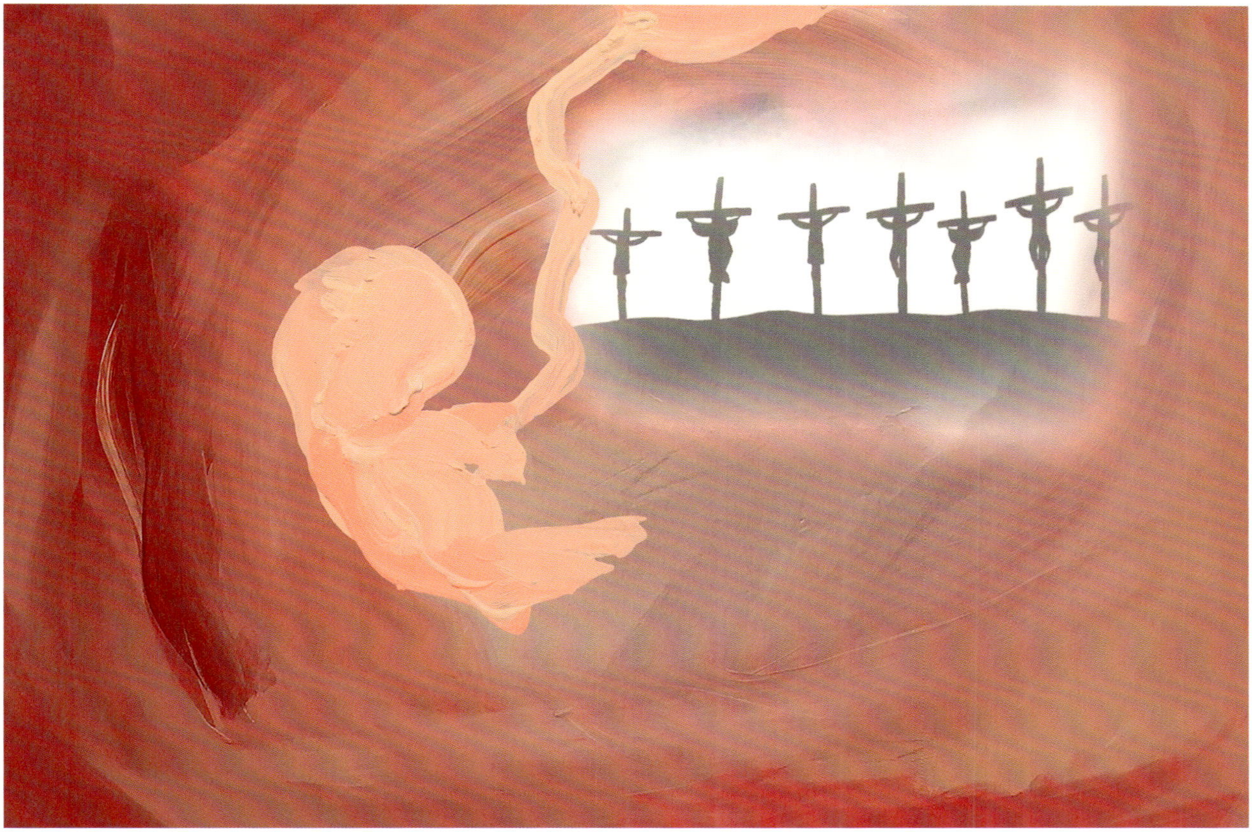

At the bottom left: cat. 124
Isis with Harpocrates?, Egypt, 3rd cent.

At the top right: cat. 121
Statuette of the goddess Isis with Horus child, unknown finding place, 1080-700 BC

cat. 122
Statuette of the goddess Isis with Horus child, possibly Egypt, 950-700 BC

Right page: cat. 140
Enthroned woman with infants, Italy, 3rd cent. BC

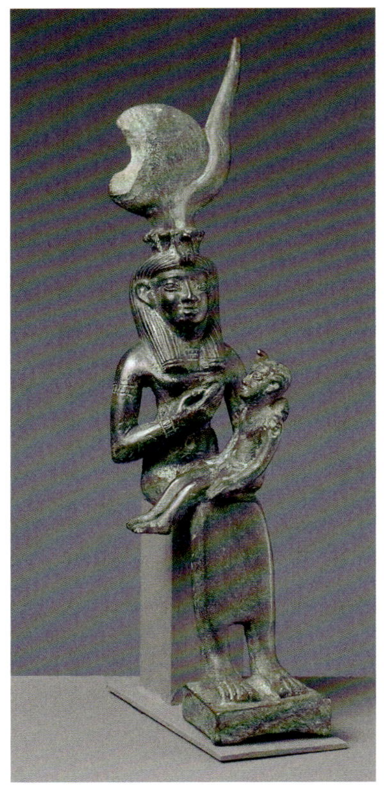

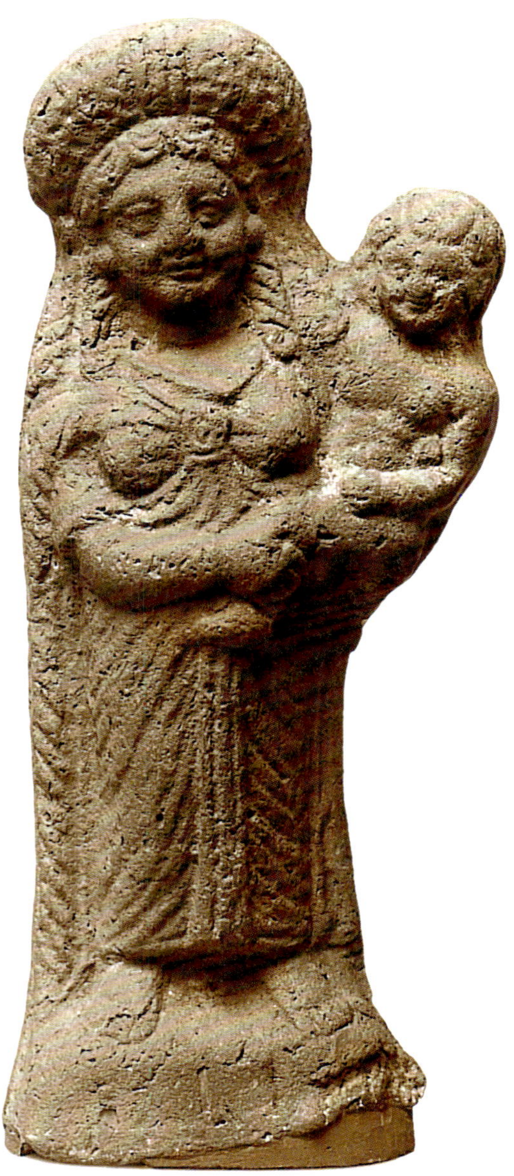

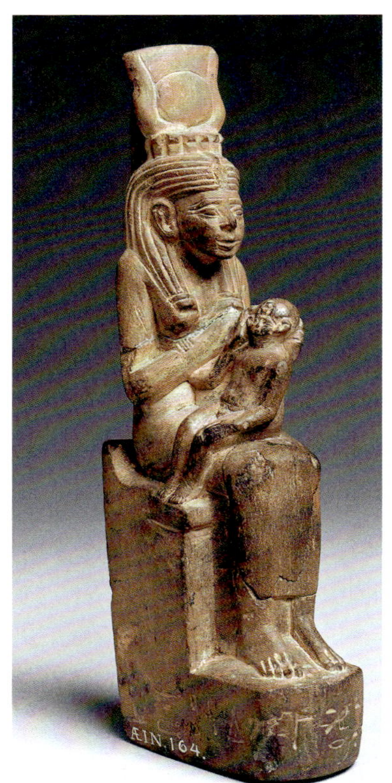

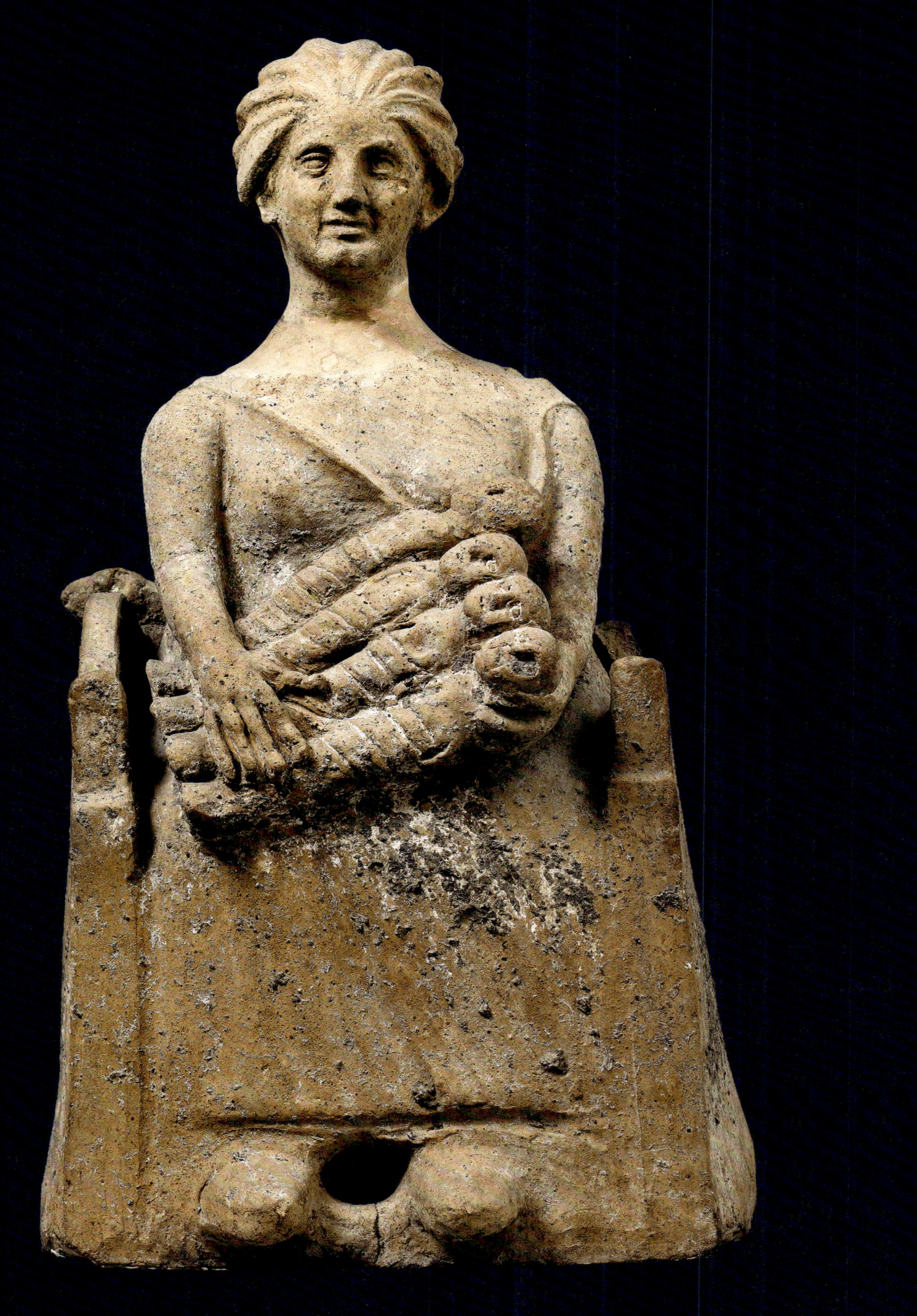

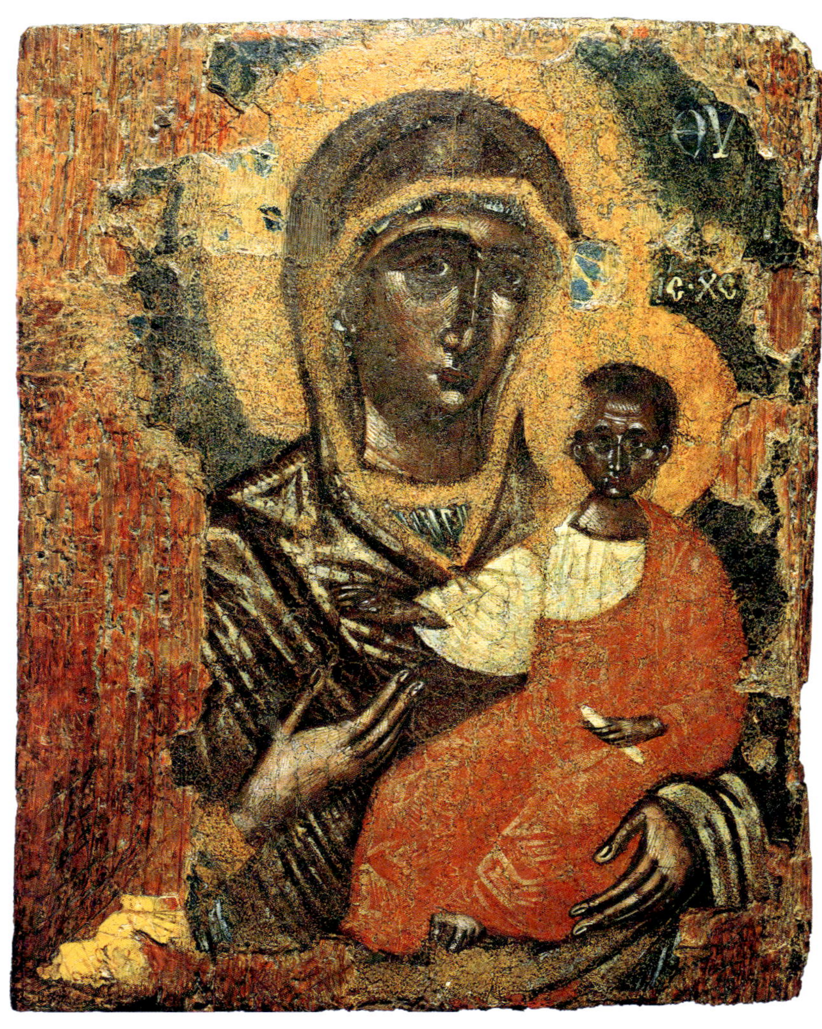

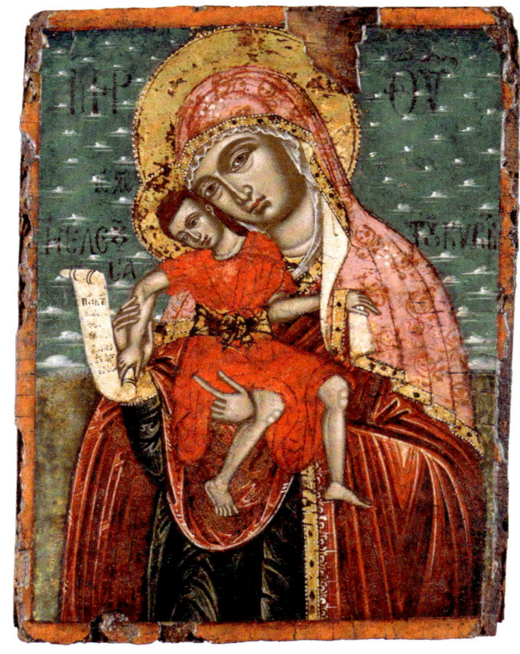

cat. 145
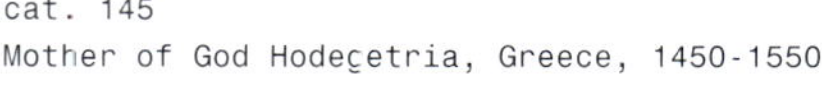
Mother of God Hodeçetria, Greece, 1450-1550

cat. 146
Mother of God from Kykkos, Greece, 1800-1850

Right page: cat. 148
Mary with child in a halo, 1470s

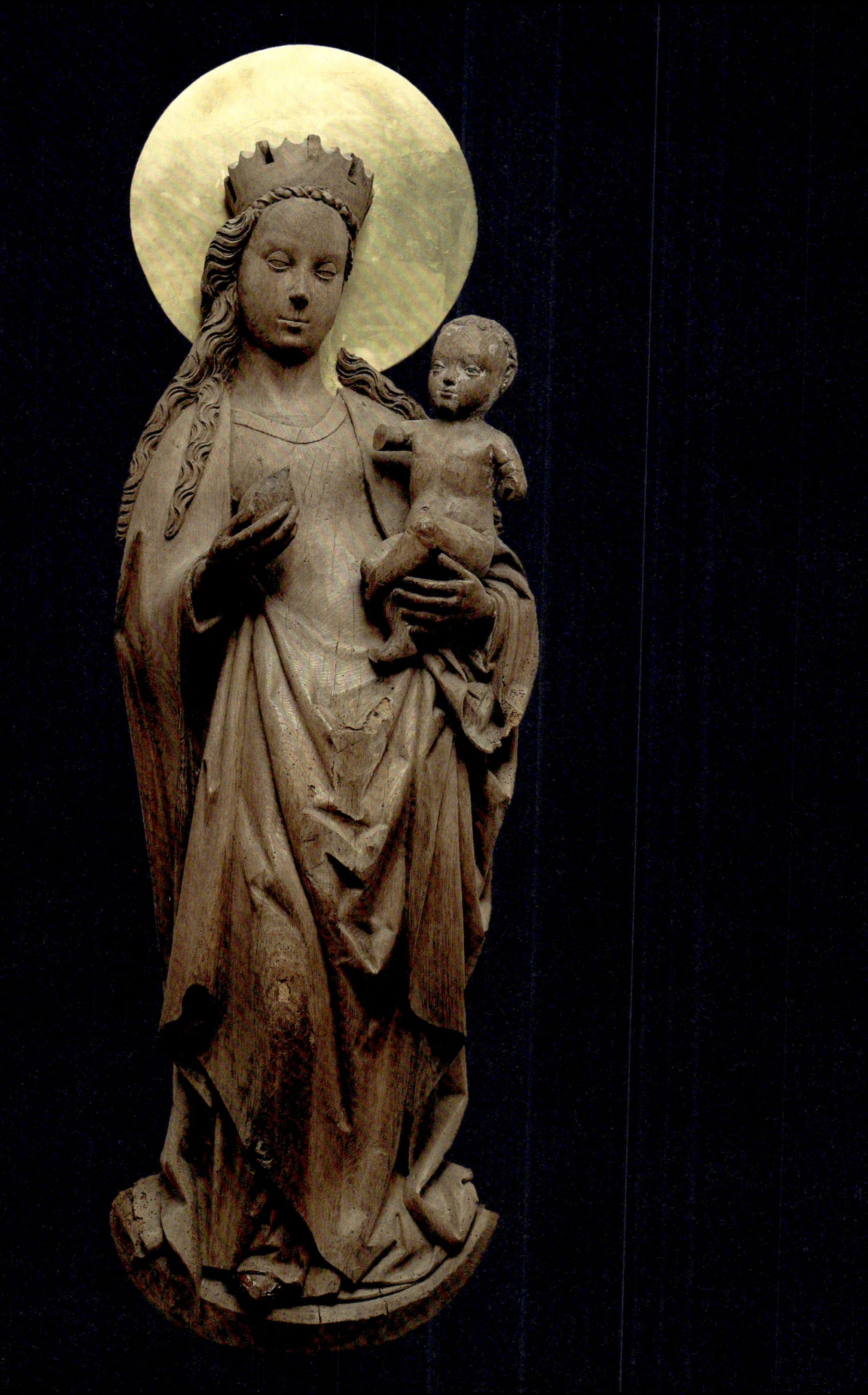

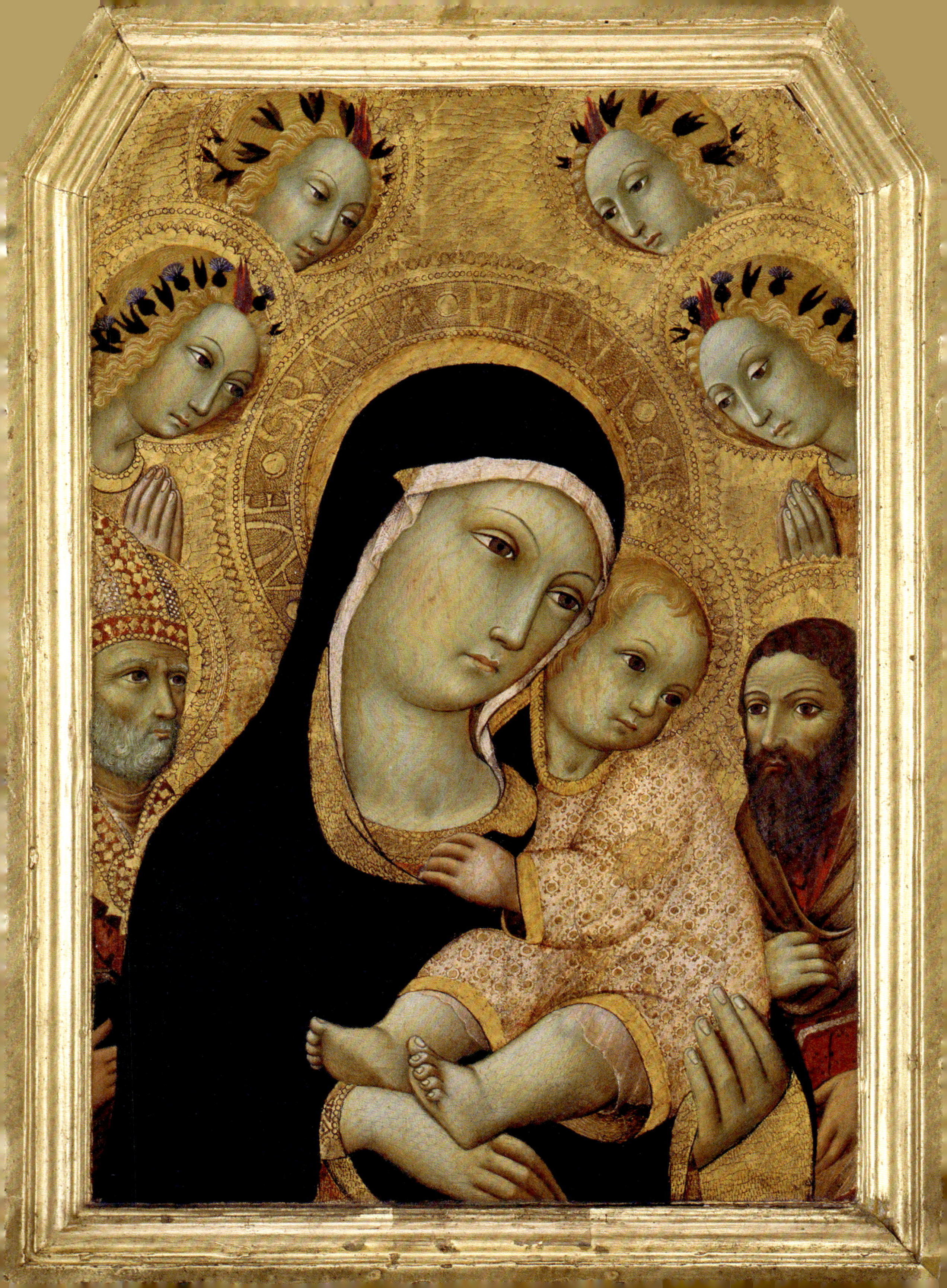

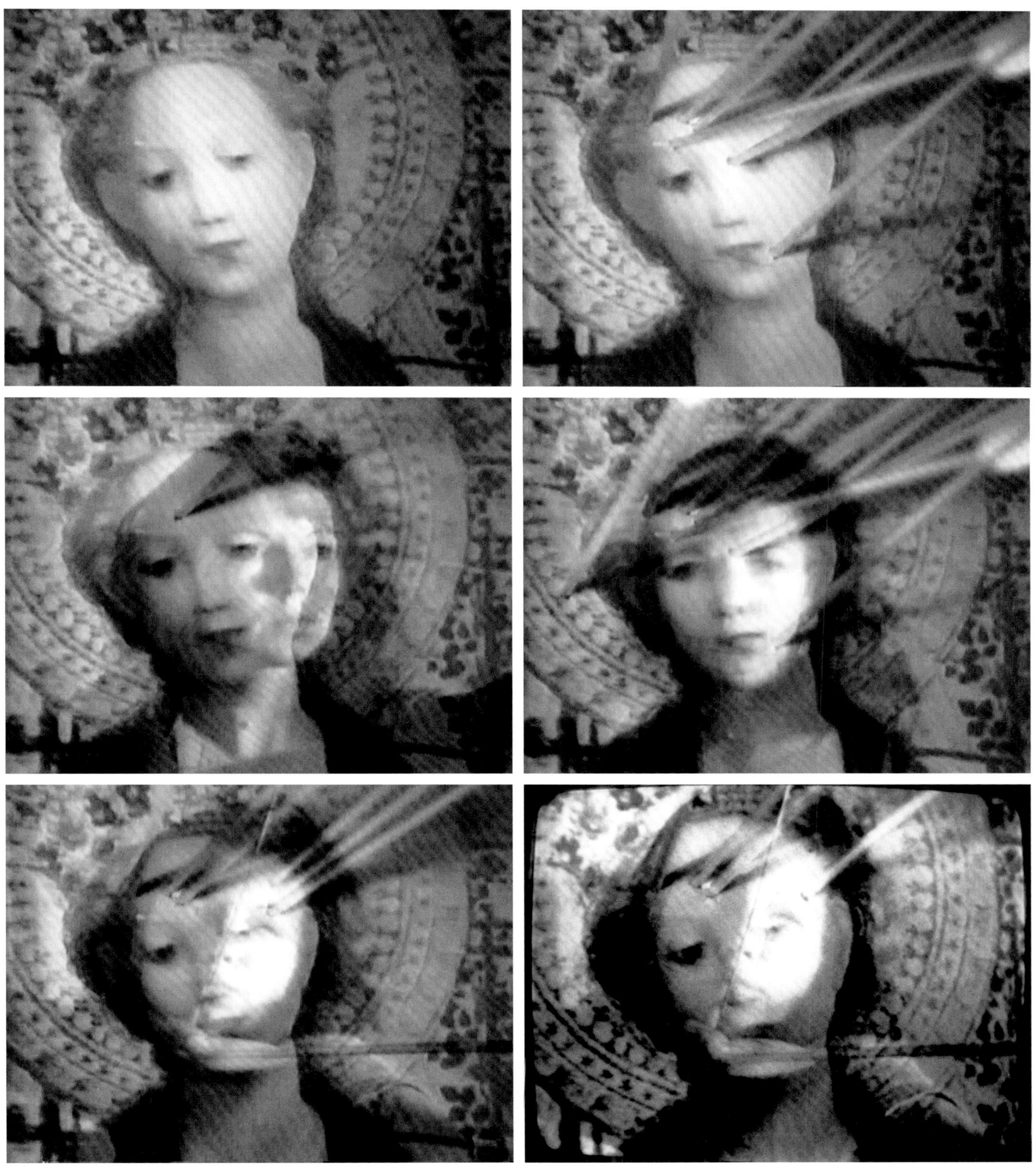

Left page: cat. 100
Sano di Pietro: *Madonna and Child, Worshipped by Angels and Saints*, c. 1450-1455

cat. 105
Ulrike Rosenbach: *Glauben Sie nicht, dass ich eine Amazone bin*, 1975. Don't Believe I'm an Amazon

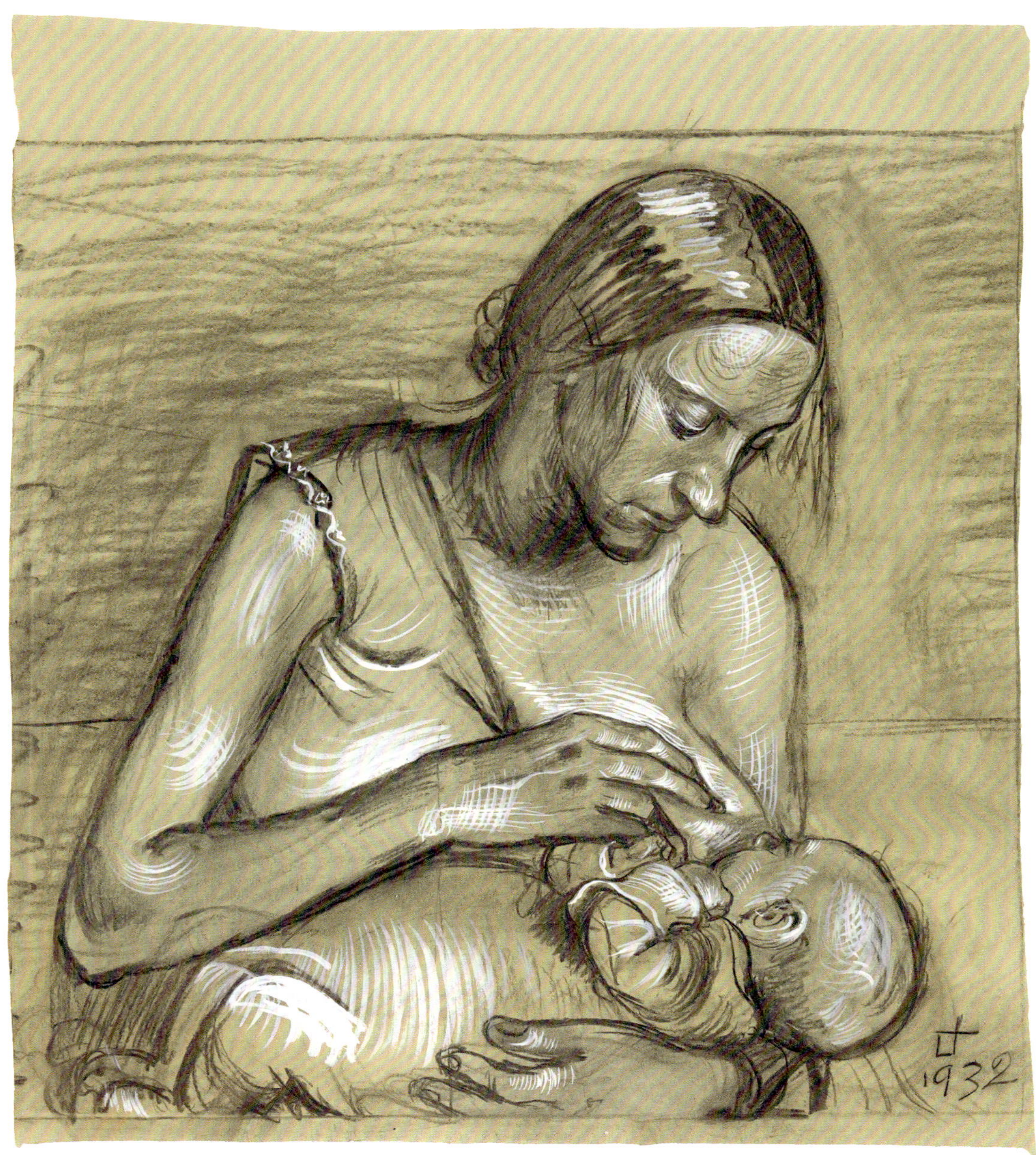

cat. 17
Otto Dix: *Mutter und Kind (Stillende Mutter)*, 1932
Mother and Child (Nursing Mother)

Right page: cat. 14
Rineke Dijkstra: *Julie, Den Haag, Netherlands, February 29 1994*, 1994

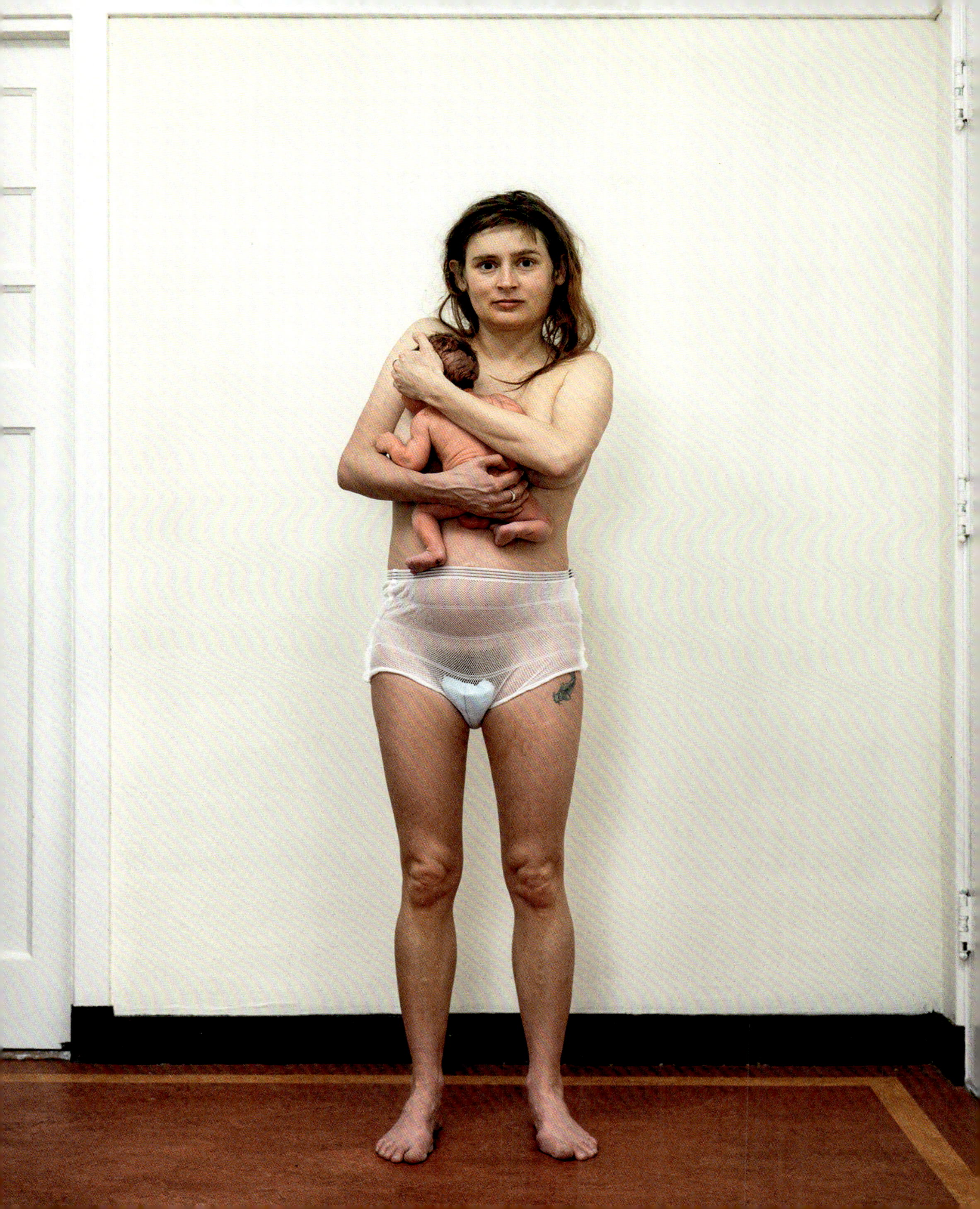

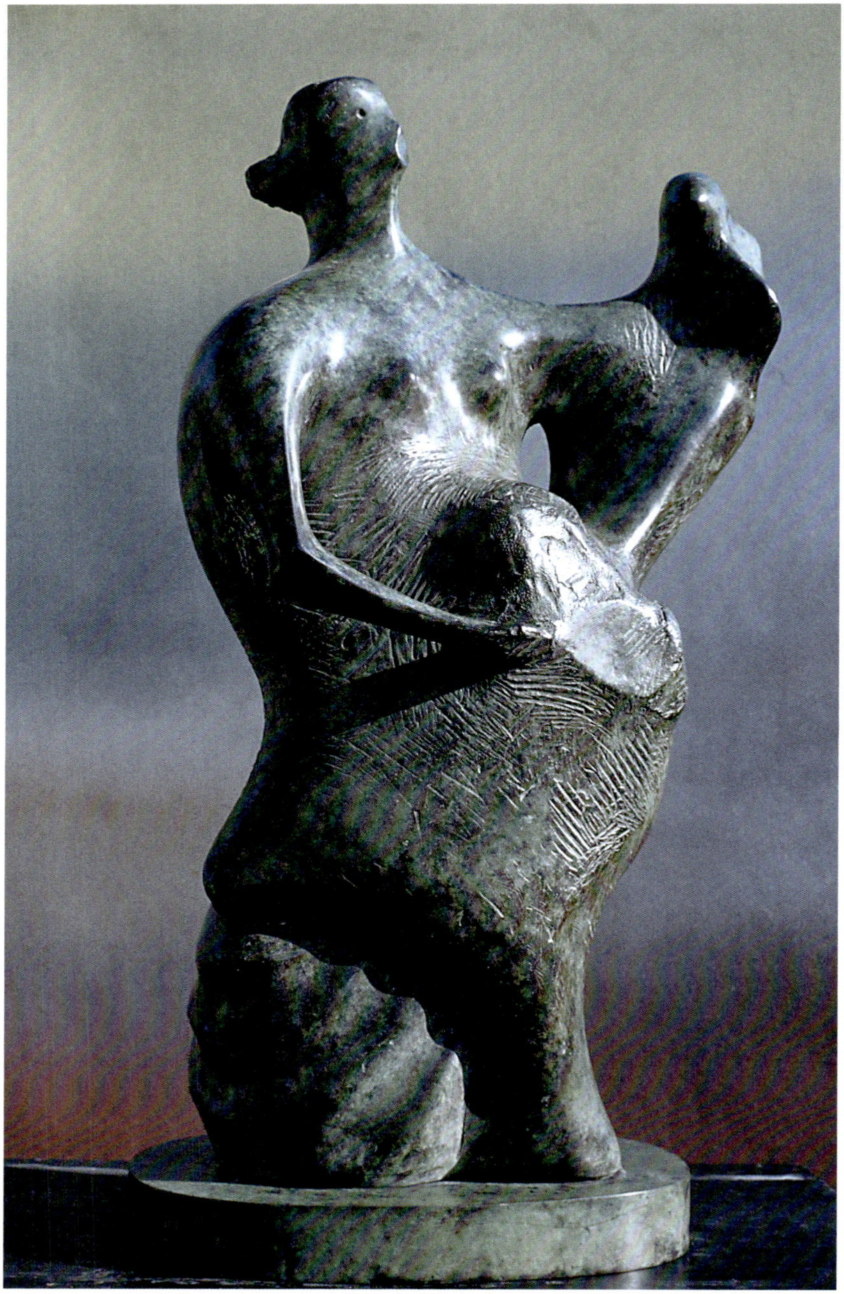

cat. 77
Henry Moore: *Maquette for "Mother and Child: Upright"*, 1977

Right page: cat. 74
Henry Moore: *Mother and Child*, 1932

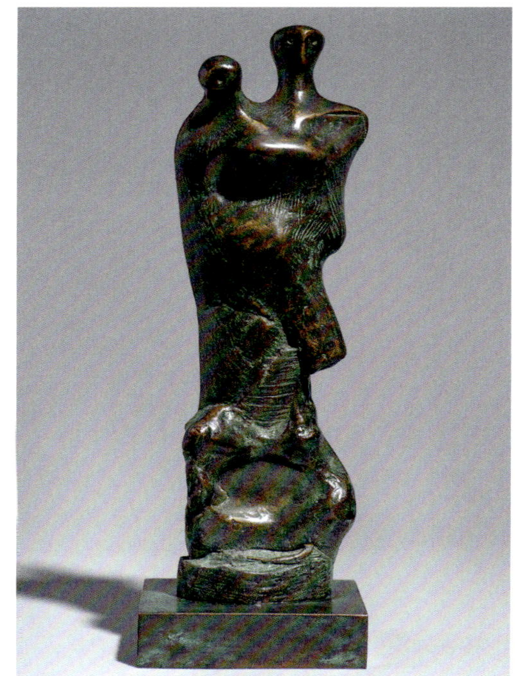

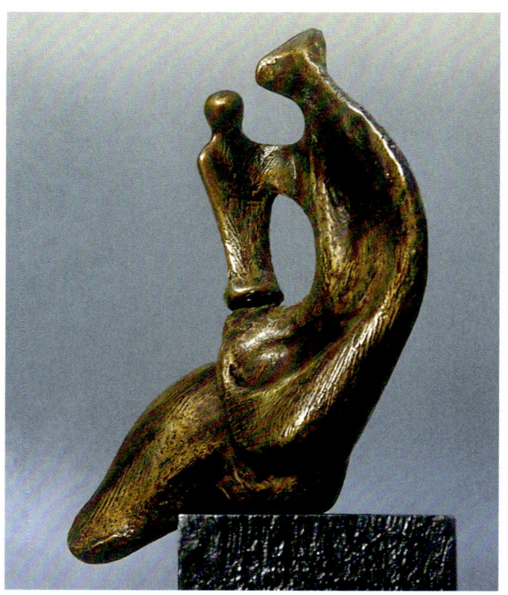

cat. 76
Henry Moore: *Standing Mother and Child*, 1975

cat. 78
Henry Moore: *Seated Mother and Child: Thin*, 1980

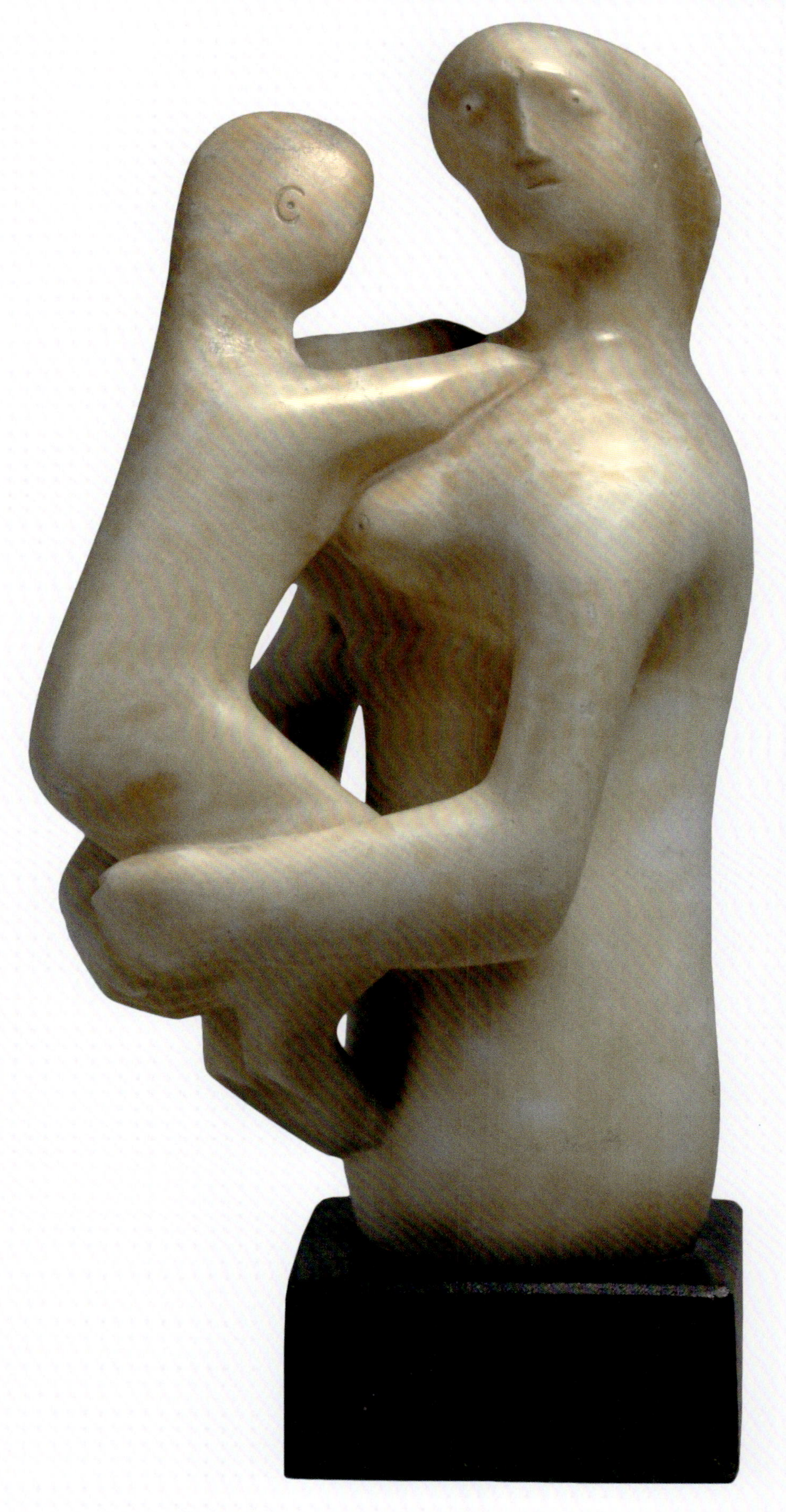

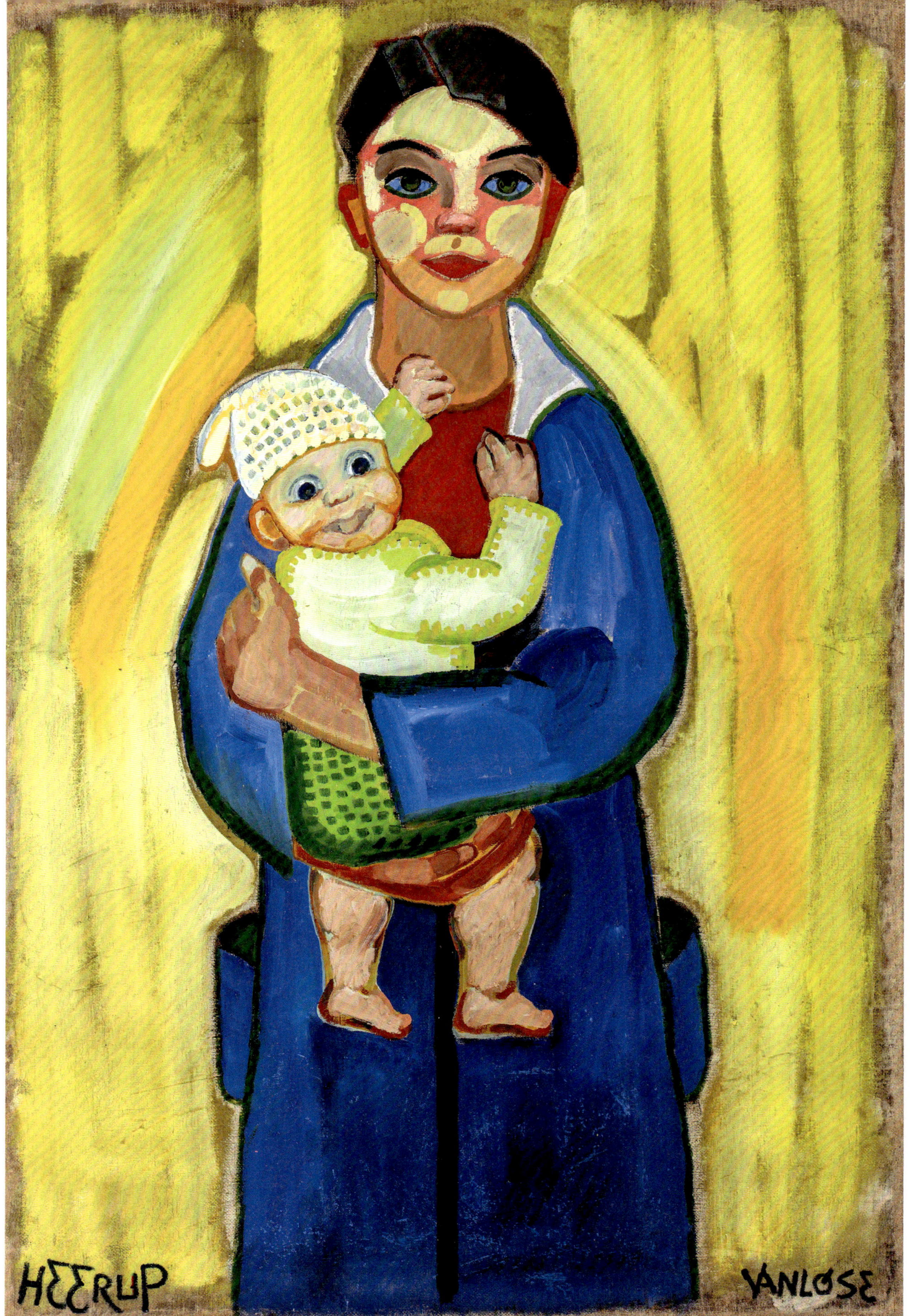
HEERUP
VANLØSE

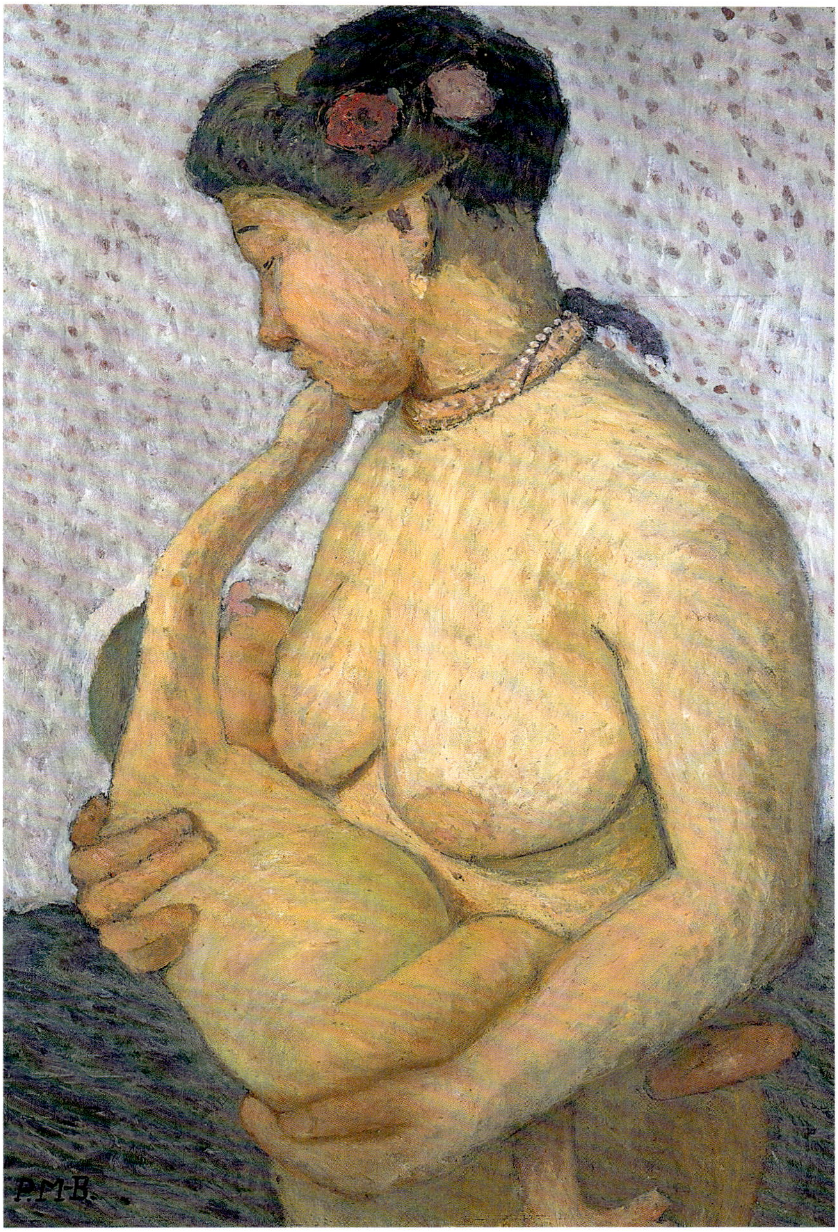

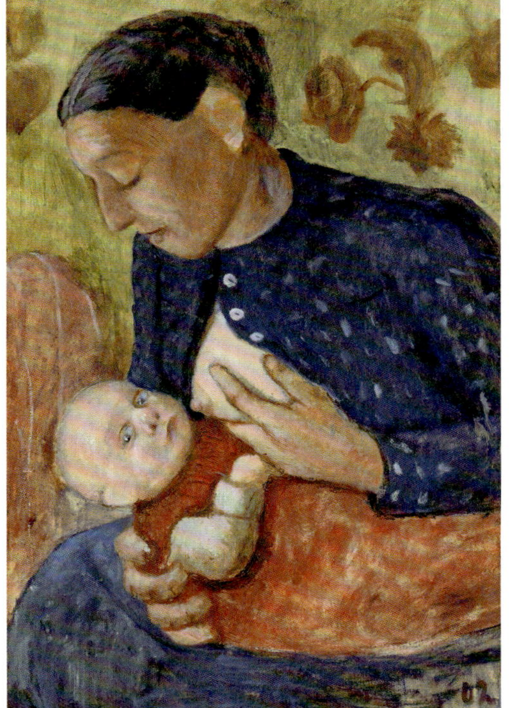

cat. 66
Paula Modersohn-Becker: *Kind an der Brust, Halbakt*, 1906
Mother Nursing Her Baby, Nude

cat. 67
Paula Modersohn-Becker: *Stillende Mutter*, 1902
Nursing Mother

Left page: cat. 28
Henry Heerup: *Vanløse-madonna*, 1934
Madonna of Vanløse

Inventing the Renaissance Madonna

By Neville Rowley

Neville Rowley is curator for Early Italian Art, Gemäldegalerie and Bode-Museum, Staatliche Museen zu Berlin and holds a Ph.D. in History of Art from Sorbonne University.

"… A soft smile brightened her lips, and her face, moved by the expectation of a pleasure, shone like that of an Italian Madonna": those are the words in which the French writer Honoré de Balzac described one of the main characters of his novel *The Search for the Absolute*, published in 1834. At the time, an "Italian Madonna" had to possess an irresistible sensual appeal, a stereotype still valid today: almost every Italian actress has to be compared to a Madonna, from Sophia Loren to Monica Bellucci. However, not every representation of the Virgin with her Child made in Italy since the Middle Ages has shown a charming face full of promise, far from it; it was only at the end of the 15th century that such a tradition was established. This article proposes to go through the genesis of this iconography, taking as examples works in two museums particularly rich in this type of production, the Gemäldegalerie and the Bode-Museum, both located in Berlin – which are simply the workplaces of the author of these lines.

The history of art as we know it was invented in the middle of the 16th century by a Tuscan artist, Giorgio Vasari, who placed his adopted city, Florence, at the center of all possible innovations. This point of view has since been widely nuanced: in fact, if our story begins in Florence at the end of the 13th century, it is not to boast the originality of the city, it is on the contrary the most perfect cultural submission to Byzantium, then capital of the Eastern Roman Empire. Let us look at the *Enthroned Madonna and Child* by the Master of the Maddalena: everything breathes monumentality in this large panel. The Virgin Mary is so gigantic that she dwarves the two angels who present her to the viewer at the very top of the painting. As the Mother of Jesus Christ, the Virgin Mary is revered by Christians as a sort of tabernacle who hosted the Messiah. This is why she sits here on a throne, privilege of kings and queens, which further accentuates her majesty. In medieval symbolism, the Virgin is often referred to as *Sedes Sapientiae*, a "throne of wisdom". No doubt she knows everything, but she seems to have forgotten that she carries Jesus Christ, the Son of God; in any case, she does not look at him. Her hands look more like pincers or claws: solemnity has killed tenderness. Moreover, the blessing Child already looks like an adult. As for the blinding presence of gold, on the background of the painting but also on the halos of the figures and on Mary's clothing, it contributes to flatten a representation little interested in the effect of relief: under her magnificent robe which seems as if spread out on the panel, Mary has the anatomy of a mannequin, and not that of a woman of flesh and bones. Admittedly, she is not yet the sensual Madonna by whom Balzac will be seduced; if her glance pierces us, it is more with fear than with admiration.

At the time when the Master of the Maddalena painted his *Virgin and Child*, a figurative revolution was taking place in Italy. It was the work of the Florentine painter Giotto (which did not displease Giorgio Vasari). The epicenter of this earthquake was not in Florence, however, but in Umbria – and more specifically on the walls of the Basilica of St. Francis in Assisi. St. Francis had invited his faithful to open their eyes to the beauty of the surrounding nature; he even spoke to the birds! On the walls of the Assisi Basilica, Giotto therefore represents a world full of life and humanity. His Madonnas are no longer frightening figures, but incarnations of protective motherhood: here is one in a panel by one of Giotto's best pupils, the Florentine Maso di Banco. Mary rises from her throne without losing her monumentality; the golden background inherited from Byzantium is still there, too. However, everything has changed: the mother has realized that she is carrying her Child; all her attention is turned towards the latter, and in particular the natural gesture

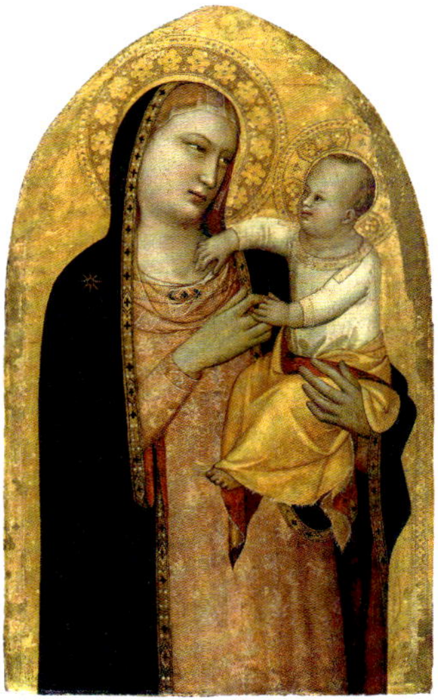

Maso di Banco:
Virgin and Child, c. 1335
Tempera and gold on panel,
81.5 × 49.2 cm
Staatliche Museen zu Berlin,
Gemäldegalerie

Master of the Maddalena:
Enthroned Virgin and Child with Angels, 1280s
Tempera and gold on panel, 167.5 × 98.4 cm
Staatliche Museen zu Berlin, Gemäldegalerie

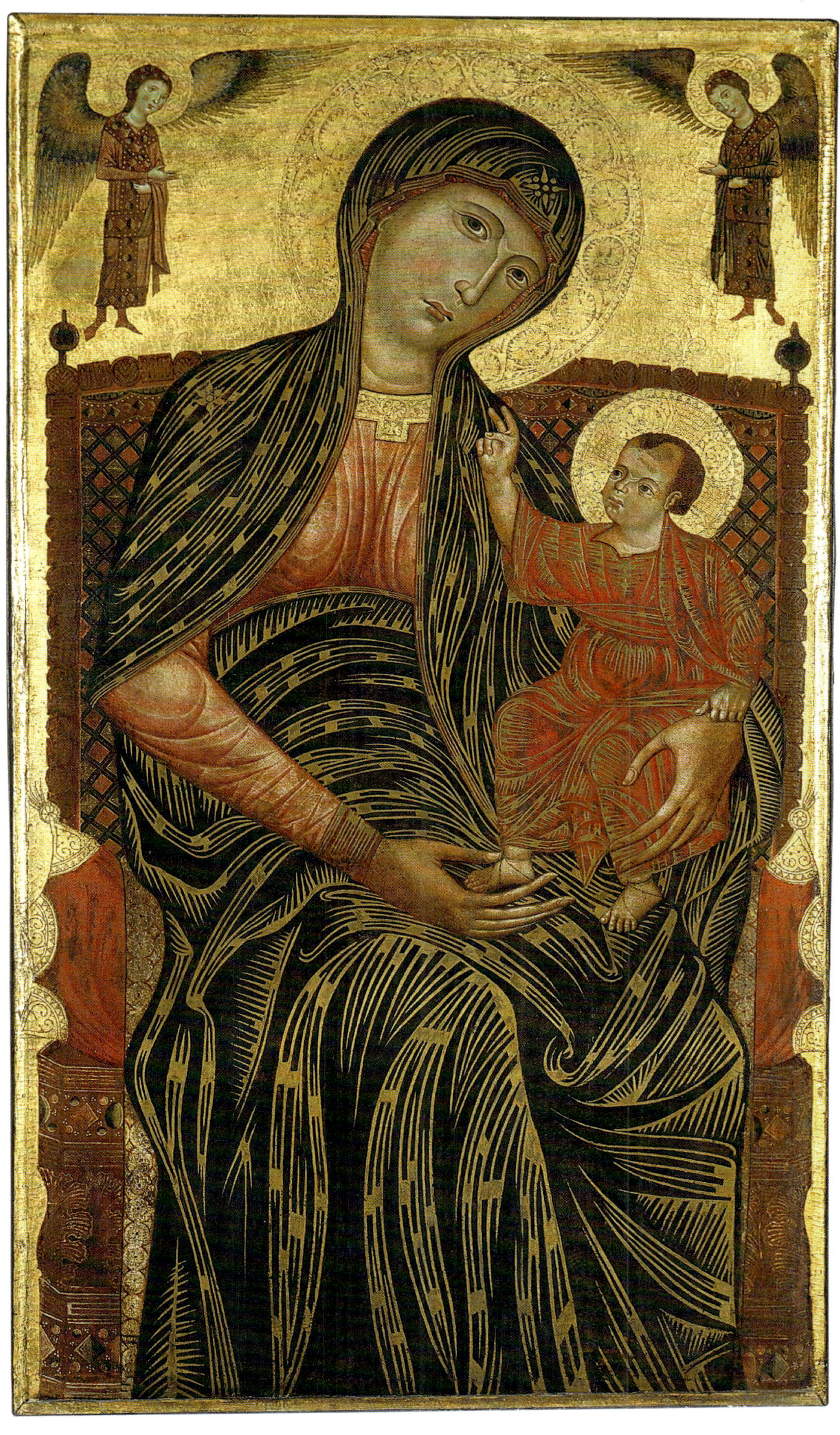

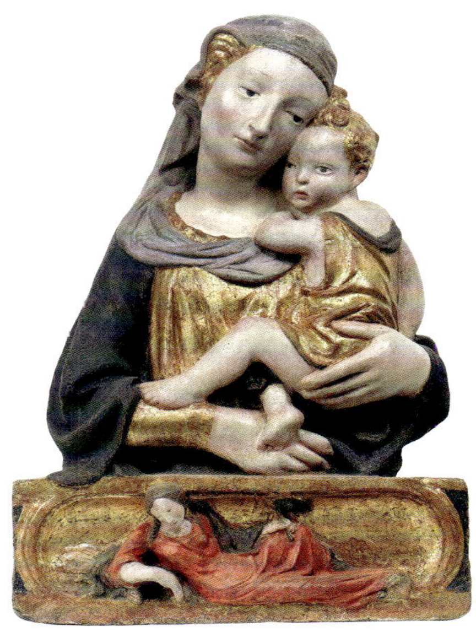

After Lorenzo Ghiberti: *Virgin and Child*, 1430s
Stucco, 80 × 56.5 × 21 cm
Staatliche Museen zu Berlin, Skulpturensammlung und Museum für Byzantinische Kunst (exhibited at the Bode-Museum)

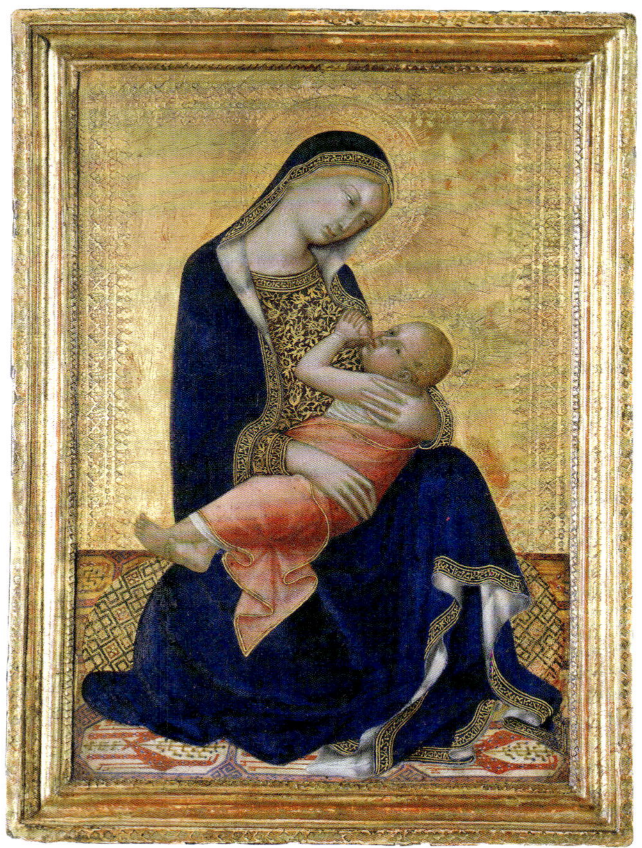

Lippo Memmi: *Virgin of Humility*, c. 1345
Tempera and gold on panel, 32.2 × 23.4 cm
Staatliche Museen zu Berlin, Gemäldegalerie

of letting the Child play with her fingers – we are far from the claws of the Byzantine Madonna, clutching the feet of her offspring. The Child, for his part, no longer makes a too serious gesture of blessing, but leans more prosaically on his mother's neck so as not to fall. All is true in this painting. It lacks, however, a sensual dimension: the Madonna has an androgynous face, while her body disappears entirely under her garment.

Shortly afterwards, an intimate part of Mary's body is surprisingly shown. We are no longer in Florence, but in Siena, in a tiny work by Lippo Memmi. The Virgin has sat back down – except that this time it is no longer on an intimidating throne, but on a cushion lying on the ground; a new iconography invented around 1340 by Lippo Memmi's brother-in-law, Simone Martini. The ambition of this imagery is clear: to show the humility of the Virgin. Mary is erected as a model not only for having given birth to Christ, but also for her submission to God's will: no doubt that the patriarchy of the time was delighted with such a compelling message. From this ideology, Lippo Memmi brings out realism by allowing himself to show Mary breastfeeding her Child. At a time when the female body is usually hidden from view, such an innovation (also due to Simone Martini) is not self-evident – besides, the viewer is only invited to see a tiny part of the nursing breast, hidden under the hand of Jesus. The Madonna was intended to gather the compassion of mothers, not the attraction of fathers; we are still far from Balzac's words.

Throughout the 14th century, every home had to have its painted Madonna hanging on the wall of the marital bedroom. Except that the objects were not always easy to get: gold was very expensive, and painters had many other public tasks to do, and the deadlines were often getting longer. At the beginning of the 15th century, the Florentine goldsmith Lorenzo Ghiberti got around this difficulty by inventing reproducible sculpted Madonnas: the version in the Bode-Museum is thus one of the dozens of known examples of a composition reproduced mechanically by means of molds, both in terracotta and in stucco. Compared to the other paintings, the protagonists are this time seen in three dimensions, which naturally makes them appear more alive: the Virgin is tenderly leaning her head over that of her Son, who is shown in a dynamic pose. Symbolism, however, is not far away: the proximity between the two heads is inherited from the Byzantine type of "Madonnas of Tenderness" (or *Glykophilousa*), while showing the sole of the Child's foot also comes from the same tradition. On the basis of Ghiberti's relief, an elongated figure makes the

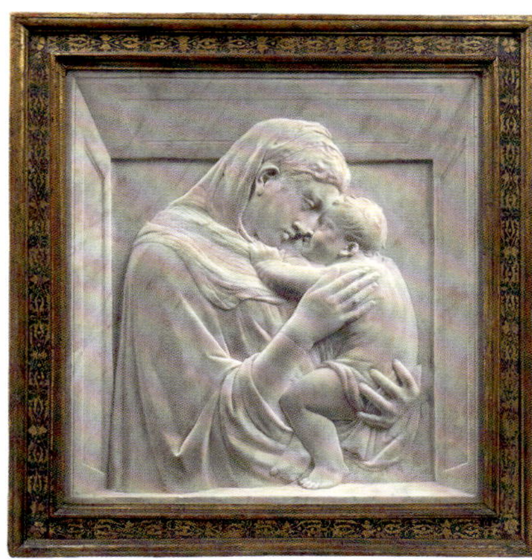

Donatello: *Virgin and Child*, called *the Pazzi Madonna*, c. 1422
Marble, 74.5 × 73 × 6.5 cm
Staatliche Museen zu Berlin, Skulpturensammlung und Museum für Byzantinische Kunst (exhibited at the Bode-Museum)

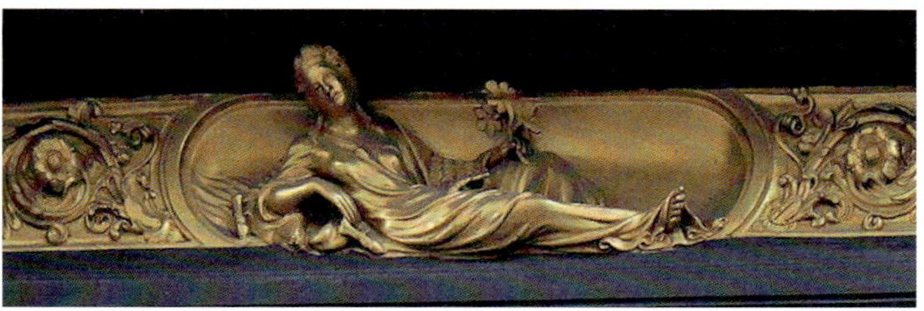

Lorenzo Ghiberti: *Eve* (detail of *the Gates of Paradise*), 1425-1452
Gilded bronze
Florence, Museo dell'Opera del Duomo

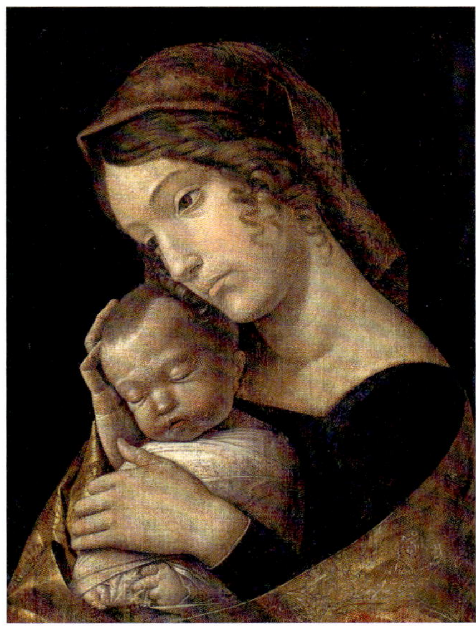

Andrea Mantegna: *Virgin and Child*, called *the James Simon Madonna*, c. 1455
Glue size on canvas, 48.4 × 32.2 cm
Staatliche Museen zu Berlin, Gemäldegalerie (exhibited at the Bode-Museum)

allegory more complex: a comparison with the artist's masterpiece, the Gates of Paradise produced for the Baptistery of Florence, tells us that this is the first woman, Eve. What is she doing here? Nothing other than highlighting Mary's role: Eve is the first woman of the Old Testament, the one who sinned by giving Adam the fruit of the forbidden tree; Mary is the first woman – and the only one – who did not sin. She is the exact opposite of Eve. At the time, the ritual prayer to the Virgin (which begins with "Hail Mary", *Ave Maria*) was explicitly interpreted in this sense: in Latin, "AVE" is the palindrome of "EVA".

Ghiberti may have been one of the greatest sculptors of Quattrocento Florence, but his glory was soon to be overshadowed by one of his pupils: Donatello. Here he is, in a youthful work that is undoubtedly the masterpiece of the Bode-Museum, the *Pazzi Madonna*. This time, there is no trace of medieval gold: for the first time since antiquity, marble is left monochrome, following the example of the Roman statues that were then fervently excavated and whose original color had been lost with time and oblivion. Donatello wants at all costs to bring the viewer into the scene he represents: the Virgin and the Child are seen in a niche that follows the new principles of mathematical perspective – as if they were both in a kind of tabernacle. Certain codes persist all the same, as the sole of Christ's foot is left visible, and the Virgin's head still lays over that of her Son. Beyond tenderness, however, there is violence in this face-to-face encounter. For the spectator of the time, this violence was quite clear to decipher: the Virgin knows that her Son was born to redeem mankind from sin and that he will have to die too soon to fulfill his destiny. Here the Madonna acquires one of the key characteristics on which her power of seduction will be based: melancholy.

Andrea Mantegna directly translated into painting the model of Donatello, who was one of his masters in Padua. This time the Child is depicted sleeping, in an incredibly realistic way, reinforced by the fact that he is dressed in swaddling clothes, in which babies were then held in the (vain) hope of improving their growth. It is difficult not to be sensitive to the prophetic dimension of such a scene: sleep prefigures Christ's death, while the swaddling clothes announce the shroud that will wrap the lifeless body of Jesus in the tomb. Mary, for her part, has the sad eyes of one who already knows all this. Locks of curly hair escape from her headdress – she has finally become seductive.

It is time to make way for the painter who will crystallize the image of the Italian Madonna: Sandro Botticelli. His *Virgin and Child with Angels* (p. 55)

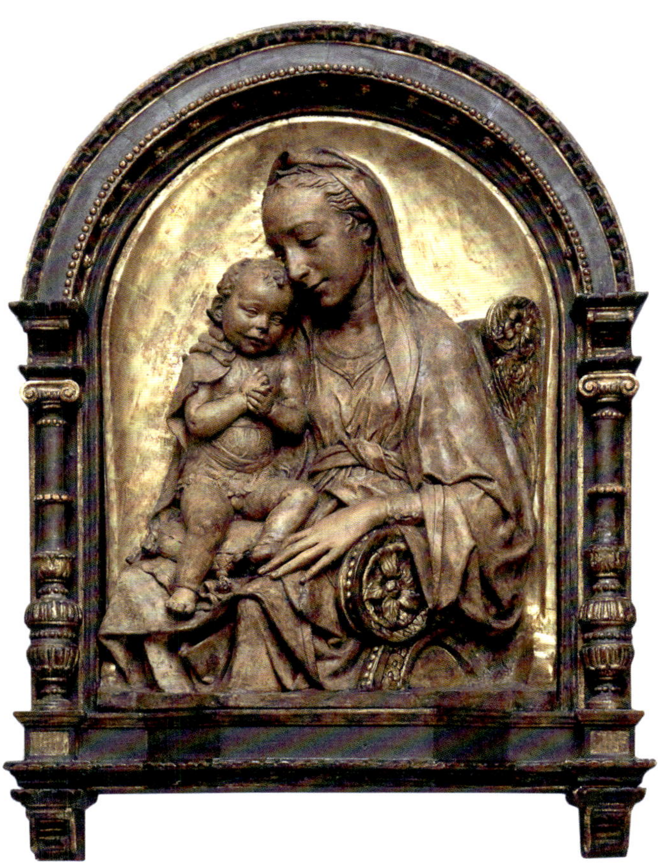

Circle of Leonardo da Vinci: *Virgin and Child*, c. 1480
Terracotta, 110 × 84 × 23 cm
Staatliche Museen zu Berlin, Skulpturensammlung und Museum für Byzantinische Kunst (exhibited at the Bode-Museum)

synthesizes all past experiences, his Madonna hesitating between the real and the symbolic. The realistic aspect of the figures cannot hide the fact that they are shown in an unreachable Paradise, where the hands of God the Father can come from the sky to crown Mary's head, together with a most Byzantine shower of gold. This gold had a symbolic as well as a mercantile function, since its brilliance was appreciated as much as its value. This aspect is also central to the understanding of why the blue color was so often used to represent the Virgin's mantle, as it was obtained from lapis lazuli, a semi-precious stone imported from present-day Afghanistan at an even higher price than gold. In Botticelli's painting, Jesus has turned towards us as if to make us accomplices in his gesture: he presses on one of his mother's breasts to make the milk come out in golden spurts (one must be very close to see such a detail!). The Virgin Mary is the chastest possible person; for this reason, she can nourish all fantasies: her empty gaze becomes an integral part of her beauty. Writers of all stripes will no longer fail to fall in love with Botticelli's Madonnas: in Marcel Proust's *In Search of Lost Time*, one of the characters will conceive a lifelong passion for a woman only because her face resembled one of Botticelli's virgins.

One last thing is missing, though: the "soft smile" described by Balzac. It is certainly not to be found in Botticelli's work – but where? Madonnas are sad, we have seen, they do not usually smile. More than any other, an artist from the same generation as Botticelli was fascinated by the representation of the smile: Leonardo da Vinci. One thinks of the *Mona Lisa*, of course – but she is not a Madonna. However, a number of *Virgin and Child* paintings by the artist exhibit this smile, sometimes frank, sometimes ineffable. Recently, a terracotta showing the seated Virgin smiling at her Child has been convincingly attributed to Leonardo; this work is in the Victoria and Albert Museum in London, and is closely linked with another terracotta *Madonna* in the Bode-Museum. The work contains elements already encountered, such as the throne and the golden background. However, Christ is much more undressed than usual: the lower part of His body is naked, including His genitals, which is a means of unambiguously showing His humanity (Hans Memling will be even more radical in that respect). Jesus is therefore cold and rubs His hands; His mother covers His shoulders with her coat. A soft smile brightens her lips, and her face seems moved by the expectation of a pleasure: we have joined Balzac. The myth has been cast. It remains to be seen who is the author of this sublime Berlin terracotta. What if it was Leonardo himself?

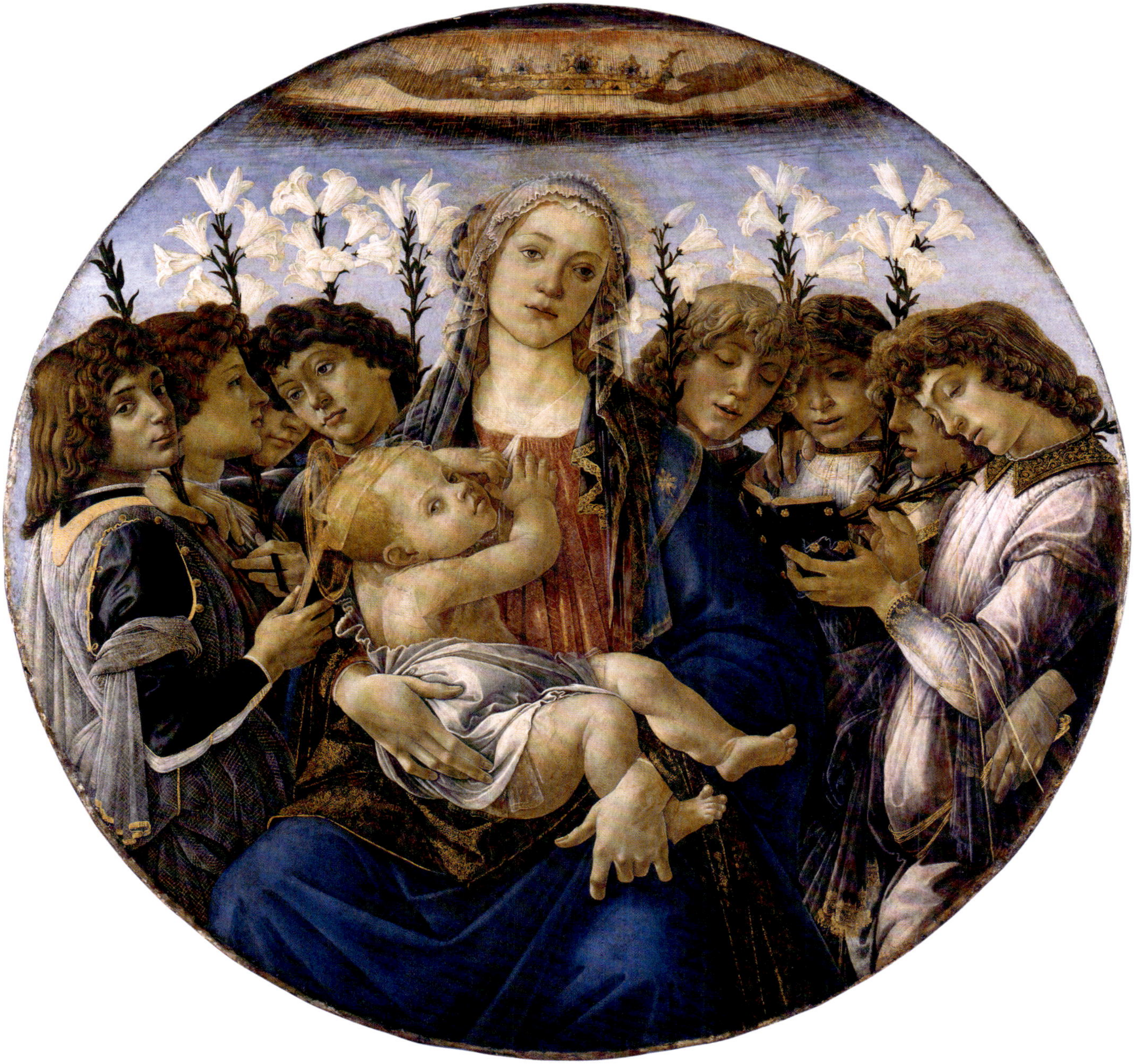

Sandro Botticelli: *Virgin and Child with Angels*,
called *the Raczynski Tondo*, 1477
Tempera and gold on panel, diam: 136.5 cm
Staatliche Museen zu Berlin, Gemäldegalerie

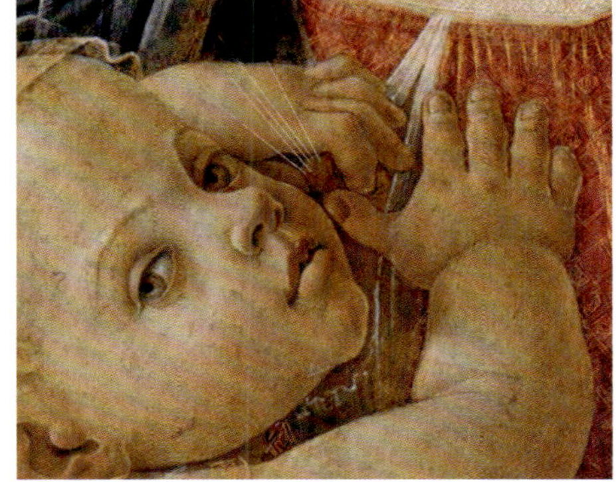

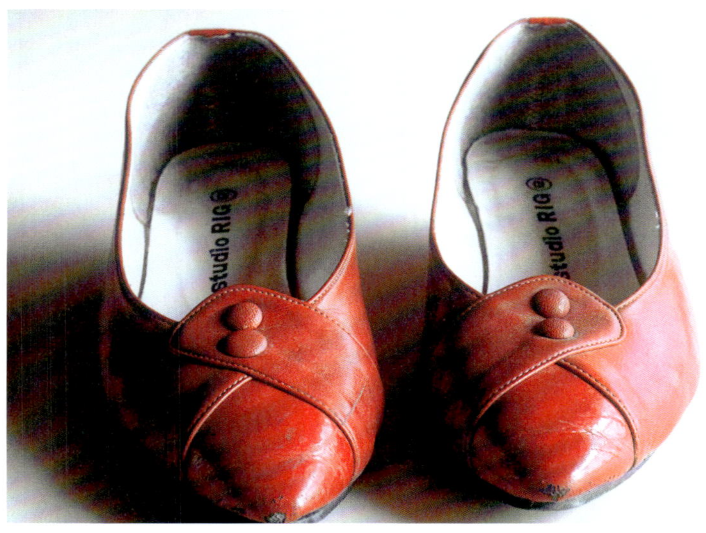

cat. 36
Miyako Ishiuchi: *Mother's #14*, 2001/2004

At the top right: cat. 43
Miyako Ishiuchi: *Mother's #57*, 2004/2005

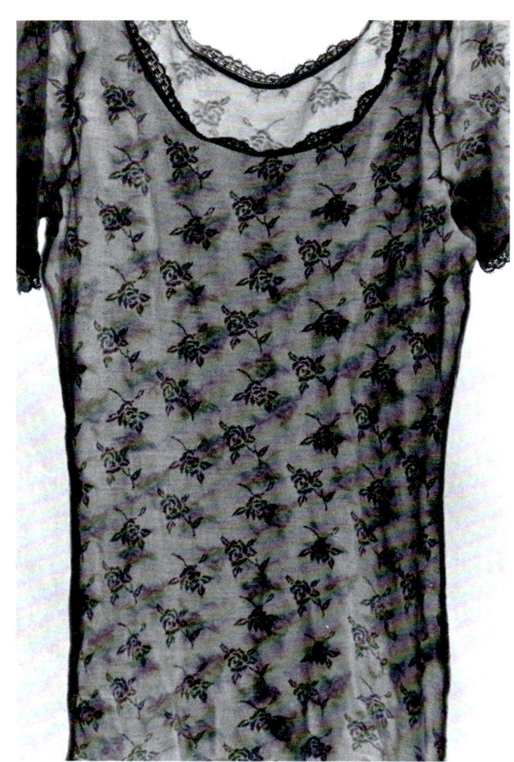

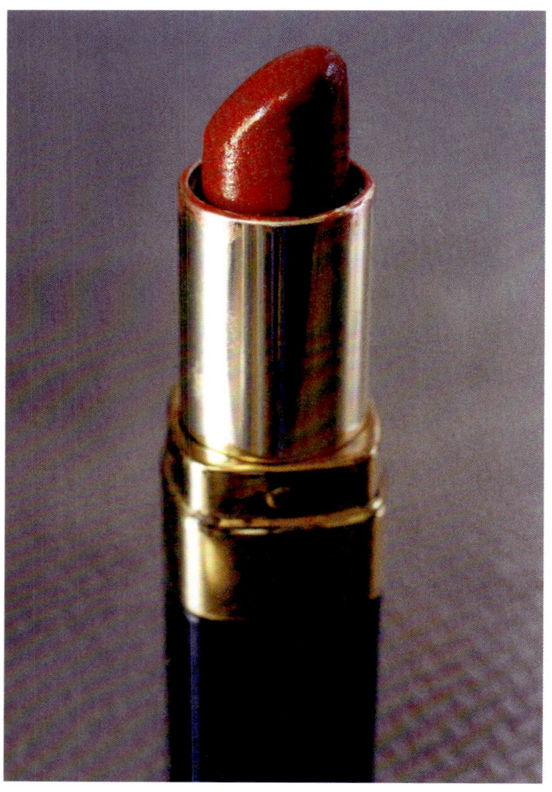

cat. 39
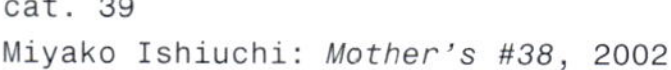
Miyako Ishiuchi: *Mother's #38*, 2002

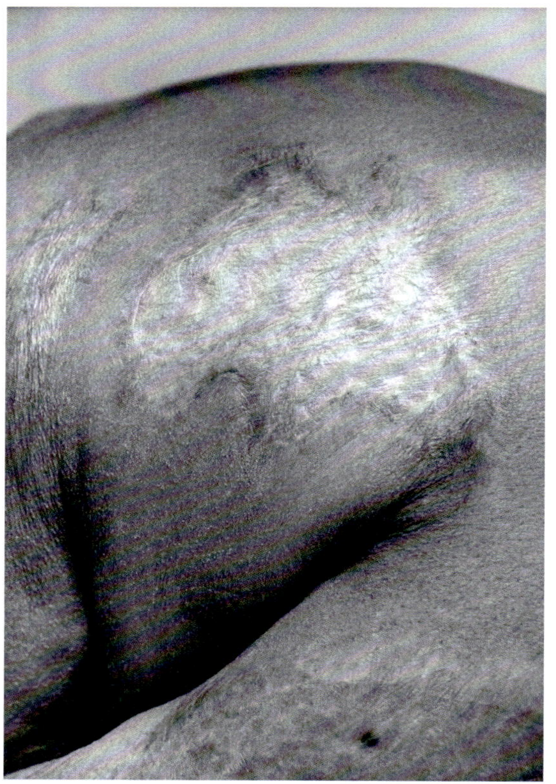

cat. 45
Miyako Ishiuchi: *Mother's 25 Mar 1916 #66*, 2000

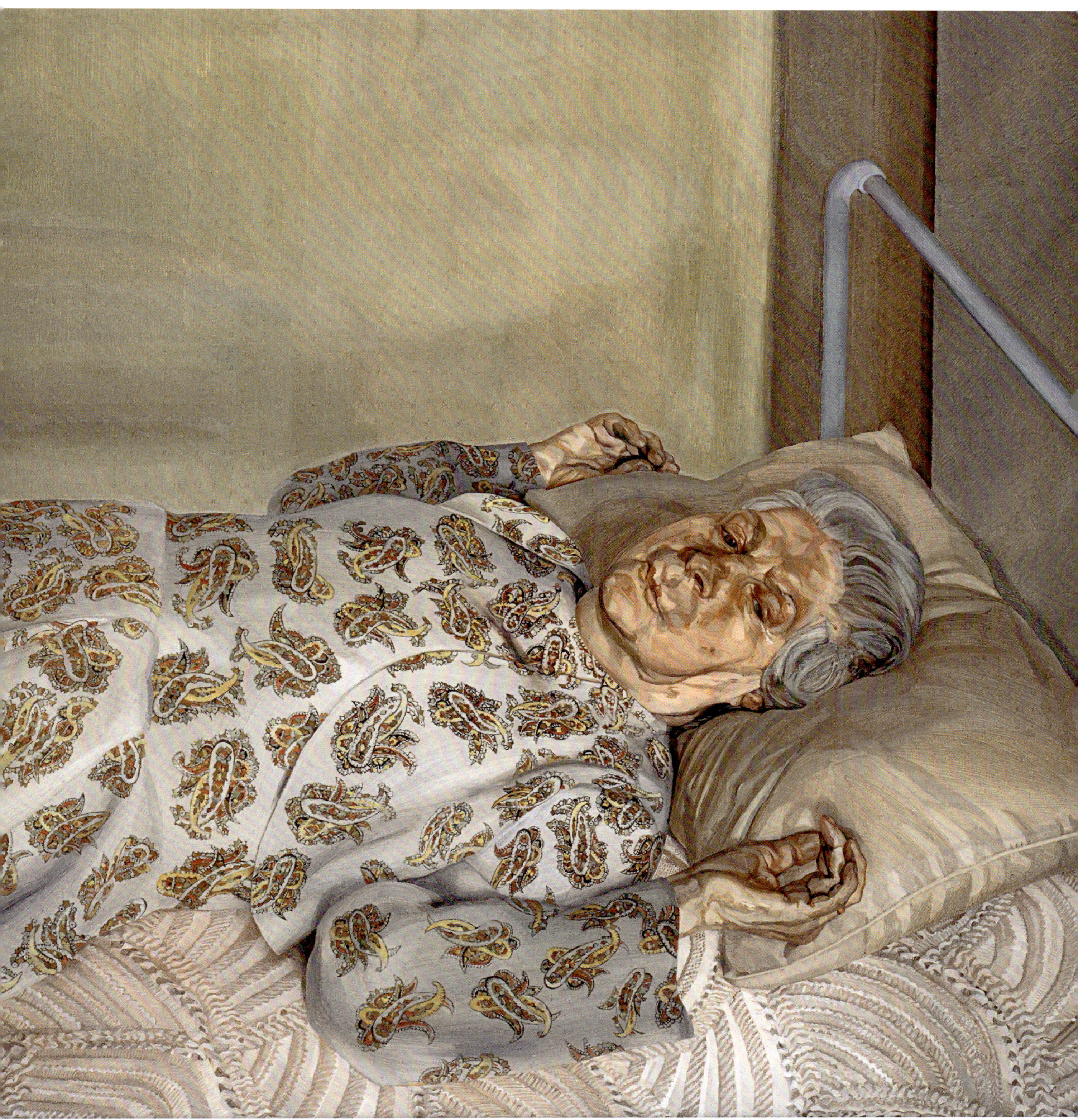

cat. 22
Lucian Freud: *The Painter's Mother, Resting I*, 1976

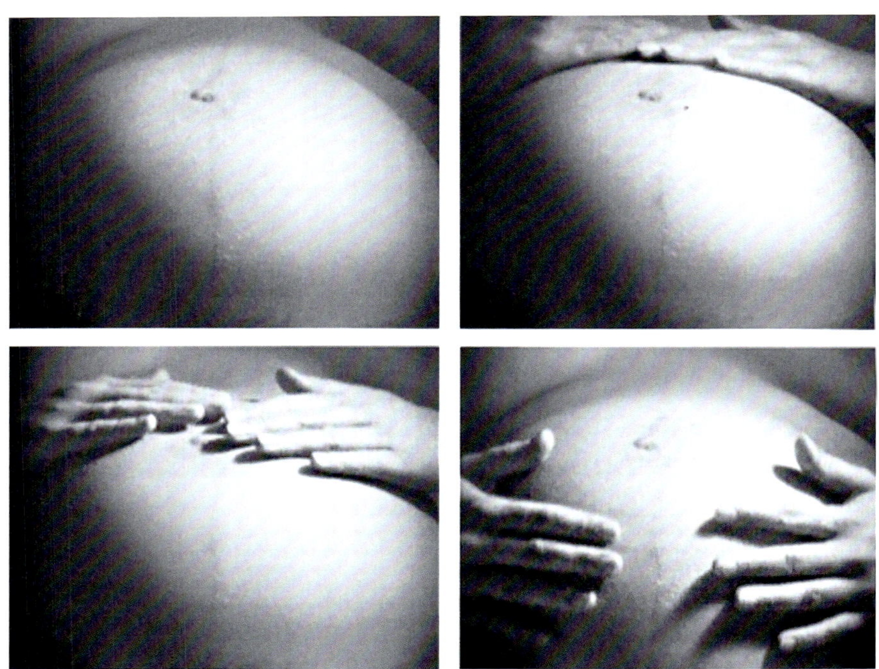

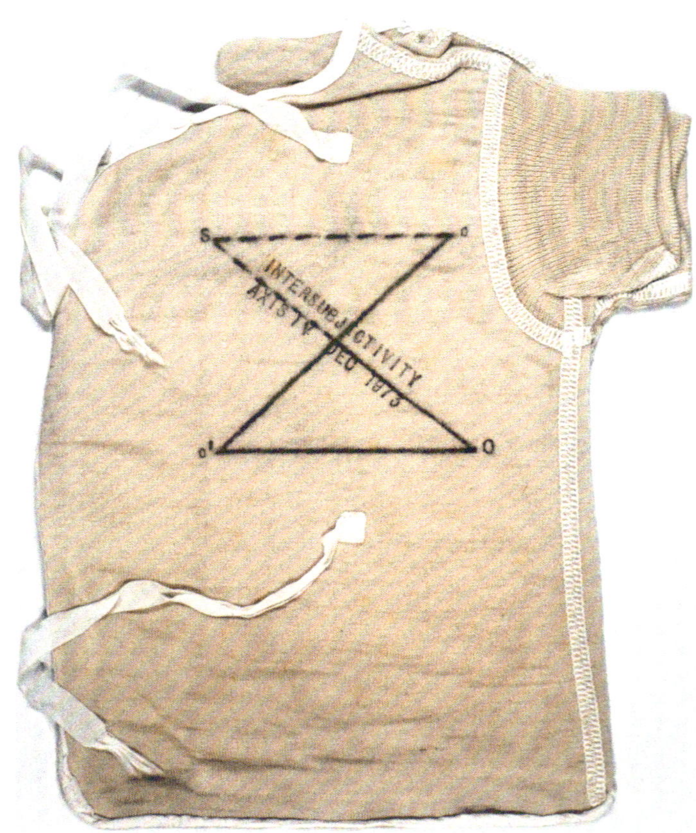

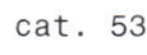
cat. 53
Mary Kelly: *Antepartum*, 1973

cat. 51
Mary Kelly: *Post-Partum Document: Introduction*, 1973

Right page: cat. 52
Mary Kelly: *Post-Partum Document: Documentation IV*, 1976

REF. 1-8T

DOCUMENTATION IV
TRANSITIONAL OBJECTS,
DIARY AND DIAGRAM

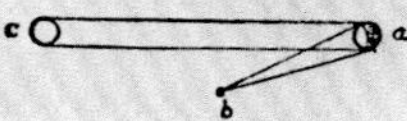

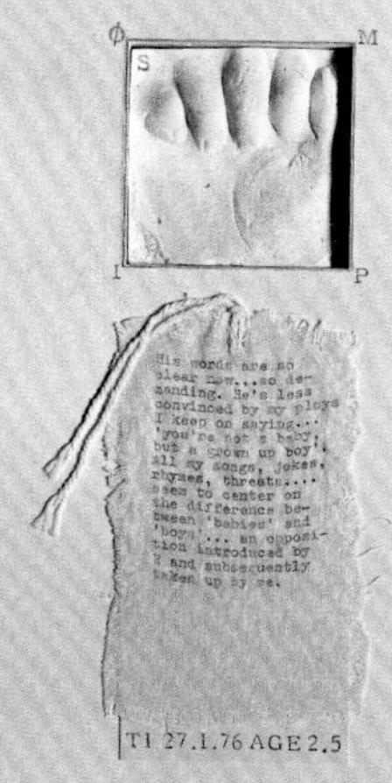

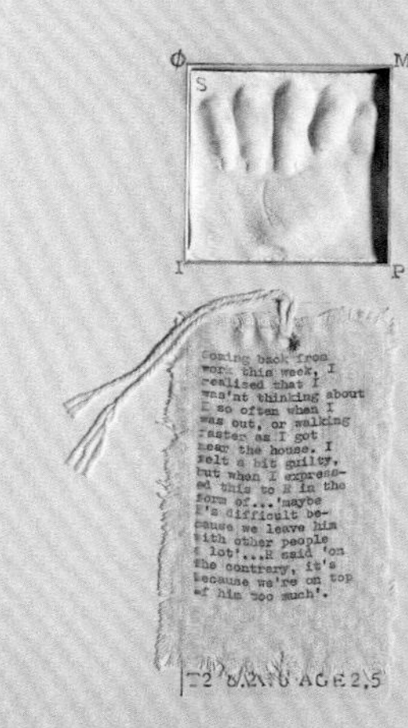

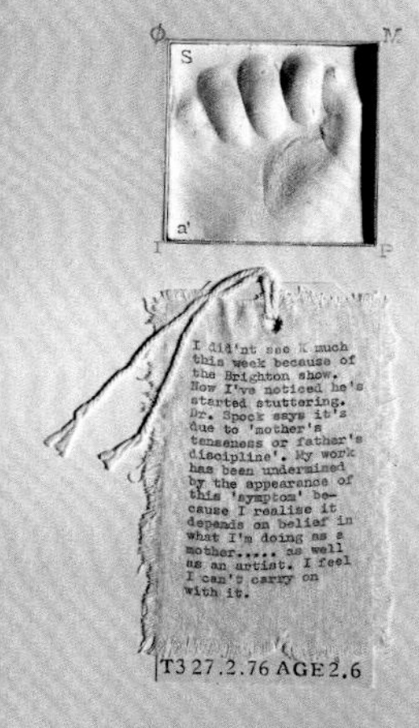

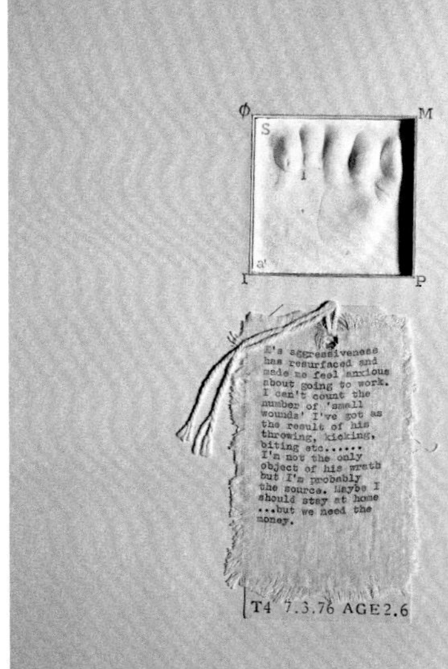

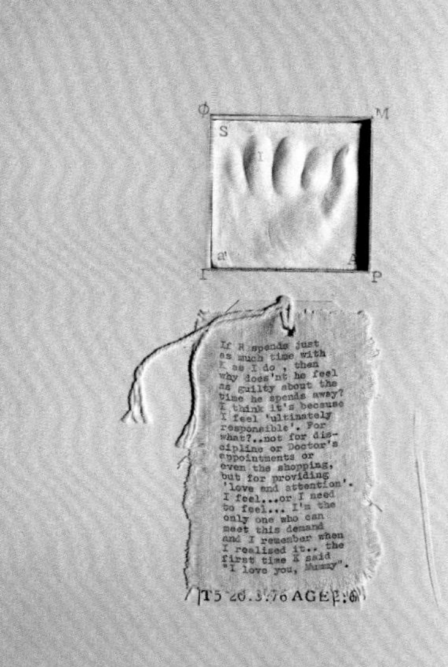

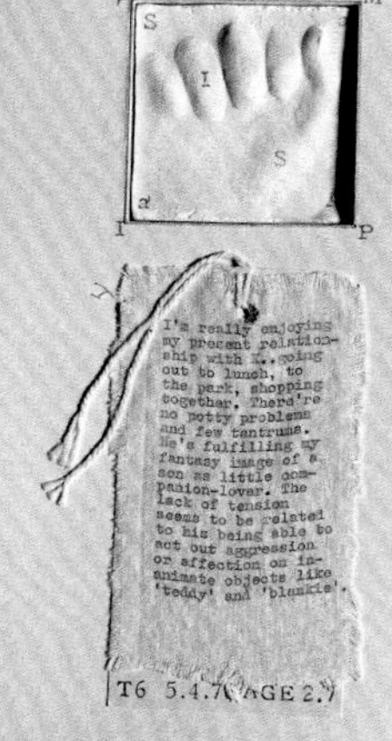

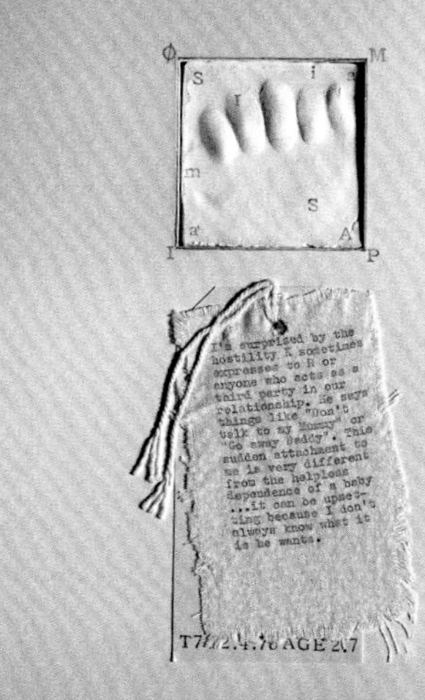

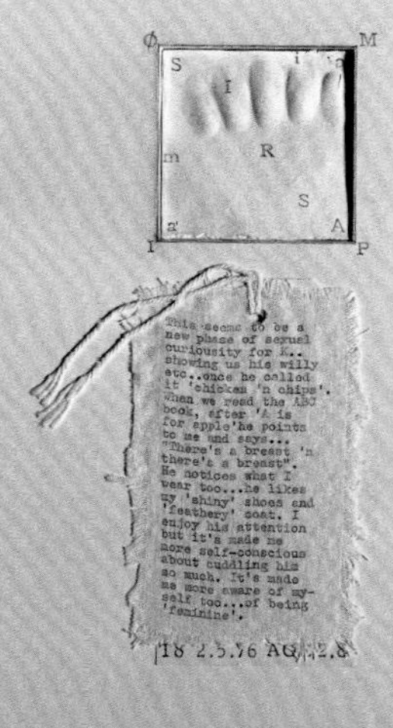

cat. 46
Chantal Joffe: *Self-portrait Combing Esme's Hair*, 2009

cat. 47
Chantal Joffe: *Self-portrait with Esme at Bedtime*, 2018

Right: cat. 48
Chantal Joffe: *Me and Esme in the Garden*, 2020

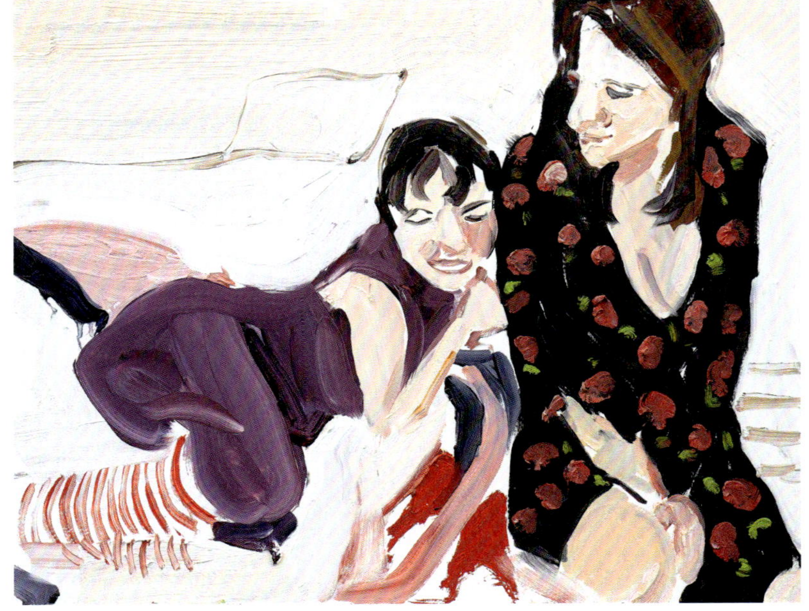

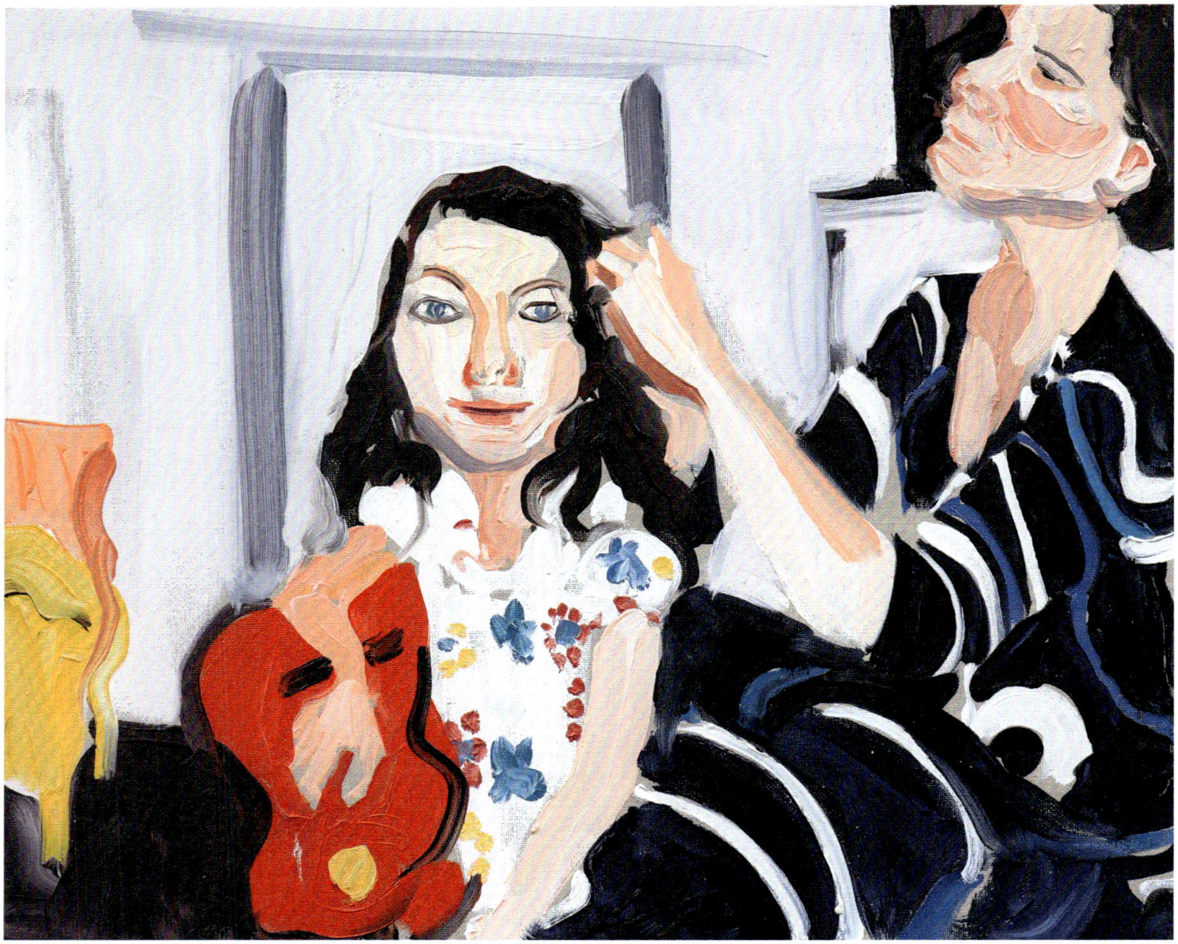

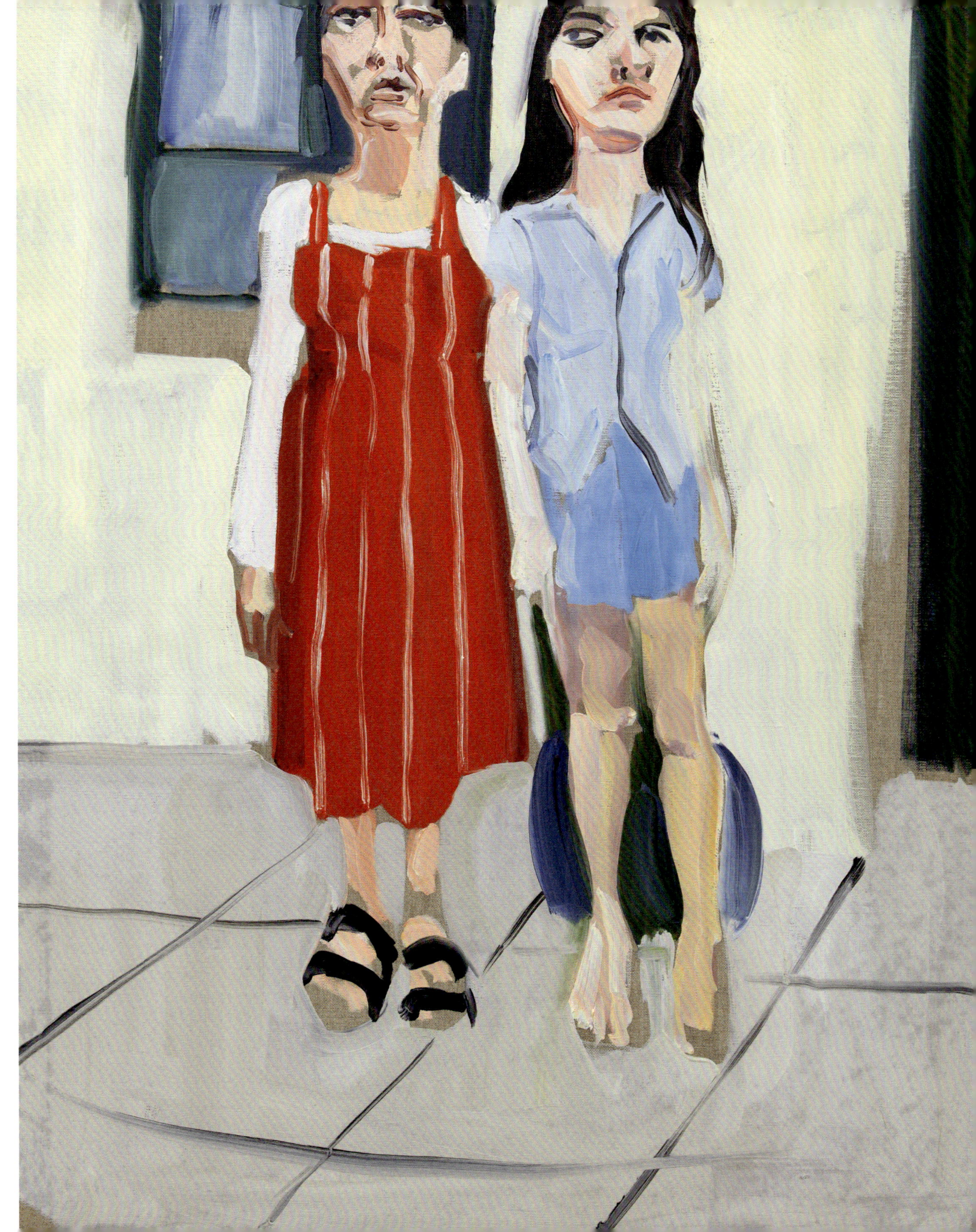

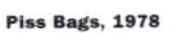

Piss Bags, 1978

Locked in the van while their mothers continued their affair, the boys were forced to piss into their chip bags.

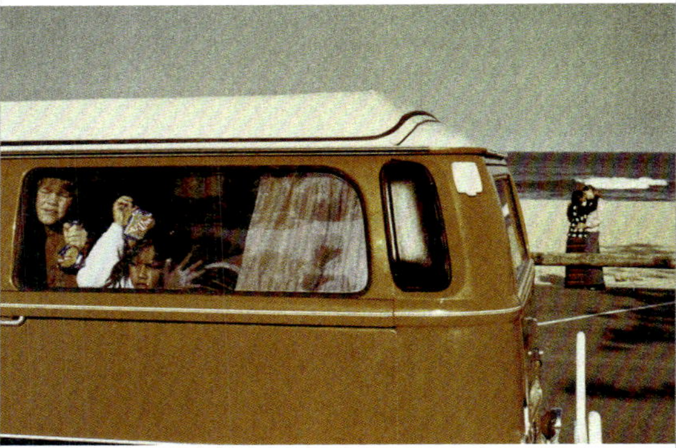

Tracey Moffatt

Homemade Hand-knit, 1958

He knew his team mates were chuckling over his mother's hand-knitted rugby uniform.

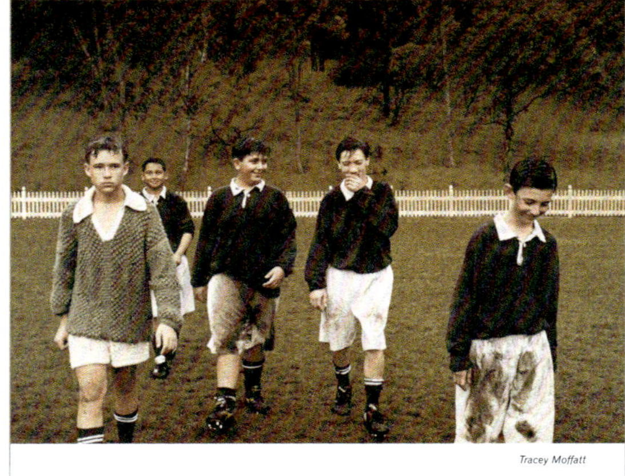

Tracey Moffatt

Mother's Reply, 1976

On the night of her first school dance, she asked her mother what she thought. She replied *"you don't dress a pig up unless ya gonna eat it."*

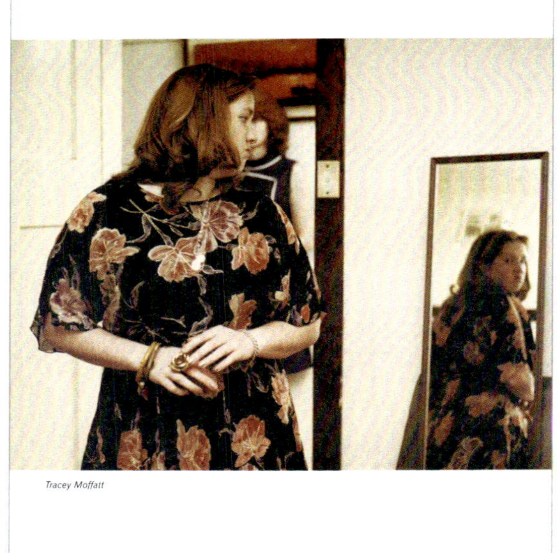

Tracey Moffatt

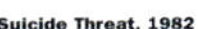

Suicide Threat, 1982

She was forty-five, single and pregnant for the first time. When her mother found out, she said *"If I wasn't Catholic I'd commit suicide."*

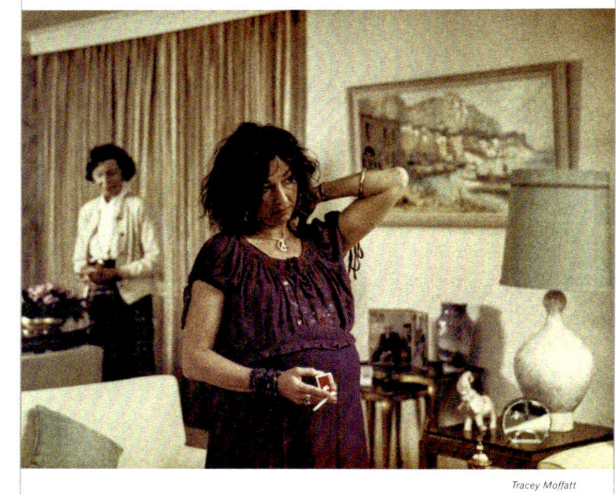

Tracey Moffatt

cat. 71
Tracey Moffatt: *Scarred for Life II: Piss Bags 1978*, 1999

cat. 70
Tracey Moffatt: *Scarreo for Life II: Mother's Reply 1976*, 1999

cat. 68
Tracey Moffatt: *Scarred for Life II: Homemade Hand Knit 1958*, 1999

cat. 73
Tracey Moffatt: *Scarred for Life II: Suicide Threat 1982*, 1999

Right: cat. 6
Candice Breitz: *MOTHER*, 2005

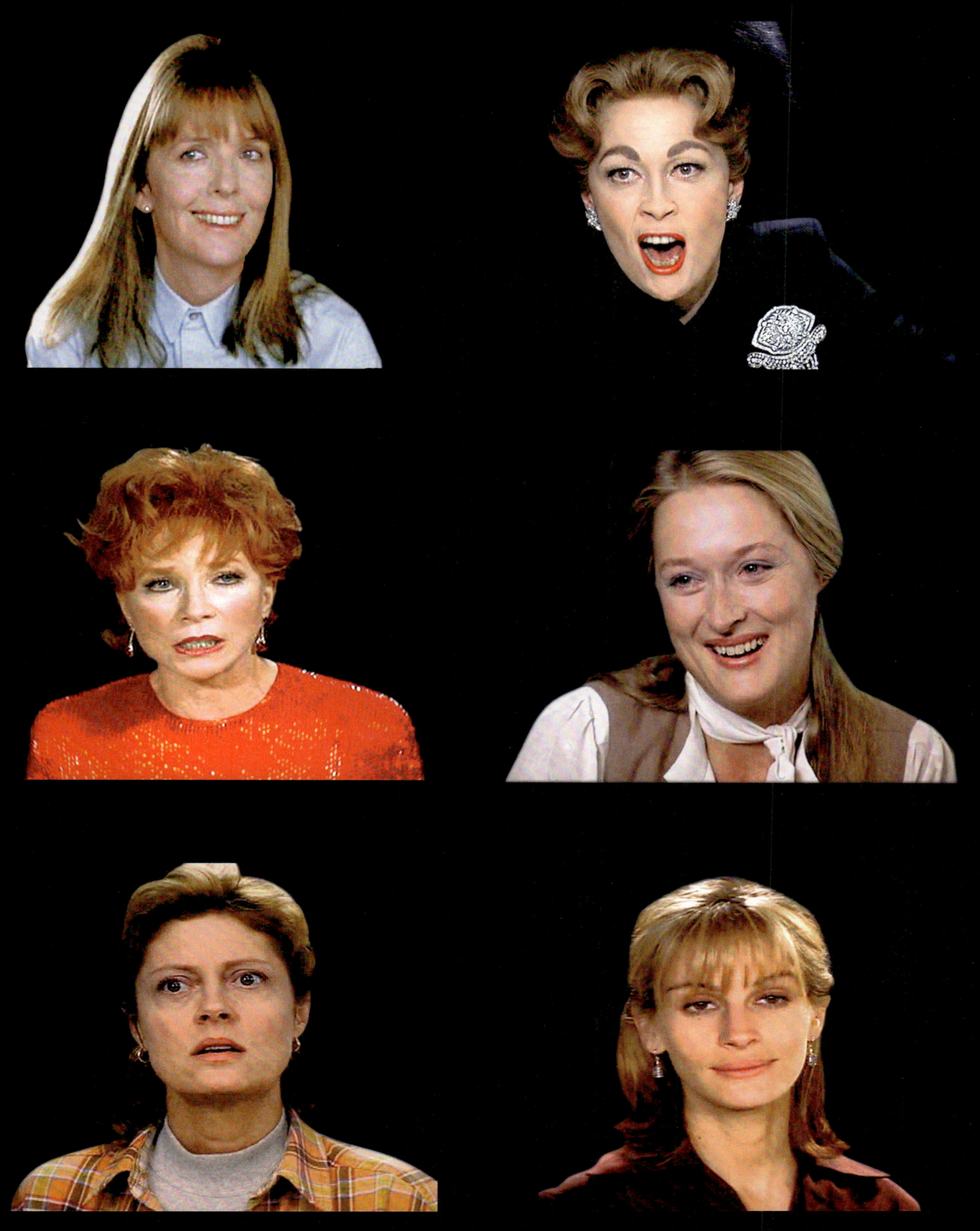

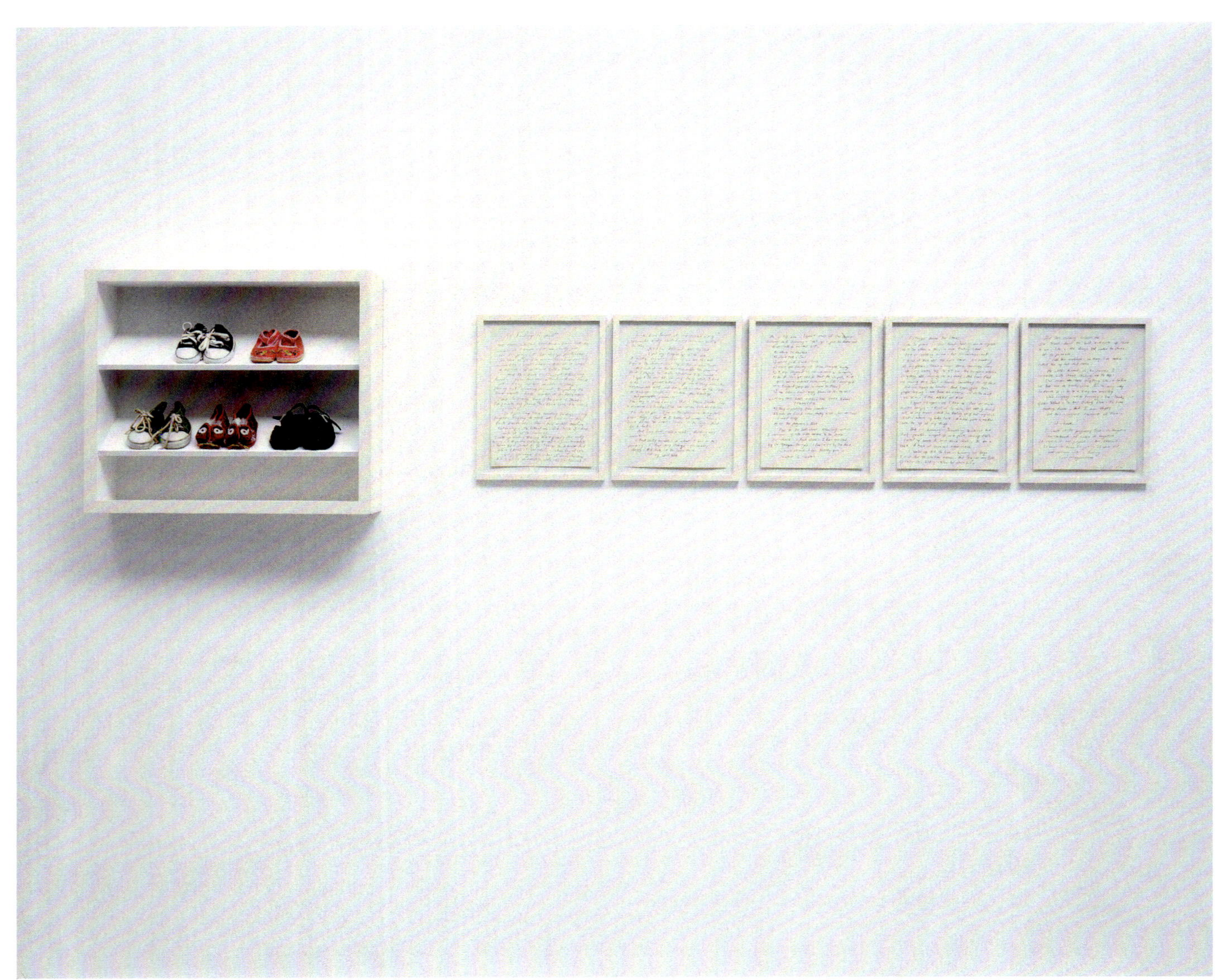

cat. 19
Tracey Emin: *Feeling Pregnant II*, 1999-2002

Marcel Proust: *In Search of Lost Time. Swann's Way* (1913)

I never took my eyes off my mother. I knew that when they were at table I should not be permitted to stay there for the whole of dinner-time, and that Mamma, for fear of annoying my father, would not allow me to kiss her several times in public, as I would have done in my room. And so I promised myself that in the dining-room, as they began to eat and drink and as I felt the hour approach, I would put beforehand into this kiss, which was bound to be so brief and furtive, everything that my own efforts could muster, would carefully choose in advance the exact spot on her cheek where I would imprint it, and would so prepare my thoughts as to be able, thanks to these mental preliminaries, to consecrate the whole of the minute Mamma would grant me to the sensation of her cheek against my lips, as a painter who can have his subject for short sittings only prepares his palette, and from what he remembers and from rough notes does in advance everything which he possibly can do in the sitter's absence. But tonight, before the dinner-bell had sounded, my grandfather said with unconscious cruelty: "The little man looks tired; he'd better go up to bed. Besides, we're dining late tonight."

And my father, who was less scrupulous than my grandmother or my mother in observing the letter of a treaty, went on: "Yes; run along; off to bed."

I would have kissed Mamma then and there, but at that moment the dinner-bell rang.

"No, no, leave your mother alone. You've said good night to one another, that's enough. These exhibitions are absurd. Go on upstairs."

And so I must set forth without viaticum; must climb each step of the staircase "against my heart," as the saying is, climbing in opposition to my heart's desire, which was to return to my mother, since she had not, by kissing me, given my heart leave to accompany me. That hateful staircase, up which I always went so sadly, gave out a smell of varnish which had, as it were, absorbed and crystallised the special quality of sorrow that I felt each evening, and made it perhaps even crueller to my sensibility because, when it assumed this olfactory guise, my intellect was powerless to resist it. When we have gone to sleep with a raging toothache and are conscious of it only as of a little girl whom we attempt, time after time, to pull out of the water, or a line of Molière which we repeat incessantly to ourselves, it is a great relief to wake up, so that our intelligence can disentangle the idea of toothache from any artificial semblance of heroism or rhythmic cadence. It was the converse of this relief which I felt when my anguish at having to go up to my room invaded my consciousness in a manner infinitely more rapid, instantaneous almost, a manner at once insidious and brutal, through the inhalation – far more poisonous than moral penetration – of the smell of varnish peculiar to that staircase.

Once in my room I had to stop every loophole, to close the shutters, to dig my own grave as I turned down the bed-clothes, to wrap myself in the shroud of my nightshirt. But before burying myself in the iron bed which had been placed there because, on summer nights, I was too hot among the rep curtains of the four-poster, I was stirred to revolt, and attempted the desperate stratagem of a condemned prisoner. I wrote to my mother begging her to come upstairs for an important reason which I could not put in writing. My fear was that Françoise, my aunt's cook who used to be put in charge of me when I was at Combray, might refuse to take my note. I had a suspicion that, in her eyes, to carry a message to my mother when there was a guest would appear as flatly inconceivable as for the door-keeper of a theatre to hand a letter to an actor upon the stage. [...]

My mother did not appear, but without the slightest consideration for my self-respect (which depended upon her keeping up the fiction that she had asked me to let her know the result of my search for something or other) told Françoise to tell me, in so many words: "There is no answer" – words I have so often, since then, heard the hall-porters in grand hotels and the flunkeys in gambling- clubs and the like repeat to some poor girl who replies in bewilderment: "What! he said nothing? It's not possible. You did give him my letter, didn't you? Very well, I shall wait a little longer." And, just as she invariably protests that she does not need the extra gas-jet which the porter offers to light for her, and sits on there, hearing nothing further except an occasional remark on the weather which the porter exchanges with a bell-hop whom he will send off suddenly, when he notices the time, to put some customer's wine on the ice, so, having declined Françoise's offer to make me some tea or to stay beside me, I let her go off again to the pantry, and lay down and shut my eyes, trying not to hear the voices of my family who were drinking their coffee in the garden.

But after a few seconds I realised that, by writing that note to Mamma, by approaching – at the risk of making her angry – so near to her that I felt I could reach out and grasp the moment in which I should see her again, I had cut myself off from the possibility of going to sleep until I actually had seen her, and my heart began to beat more and more painfully as I increased my agitation by ordering myself to keep calm and to acquiesce in my ill-fortune. Then, suddenly, my anxiety subsided, a feeling of intense happiness coursed through me, as when a strong medicine begins to take effect and one's pain vanishes: I had formed a resolution to abandon all attempts to go to sleep without seeing Mamma, had made up my mind to kiss her at all costs, even though this meant the certainty of being in disgrace with her for long afterwards – when she herself came up to bed. The calm which succeeded my anguish filled me with extraordinary exhilaration, no less than my sense of expectation, my thirst for and my fear of danger. [...]

My mother opened the latticed door which led from the hall to the staircase. Presently I heard her coming upstairs to close her window. I went quietly into the passage; my heart was beating so violently that I could hardly move, but at least it was throbbing no longer with anxiety, but with terror and joy. I saw in the well of the stair a light coming upwards, from Mamma's candle. Then I saw Mamma herself and I threw myself upon her. For an instant she looked at me in astonishment, not realising what could have happened. Then her face assumed an expression of anger. She said not a single word to me; and indeed I used to go for days on end without being spoken to, for far more venial offences than this. A single word from Mamma would have been an admission that further intercourse with me was within the bounds of possibility, and that might perhaps have appeared to me more terrible still, as indicating that, with such a punishment as was in store for me, mere silence and black looks would have been puerile. A word from her then would have implied the false calm with which one addresses a servant to whom one has just decided to give notice; the kiss one bestows on a son who is being packed off to enlist, which would have been denied him if it had merely been a matter of being angry with him for a few days. But she heard my father coming from the dressing- room, where he had gone to take off his clothes, and, to avoid the scene which he would make if he saw me, she said to me in a voice half-stifled with anger: “Off you go at once. Do you want your father to see you waiting there like an idiot?” But I implored her again: “Come and say good night to me,” terrified as I saw the light from my father’s candle already creeping up the wall, but also making use of his approach as a means of blackmail, in the hope that my mother, not wishing him to find me there, as find me he must if she continued to refuse me, would give in and say: “Go back to your room. I will come.”

Too late: my father was upon us. Instinctively I murmured, though no one heard me, “I’m done for!”

I was not, however. My father used constantly to refuse to let me do things which were quite clearly allowed by the more liberal charters granted me by my mother and grandmother, because he paid no heed to “principles,” and because for him there was no such thing as the “rule of law.” For some quite irrelevant reason, or for no reason at all, he would at the last moment prevent me from taking some particular walk, one so regular, so hallowed, that to deprive me of it was a clear breach of faith; or again, as he had done this evening, long before the appointed hour he would snap out: “Run along up to bed now; no excuses!” But at the same time, because he was devoid of principles (in my grandmother’s sense), he could not, strictly speaking, be called intransigent. He looked at me for a moment with an air of surprise and annoyance, and then when Mamma had told him, not without some embarrassment, what had happened, said to her: “Go along with him, then. You said just now that you didn’t feel very sleepy, so stay in his room for a little. I don’t need anything.”

“But, my dear,” my mother answered timidly, “whether or not I feel sleepy is not the point; we mustn’t let the child get into the habit ...”

“There’s no question of getting into a habit,” said my father, with a shrug of the shoulders; “you can see quite well that the child is unhappy. After all, we aren’t gaolers. You’ll end by making him ill, and a lot of good that will do. There are two beds in his room; tell Françoise to make up the big one for you, and stay with him for the rest of the night. Anyhow, I’m off to bed; I’m not so nervy as you. Good night.” [...]

Mamma spent that night in my room: when I had just committed an offence for which I expected to be banished from the household, my parents gave me a far greater concession than I could ever have won as the reward of a good deed. Even at the moment when it manifested itself in this crowning mercy, my father’s behaviour towards me still retained that arbitrary and unwarranted quality which was so characteristic of him and which arose from the fact that his actions were generally dictated by chance expediencies rather than based on any formal plan. And perhaps even what I called his severity, when he sent me off to bed, deserved that title less than my mother’s or my grandmother’s attitude, for his nature, which in some respects differed more than theirs from my own, had probably prevented him from realising until then how wretched I was every evening, something which my mother and grandmother knew well; but they loved me enough to be unwilling to spare me that suffering, which they hoped to teach me to overcome, so as to reduce my nervous sensibility and to strengthen my will. Whereas my father, whose affection for me was of another kind, would not, I suspect, have had the same courage, for as soon as he had grasped the fact that I was unhappy he had said to my mother: "Go and comfort him."

Mamma stayed that night in my room, and it seemed that she did not wish to mar by recrimination those hours which were so different from anything that I had had a right to expect, for when Françoise (who guessed that something extraordinary must have happened when she saw Mamma sitting by my side, holding my hand and letting me cry unchided) said to her: "But, Madame, what is young master crying for?" she replied: "Why, Françoise, he doesn't know himself: it's his nerves. Make up the big bed for me quickly and then go off to your own." And thus for the first time my unhappiness was regarded no longer as a punishable offence but as an involuntary ailment which had been officially recognised, a nervous condition for which I was in no way responsible: I had the consolation of no longer having to mingle apprehensive scruples with the bitterness of my tears; I could weep henceforth without sin. I felt no small degree of pride, either, in Françoise's presence at this return to humane conditions which, not an hour after Mamma had refused to come up to my room and had sent the snubbing message that I was to go to sleep, raised me to the dignity of a grown-up person, brought me of a sudden to a sort of puberty of sorrow, a manumission of tears. I ought to have been happy; I was not. It struck me that my mother had just made a first concession which must have been painful to her, that it was a first abdication on her part from the ideal she had formed for me, and that for the first time she who was so brave had to confess herself beaten. It struck me that if I had just won a victory it was over her, that I had succeeded, as sickness or sorrow or age might have succeeded, in relaxing her will, in undermining her judgment; and that this evening opened a new era, would remain a black date in the calendar. And if I had dared now, I should have said to Mamma: "No, I don't want you to, you mustn't sleep here." But I was conscious of the practical wisdom, of what would nowadays be called the realism, with which she tempered the ardent idealism of my grandmother's nature, and I knew that now the mischief was done she would prefer to let me enjoy the soothing pleasure of her company, and not to disturb my father again. Certainly my mother's beautiful face seemed to shine again with youth that evening, as she sat gently holding my hands and trying to check my tears; but this was just what I felt should not have been; her anger would have saddened me less than this new gentleness, unknown to my childhood experience; I felt that I had with an impious and secret finger traced a first wrinkle upon her soul and brought out a first white hair on her head. This thought redoubled my sobs, and then I saw that Mamma, who had never allowed herself to indulge in any undue emotion with me, was suddenly overcome by my tears and had to struggle to keep back her own. When she realised that I had noticed this, she said to me with a smile: "Why, my little chick, my little canary, he's going to make Mamma as silly as himself if this goes on. Look, since you can't sleep, and Mamma can't either, we mustn't go on in this stupid way; we must do something; I'll get one of your books." But I had none there. "Would you like me to get out the books now that your grandmother is going to give you for your birthday? Just think it over first, and don't be disappointed if there's nothing new for you then."

Marcel Proust: *In Search of Lost Time. Swann's Way*, Volume 1, pp. 35-52
Translated by C.K. Scott Moncrieff & Terence Kilmartin, revised by D.J. Enright. Modern Library, 1992

Sylvia Plath:
Morning Song (1965)

Love set you going like a fat gold watch.
The midwife slapped your footsoles, and your bald cry
Took its place among the elements.

Our voices echo, magnifying your arrival. New statue.
In a drafty museum, your nakedness
Shadows our safety. We stand round blankly as walls.

I'm no more your mother
Than the cloud that distills a mirror to reflect its own slow
Effacement at the wind's hand.

All night your moth-breath
Flickers among the flat pink roses. I wake to listen:
A far sea moves in my ear.

One cry, and I stumble from bed, cow-heavy and floral
In my Victorian nightgown.
Your mouth opens clean as a cat's. The window square

Whitens and swallows its dull stars. And now you try
Your handful of notes;
The clear vowels rise like balloons.

Sylvia Plath: *Ariel: The Restored Edition*, p. 5
Faber & Faber, 2007

Lydia Davis:
The Old Dictionary (1999)

I have an old dictionary, about one hundred and twenty years old, that I need to use for a particular piece of work I'm doing this year. Its pages are brownish in the margins and brittle, and very large. I risk tearing them when I turn them. When I open the dictionary I also risk tearing the spine, which is already split more than halfway up. I have to decide, each time I think of consulting it, whether it is worth damaging the book further in order to look up a particular word. Since I need to use it for this work, I know I will damage it, if not today, then tomorrow, and that by the time I am done with this work it will be in poorer condition than it was when I started, if not completely ruined. When I took it off the shelf today, though, I realized that I treat it with a good deal more care than I treat my young son. Each time I handle it, I take the greatest care not to harm it: my primary concern is not to harm it. What struck me today was that even though my son should be more important to me than my old dictionary, I can't say that each time I deal with my son, my primary concern is not to harm him. My primary concern is almost always something else, for instance to find out what his homework is, or to get supper on the table, or to finish a phone conversation. If he gets harmed in the process, that doesn't seem to matter to me as much as getting the thing done, whatever it is. Why don't I treat my son at least as well as the old dictionary? Maybe it is because the dictionary is so obviously fragile. When a corner of a page snaps off, it is unmistakable. My son does not look fragile, bending over a game or manhandling the dog. Certainly his body is strong and flexible, and is not easily harmed by me. I have bruised his body and then it has healed. Sometimes it is obvious to me when I have hurt his feelings, but it is harder to see how badly they have been hurt, and they seem to mend. It is hard to see if they mend completely or are forever slightly damaged. When the dictionary is hurt, it can't be mended. Maybe I treat the dictionary better because it makes no demands on me, and doesn't fight back. Maybe I am kinder to things that don't seem to react to me. But in fact my houseplants do not seem to react much and yet I don't treat them very well. The plants make one or two demands. Their demand for light has already been satisfied by where I put them. Their second demand is for water. I water them but not regularly. Some of them don't grow very well because of that and some of them die. Most of them are strange-looking rather than nice-looking. Some of them were nice-looking when I bought them but are strange-looking now because I haven't taken very good care of them. Most of them are in pots that are the same ugly plastic pots they came in. I don't actually like them very much. Is there any other reason to like a houseplant, if it is not nice-looking? Am I kinder to something that is nice-looking? But I could treat a plant well even if I didn't like its looks. I should be able to treat my son well when he is not looking good and even when he is not acting very nice. I treat the dog better than the plants, even though he is more active and more demanding. It is simple to give him food and water. I take him for walks, though not often enough. I have also sometimes slapped his nose, though the vet told me never to hit him anywhere near the head, or maybe he said anywhere at all. I am only sure I am not neglecting the dog when he is asleep. Maybe I am kinder to things that are not alive. Or rather if they are not alive there is no question of kindness. It does not hurt them if I don't pay attention to them, and that is a great relief. It is such a relief it is even a pleasure. The only change they show is that they gather dust. The dust won't really hurt them. I can even get someone else to dust them. My son gets dirty, and I can't clean him, and I can't pay someone to clean him. It is hard to keep him clean, and even complicated trying to feed him. He doesn't sleep enough, partly because I try so hard to get him to sleep. The plants need two things, or maybe three. The dog needs five or six things. It is very clear how many things I am giving him and how many I am not, therefore how well I'm taking care of him. My son needs many other things besides what he needs for his physical care, and these things multiply or change constantly. They can change right in the middle of a sentence. Though I often know, I do not always know just what he needs. Even when I know, I am not always able to give it to him. Many times each day I do not give him what he needs. Some of what I do for the old dictionary, though not all, I could do for my son. For instance, I handle it slowly, deliberately, and gently. I consider its age. I treat it with respect. I stop and think before I use it. I know its limitations. I do not encourage it to go farther than it can go (for instance, to lie open flat on the table). I leave it alone a good deal of the time.

Lydia Davis: *The Collected Stories of Lydia Davis*,
pp. 374-376
Penguin, 2011

The Old Testament:
The Judgment of Solomon

Now two women who were harlots came to the king, and stood before him. And one woman said, "O my lord, this woman and I dwell in the same house; and I gave birth while she was in the house. Then it happened, the third day after I had given birth, that this woman also gave birth. And we were together; no one was with us in the house, except the two of us in the house. And this woman's son died in the night, because she lay on him. So she arose in the middle of the night and took my son from my side, while your maidservant slept, and laid him in her bosom, and laid her dead child in my bosom. And when I rose in the morning to nurse my son, there he was, dead. But when I had examined him in the morning, indeed, he was not my son whom I had borne." Then the other woman said, "No! But the living one is my son, and the dead one is your son." And the first woman said, "No! But the dead one is your son, and the living one is my son." Thus they spoke before the king. And the king said, "The one says, 'This is my son, who lives, and your son is the dead one'; and the other says, 'No! But your son is the dead one, and my son is the living one.'" Then the king said, "Bring me a sword." So they brought a sword before the king. And the king said, "Divide the living child in two, and give half to one, and half to the other." Then the woman whose son was living spoke to the king, for she yearned with compassion for her son; and she said, "O my lord, give her the living child, and by no means kill him!" But the other said, "Let him be neither mine nor yours, but divide him." So the king answered and said, "Give the first woman the living child, and by no means kill him; she is his mother."

The Bible: The Old Testament,
The First Book of Kings, chapter 3: 16-27

Gustave Flaubert: *Madame Bovary* (1857)

The fire was out, the clock ticked on, and Emma vaguely marveled that these things should be so calm while within herself she felt such turmoil. But between the window and the sewing table, there was little Berthe, tottering in her knitted booties, trying to reach her mother, to catch hold of the ends of her apron strings.

"Leave me alone!" said Emma, putting her away with her hand.

The little girl soon came back, even closer to her knees; and, leaning on them with her arms, she looked up at her with her big blue eyes, while a thread of clear saliva dropped from her lip onto the silk of the apron.

"Leave me alone!" the young woman said again, very irritated.

Her face terrified the child, who began screaming.

"Oh, leave me alone, won't you!" she said, thrusting her off with her elbow. Berthe fell at the foot of the chest of drawers, against the brass fittings; she cut her cheek; the blood ran. Madame Bovary rushed to pick her up, broke the bellpull, called the servant at the top of her voice, and she was about to begin cursing herself when Charles appeared. It was the dinnertime, he had come home.

"Look, my dear," Emma said to him calmly, "the baby was playing and has just fallen and hurt herself."

Charles reassured her that it was not at all serious, and he went off to find some diachylon.

Madame Bovary did not go down to the dining room; she insisted on remaining alone to look after her child. Then, as she watched her sleeping, the worry that she still felt dissipated gradually, and she appeared in her own eyes quite foolish and quite good to have allowed herself to be upset over so unimportant a thing. Berthe, indeed, was no longer sobbing. Her breathing, now, was barely perceptible as it lifted the cotton coverlet. A few large teardrops had gathered in the corners of her half-closed eyelids, through whose lashes one could glimpse two pale, sunken pupils; the adhesive plaster, stuck to her cheek, pulled the stretched skin to one side.

"How strange," thought Emma. "The child is so ugly."

Gustave Flaubert: *Madame Bovary*
Translated by Lydia Davis
Penguin Classics Deluxe Edition, 2012

Rachel Cusk:
A Life's Work (2001)

The baby and I are conveyed home through the streets of London in a taxi; like a cortège after a royal wedding driving through cheering crowds, a conventionally great moment underpinned by the suspicion of deep unfamiliarity, entertained in the glare of the utterly inescapable. We are, I have no doubt, a couple, a pair. I have not written off the many fleshly associations she has with others, but they have yet to make themselves real. All that is clear at this point is that I have replicated, like a Russian doll. I left home one; I have come back two.

It is only when I walk through the front door to my house that I realise things have changed. It is as if I have come to the house of someone who has just died, someone I loved, someone I can't believe has gone. The rooms, the furniture, the pictures and possessions all wear an unbearable patina of familiarity: standing there I feel bludgeoned by tragedy, as though I were standing in the irretrievable past. Minutes later the same rooms, the same possessions arouse in me a terrible panic, the panic of confinement. A violent anger seizes me at the sight of them; I recoil from their closeness as if in dislike. I feel burdened with secrets; an adulterous desire sets me apart from myself, fills me with both longing and revulsion for that which I have betrayed. I cannot explain these feelings. Instead I sit on the sofa and cry.

The baby is very small, I am repeatedly told. Her skin is brushed with blue. Her eyes remain closed. I, meanwhile, am disabled by my scar and can barely walk. We are still so close to our sundering that neither of us seems entire: the painful stump of our jointness, livid and fresh, remains. I don't quite understand what has happened and therefore I determine to conduct myself as though nothing had. I make tea and phone calls; I invite people round. They exclaim when I open the door, fully dressed, normal: at the returned fact of me, like an undelivered letter. Where's it gone? they laugh, pointing at my stomach. Pregnancy is a hallucination now. The mystery of the baby inside me has passed unsolved.

My ownership of my daughter is preoccupying, uncertain and fraught. In hospital I felt immediately a sort of animal-like habituation with her presence; at home I am in transactional shock, as if I had gone out and bought something extremely expensive, something for which in the shop I felt the fiercest, most private desire, and were now regarding it with shrivelled courage in my sitting room. I show it to other people, fearing their assessment. I let them touch and even hold it, silently frantic at the damage they might do, desperate to have it back. I both want and fear it, and yet can consummate neither my desire nor my fear, can neither use nor relinquish this precious purchase, for my feelings obstruct each other and hold me in a kind of deadlock. My daughter sleeps on, pale and silent.

Rachel Cusk: *A Life's Work. On Becoming a Mother*, pp. 56-58
Faber & Faber, 2019

Audre Lorde:
Now that I Am Forever with Child (1963)

How the days went
While you were blooming within me
I remember each upon each –
The swelling changed planes of my body –
And how you first fluttered, then jumped
And I thought it was my heart.

How the days wound down
And the turning of winter
I recall, with you growing heavy
Against the wind. I thought
Now her hands
Are formed, and her hair
Has started to curl
Now her teeth are done
Now she sneezes.
Then the seed opened.
I bore you one morning just before spring –
My head rang like a fiery piston
My legs were towers between which
A new world was passing.

From then
I can only distinguish
One thread within running hours
You ... flowing through selves
Toward you.

Audre Lorde: *The Collected Poems of Audre Lorde,* p. 8
W.W. Norton & Company Inc., 2000

Euripides:
Medea (431 BC)

My friends, I have decided what to do:
I'll kill my children now, at once, then flee
This land, for if I linger, hands less kind
Will bring them far more crudely to their deaths.
No way around the facts: since they must die,
The one who bore them will now take their lives.
– Steel yourself to do it now, my heart!
There is no point in putting this deed off:
However terrible, it must be done!
And you, unhappy hand, take up the blade,
And hasten to the starting line of grief!
Do not break down, do not remember how
You love your boys and how you gave them life!
Forget them rather, for this single day,
And mourn them every day that follows this one,
For they are still your darlings, even though
You murder them. I am a wretched woman.

Euripides: *Medea. A New Translation*, pp. 81-82
Translated by Charles Martin
University of California Press, 2019

Hans Christian Andersen: *The Story of a Mother* (1847)

A mother sat by her little child. She was so sad, so afraid he would die. The child's face was pallid. His little eyes were shut. His breath came faintly now, and then heavily as if he were sighing, and the mother looked more sadly at the dear little soul.

There came a knocking at the door, and a poor old man hobbled into the house. He was wrapped in a thick horseblanket. It kept him warm and he needed it to keep out the wintry cold, for outside the world was covered with snow and ice, and the wind cut like a knife.

As the child was resting quietly for a moment, and the old man was shivering from the cold, the mother put a little mug of beer to warm on the stove for him. The old man rocked the cradle and the mother sat down near it to watch her sick child, who labored to draw each breath. She lifted his little hand, and asked:

"You don't think I shall lose him, do you? Would the good Lord take him from me?"

The old man was Death himself. He jerked his head strangely, in a way that might mean yes or might mean no. The mother bowed her head and tears ran down her cheeks. Her head was heavy.

For three days and three nights she had not closed her eyes. Now she dozed off to sleep, but only a moment. Something startled her and she awoke, shuddering in the cold.

"What was that?" she said, looking everywhere about the room. But the old man had gone and her little child had gone. Death had taken the child away. The old clock in the corner whirred and whirred. Its heavy lead weight dropped down to the floor with a thud. Bong! the clock stopped. The poor mother rushed wildly out of the house, calling for her child.

Out there in the snow sat a woman, dressed in long black garments. "Death," she said, "has been in your house. I just saw him hurrying away with your child in his arms. He goes faster than the wind. And he never brings back what he has taken away."

"Tell me which way he went," said the mother. "Only tell me the way, and I will find him."

"I know the way," said the woman in black, "but before I tell you, you must sing to me all those songs you used to sing to your child. I am night. I love lullabies and I hear them often. When you sang them I saw your tears."

"I shall sing them again – you shall hear them all," said the mother, "but do not stop me now. I must catch him. I must hurry to find my child."

Night kept silent and still, while the mother wrung her hands, and sang, and wept. She sang many songs, but the tears that she shed were many, many more. At last Night said to her, "Go to the right. Go into the dark pine woods. I saw Death go there with your child."

Deep into the woods the mother came to a crossroad, where she was at a loss which way to go. At the crossroad grew a blackthorn bush, without leaf or flower, for it was wintertime and its branches were glazed with ice.

"Did you see Death go by with my little child?"

"Yes," said the blackthorn bush. "But I shall not tell you which way he went unless you warm me against your heart. I am freezing to death. I am stiff with ice."

She pressed the blackthorn bush against her heart to warm it, and the thorns stabbed so deep into her flesh that great drops of red blood flowed. So warm was the mother's heart that the blackthorn bush blossomed and put forth green leaves on that dark winter's night. And it told her the way to go.

Then she came to a large lake, where there was neither sailboat nor rowboat. The ice on the lake was too thin to hold her weight, and yet not open or shallow enough for her to wade. But across the lake she must go if ever she was to find her child. She stooped down to drink the lake dry, and that of course was impossible for any human being, but the poor woman thought that maybe a miracle would happen.

"No, that would never do," the lake objected. "Let us make a bargain between us. I collect pearls, and your two eyes are the clearest I've ever seen. If you will cry them out for me, I shall carry you over to the great greenhouse where Death lives and tends his trees and flowers. Each one of them is a human life."

"Oh, what would I not give for my child," said the crying mother, and she wept till her eyes dropped down to the bottom of the lake and became two precious pearls. The lake took her up as if in a swing, and swept her to the farther shore.

Here stood the strangest house that ever was. It rambled for many a mile. One wouldn't know whether it was a cavernous, forested mountain, or whether it was made of wood. But the poor mother could not see this, for she had cried out her eyes.

"Where shall I find Death, who took my child from me?" she cried.

"He has not come back yet," said the old woman who took care of the great greenhouse while Death was away. "How did you find your way here? Who helped you?"

"The Lord helped me," she said. "He is merciful, and so must you be. Where can I find my child?"

"I don't know him," said the old woman, "and you can't see to find him. But many flowers and trees have withered away in the night, and Death will be along soon to transplant them. Every human being, you know, has his tree or his flower of life, depending on what sort of person he is. These look like other plants, but they have a heart that beats. A child's heart beats too. You know the beat of your own child's heart. Listen and you may hear it. But what will you give me if I tell you what else you must do?"

"I have nothing left," the poor mother said, "but I will go to the ends of the earth for you."

"I have nothing to do there," said the old woman, "but you can give me your long black hair. You know how beautiful it is, and I like it. I'll give you my white hair for it. White hair is better than none."

"Is that all you ask?" said the mother. "I will gladly give it to you." And she gave her beautiful long black tresses in exchange for the old woman's white hair.

Then they went into Death's great greenhouse, where flowers and trees were strangely intertwined. In one place delicate hyacinths were kept under glass bells, and around them great hardy peonies flourished. There were water plants too, some thriving where the stalks of others were choked by twisting water snakes, or gnawed away by black crayfish. Tall palm trees grew there, and plane trees, and oaks. There grew parsley and sweet-smelling thyme. Every tree or flower went by the name of one particular person, for each was the life of someone still living in China, in Greenland, or in some other part of the world. There were big trees stunted by the small pots which their roots filled to bursting, and elsewhere grew languid little flowers that came to nothing, for all the care that was lavished upon them, and for all the rich earth and the mossy carpet where they grew. The sad, blind mother bent over the tiniest plants and listened to the beat of their human hearts, and among so many millions she knew her own child's heartbeat.

"This is it," she cried, groping for a little blue crocus, which had wilted and dropped to one side.

"Don't touch that flower," the old woman said. "Stay here. Death will be along any minute now, and you may keep him from pulling it up. Threaten him that, if he does, you will pull up other plants. That will frighten him, for he has to account for them to the Lord. Not one may be uprooted until God says so."

Suddenly an icy wind blew through the place, and the blind mother felt Death come near.

"How did you find your way here?" he asked her. "How did you ever get here before me?"

"I am a mother," she said.

Then Death stretched out his long hand toward the wilted little flower, but she held her hands tightly around it, in terror lest he touch a single leaf. Death breathed upon her hands, and his breath was colder than the coldest wind. Her hands fell, powerless.

"You have no power to resist me," Death told her.

"But our Lord has," she said.

"I only do his will," said Death, "I am His gardener. I take His flowers and trees and plant them again in the great Paradise gardens, in the unknown land. But how they thrive, and of their life there, I dare not speak."

"Give me back my child," the mother wept and implored him. Suddenly she grasped a beautiful flower in each hand and as she clutched them she called to Death: "I shall tear out your flowers by the roots, for I am desperate."

"Do not touch them!" Death told her. "You say you are desperate, yet you would drive another mother to the same despair."

"Another mother!" The blind woman's hands let go the flowers.

"Behold," said Death, "you have your eyes again. I saw them shining as I crossed the lake, and fished them up, but I did not know they were yours. They are clearer than before. Take them and look deep into this well. I shall tell you the names of the flowers you were about to uproot and you shall see the whole future of those human lives that you would have destroyed and disturbed."

She looked into the well, and it made her glad to see how one life became a blessing to the world, for it was so kind and happy. Then she saw the other life, which held only sorrow, poverty, fear, and woe.

"Both are the will of God," said Death.

"Which one is condemned to misery, and which is the happy one?" she asked.

"That I shall not tell you," Death said. "But I tell you this. One of the flowers belongs to your own child. One life that you saw was your child's fate, your own child's future."

Then the mother shrieked in terror, "Which was my child? Tell me! Save my innocent child. Spare him such wretchedness. Better that he be taken from me. Take him to God's kingdom. Forget my tears. Forget the prayers I have said, and the things I have done."

"I do not understand," Death said. "Will you take your own child back or shall I take him off to a land unknown to you?"

Then the mother wrung her hands, fell on her knees, and prayed to God:

"Do not hear me when I pray against your will. It is best. Do not listen, do not listen!" And she bowed her head, as Death took her child to the unknown land.

Hans Christian Andersen: *The Story of a Mother*
Translated by Jean Hersholt

Maggie Nelson:
The Argonauts (2015)

Suddenly, the urge to push. Everyone is thrilled. Push, they say. They teach me. Hold it in, hold in the air, bear down wildly, don't waste the end of the push. The midwife puts her hand in to see if I need help pushing. She says I am a good pusher and don't need any help. I am happy I am a good pusher. I want to try.

On the fourth or so contraction, he starts to come. I don't know for sure if it's him, but I can feel the change. I push hard. One push turns into another kind of push – I feel it outside.

Commotion. I am gone but happy, something is happening. The doctor rushes in, I can see him throwing on his gear: a visor, an apron. He seems agitated but who cares. New lights come on, yellow, directed lights. People around me are moving quickly. My baby is being born.

Everyone is watching down there intently, in a kind of happy panic. Someone asks if I want to feel the baby's head, and I don't, I don't know why. Then a minute later, I do. Here he comes. It feels big but I feel big enough.

Then suddenly they tell me to stop pushing. I don't know why. Harry tells me that the doctor is stretching my perineum in circles around the baby's head, trying to keep the skin from tearing. Hold, they say, don't push, but "puff." Puff puff puff.

Then they say I can push. I push. I feel him come out, all of him, all at once. I also feel the shit that had been bedeviling me all through pregnancy and labor come out too. My first feeling is that I could run a thousand miles, I feel amazing, total and complete relief, like everything that was wrong is now right.

And then, suddenly, Iggy. Here he comes onto me, rising. He is perfect, he is right. I notice he has my mouth, incredible. He is my gentle friend. He is on me, screaming.

Maggie Nelson: *The Argonauts*, pp. 132-133
Graywolf Press, 2015

My Mommy Is Beautiful

Write your thoughts
of your mother.
Or pin a photograph
of her on to the canvas.

y.o. 2011

cat. 95
Yoko Ono: *My Mommy Is Beautiful*, 2004/2021

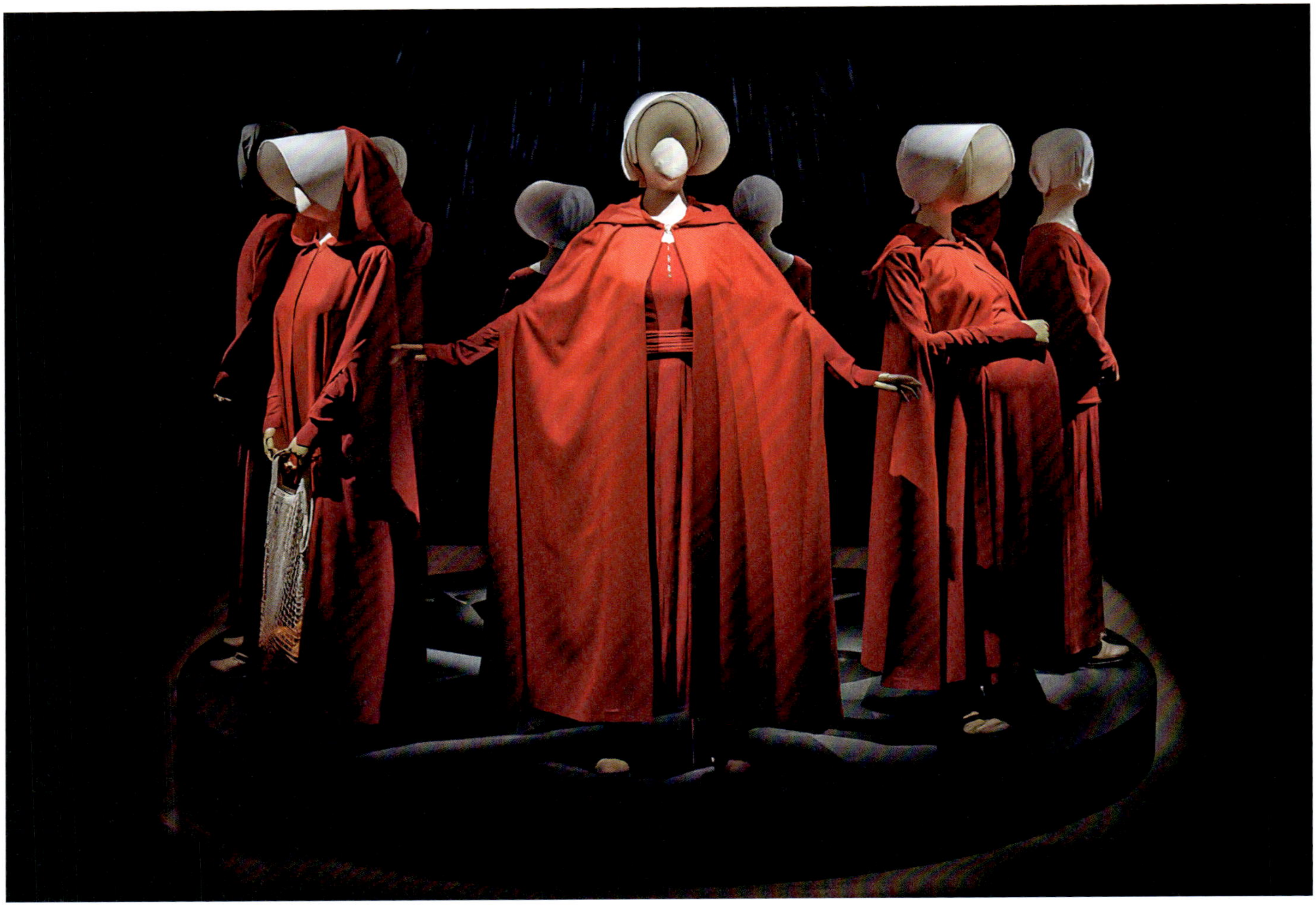

cat. 13
Ane Crabtree: Costume of the handmaids, from the TV series based on the novel by Margaret Atwood, "The Handmaid's Tale" of 1985, 2016

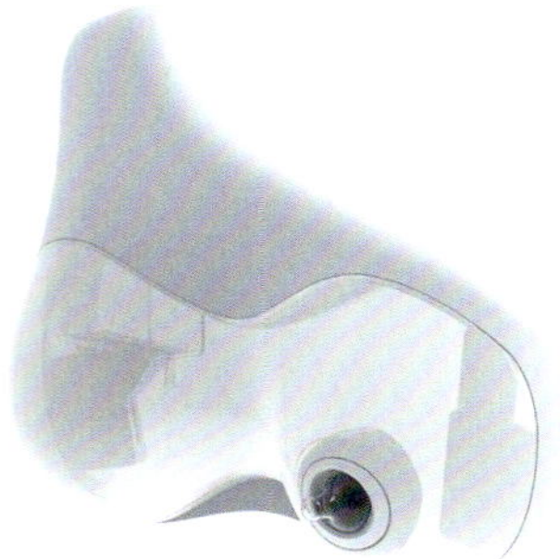

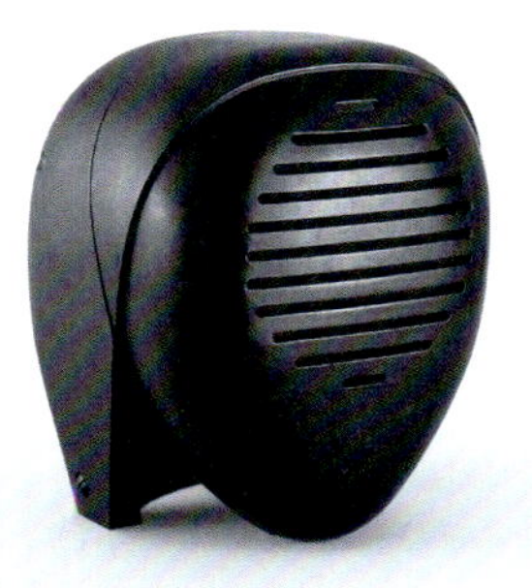

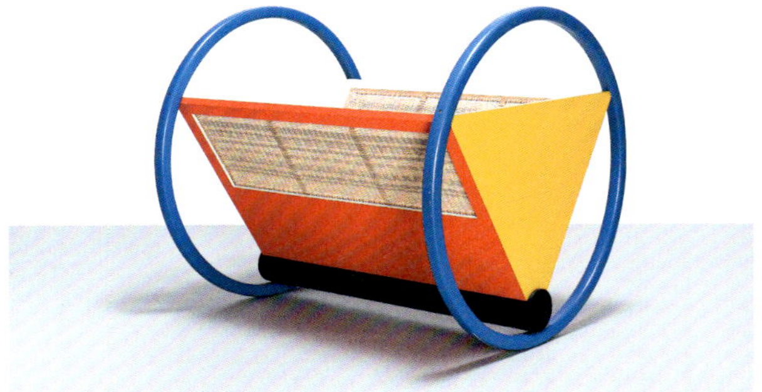

cat. 115
Osamu Takahashi in collaboration with Taikan Hoshino, Masaharu Kurosu, Kyoko Kita and Madoka Yoshio: *Fether's Nursing Assistant*, 2019

In the centre:
cat. 94
Isamu Noguchi: *Radio Nurse*, 1937

cat. 50
Peter Keler: *Bauhaus-Wiege*, 1922 (copy: 1996, Henning Seilkopf). Bauhaus cradle

Right page: cat. 24
Jean-Paul Goude in collaboration with Antonio Lopez: The Grace Jones Show: Constructivist maternity costume, New York, 1979

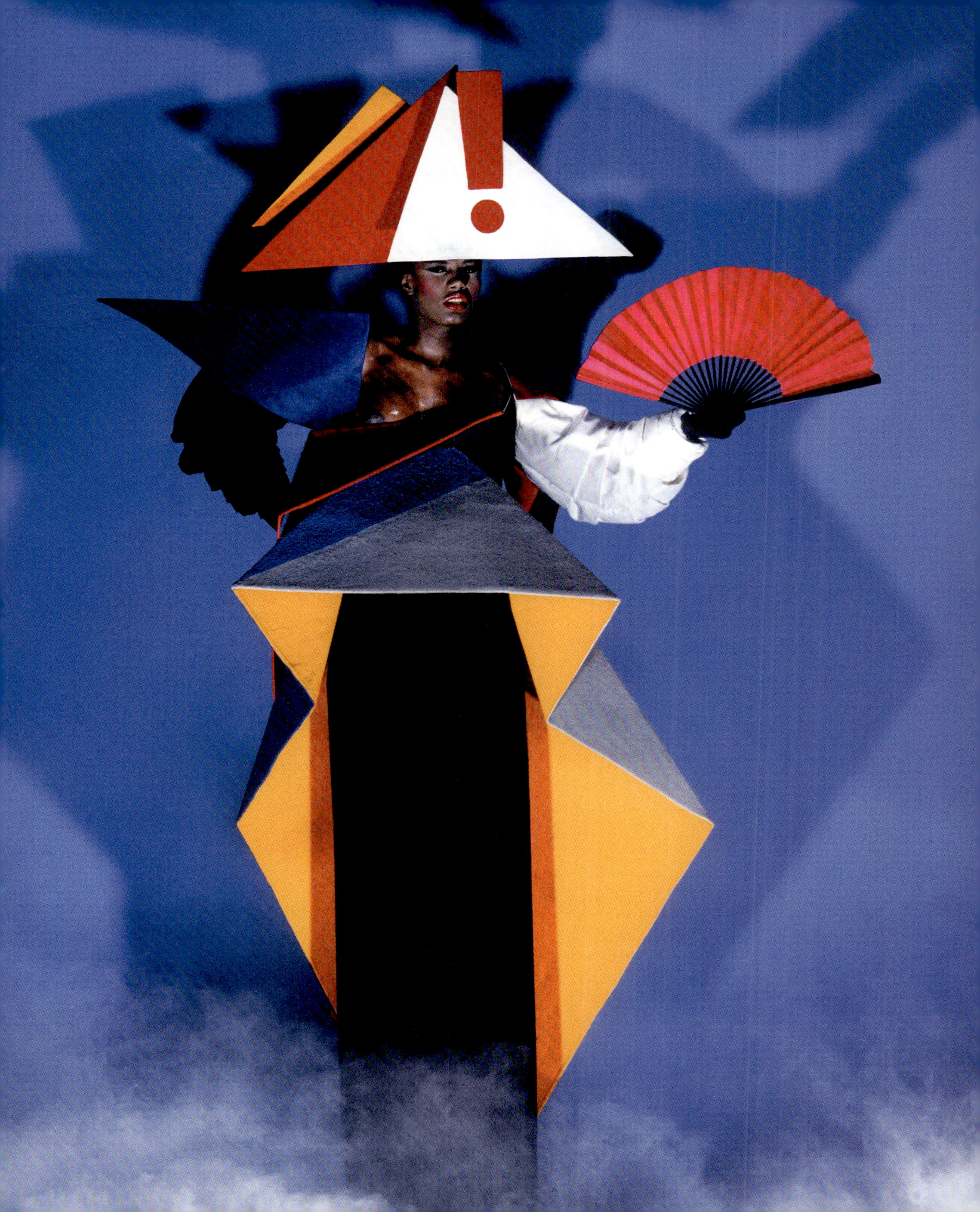

The Good Mother

– A Shifting Historical Ideal

By Pia Fris Laneth

Pia Fris Laneth holds an MA in Political Science and is the award-winning author of multiple books on the history of women in Denmark.

In his autobiography *My Childhood on Funen*[1] the Danish composer Carl Nielsen (1865-1931) reminisces about his mother's breasts: "We were allowed to suckle until we were a couple of years old, and I can clearly recall the sensation of her skin and a certain discomfort when my turned-up nose got in the way ... My mother's nipple was pink against her white skin, and when we suckled we could feel all the small rough spots and cracks." As the seventh of 13 children, Carl had both older and younger siblings and remembered breastfeeding in the home as a happy time: "When my mother sat with the youngest at her breast she was usually content, almost jolly. She would sometimes take the baby away, toy with her breast a little, then put it in the mouth of one of the slightly older children saying: 'Do you want a bit as well?' I too have stood in my clogs in front of my mother and had my share of the delights." Carl Nielsen's memories symbolise motherly love. Far into the 19th century, however, women could easily be good mothers without breastfeeding their children, changing their nappies, or feeding and bathing them. Wealthy women handed all this time-consuming and often dirty work over to nannies and wet nurses with a clear conscience. The baby manuals of the past recommended mother's milk as the best source of nourishment, the milk of other women as second best, whereas the milk of animals came third.

Whether a child reached adulthood was not thanks to the skills of the mother, but the will of God. This was common knowledge until the 1880s, when Professor of Statistics Harald Westergaard discovered that more infants survived on the islands of Funen and Bornholm than in the rest of Denmark.[2] Less than eight percent of babies died here, versus twice as many in a town like Randers. Copenhagen held the grim national record, with more than 20 percent of the capital's infants dying before their first birthday. Harald Westergaard was deeply religious, but he did not believe God intended more children to die in Randers than on Funen. Something else had to be at stake, and true enough it emerged that Danish mothers in different places had very different ideas about caring for infants. In Randers they did not consider breast milk sufficiently nourishing. A few months after being born, babies were given additional food: porridge with a knob of butter, salted pork – prechewed by an adult – that infant intestines could not digest and that contained potentially lethal bacteria. On Funen and Bornholm, on the other hand, mothers were sure that their own milk was the best their babies could get. Here infants were only given breast milk until they reached out for other food, and were not fully weaned until they could sit at the table at the age of two or three. So in Carl Nielsen's poor farmhand's home on Funen his mother's joy at breastfeeding her children was life-giving in more sense than one.

Breastfeeding Politics

The 19th-century interest in infant mortality was related to the spread of new ideas about children as innocent beings with the right to a loving, healthy and secure upbringing. The gap between upper-class and middle-class ideals and the realities of life for the lower classes led to a flood of philanthropic societies to help children. The survival of children born into poverty became society's moral responsibility. It was for the sake of their children that society chose to assist poor mothers. Unmarried mothers were those most obviously in need. They had to work for a living, so many of their new-born babies were adopted or placed with a foster mother. Given the lack of knowledge about bacteria in cow's milk and feeding bottles this solution was often a death sentence. Other unmarried mothers resorted to even more desperate measures. Almost daily the newspapers reported the discovery of dead babies or infants left outside in the hope that someone would take care of them. The philanthropists, however, did not see unmarried mothers as being 'deserving' poor, and were reluctant to help them. Imagine if they were seen to be encouraging fornication!

Children's home superintendent Rosalie Petersen was one of the first to tackle this moral dilemma.[3] In 1890 she opened a mother-and-baby home in Copenhagen in accordance with the latest principles for hygiene and with space for 18 mothers and 36 infants. Each woman had their own room – an unheard-of luxury for the majority of people in Denmark at the time – and breastfed her own child and one or more of the other children in care. It was Rosalie Petersen's hope that through breastfeeding, the unmarried mothers would bond so closely with their babies that they would not have the heart to put them up for adoption.

Only a few decades later views on the relationship between wet nurse and child had changed, and using a

At 27 Kapelvej in Copenhagen Hans Scherfig's buxom mother of twins promotes Copenhagen dairies. When it was painted in 1962 the mural scandalised some, but delighted many more. The increased prosperity and liberation of the body of the 1960s had begun.

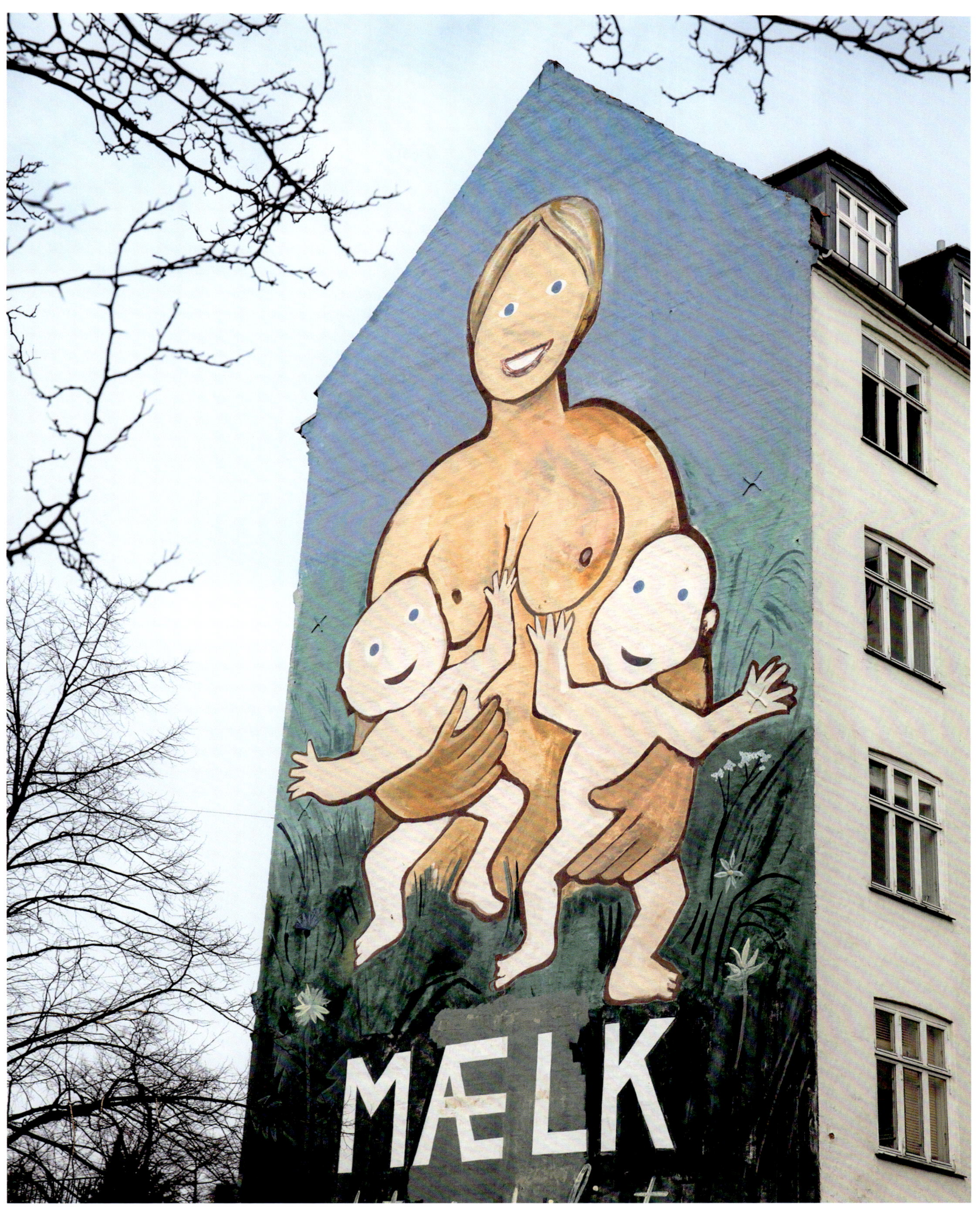
MÆLK

wet nurse was now seen as unhygienic, aesthetically offensive and socially objectionable. In *The Mother's Book*, 1916, one of the most popular handbooks at the time, Chief Physician Svenn Monrad called it "inhuman" to hire a wet nurse "because this would rob the wet nurse's own child of its natural source of nourishment, add to the risk of infection ... and finally, for many mothers seeing their child draw nourishment from the breast of a stranger is a highly embarrassing and repugnant sight".[4] Svenn Monrad recommended that women breastfed their children for at least six months. Six years later, in 1921, the state followed suit by providing advice on breastfeeding in the Danish Health Authority's first pamphlet on infant care. These efforts worked, and the rate of child mortality started to fall. Breastfeeding had now become a focus of state policy, and has been a virtually sacred maternal duty in Denmark ever since.

Miracle and Submission

The capacity of the female body to perform the greatest miracle of existence, creating a new human life, has over the centuries been idealised and romanticised as the natural and divine meaning of women's lives. Parallel to this, the same will of God and nature has been used to deny women personal and political rights: "The legislator assumes that the wife is subordinate to her husband and owes him obedience," as Professor J. H. Deuntzer wrote in the book *Danish Family Law* in 1882. The husband was his wife's legal guardian, and had absolute control of the family finances – including any fortune or inheritance belonging to his wife. He also had sole right of custody over their children.

Until 1912 the Church of Denmark, to which the vast majority of Danes belong, institutionalised women's duty of submission in the marriage ceremony, during which a bride in Denmark had to agree to the following: "Wives, submit to your own husbands, as to the Lord. For the husband is the head of his wife as Christ is the head of the church."[5] Ideas about freedom, equality and democracy were, however, contagious. After decades of tireless work, in 1915 women were given the same political rights as men. After this the pace of reform increased: equal pay for government officials was introduced in 1919, and two years later women and men were officially granted equal access to state positions – the clergy and military being notable exceptions. Legislators, however, dragged their heels when it came to equality within the home, and not until 1922 were women granted custody of their own children. As head of the family, however, the husband remained their children's guardian in financial matters right up until 1956. Finally, in 1925 married women were granted joint control of matrimonial property, something the husband had previously had a monopoly on.

Once these laws on marital and custodial rights had been passed, Danish women had achieved a high degree of formal, legal equality with men. Motherhood was, however, still only regarded as morally and socially acceptable under the guardianship of a husband, and women were still a long way off achieving the right to decide over their own bodies and sexuality. This lack of self-determination was reflected in the ban on advertisements for contraception, the ban on abortion and the lack of access to information on sex and sexuality. Very few doctors were willing to tell married women – let alone unmarried women – how to avoid pregnancy. The consequences were heart-breaking: "I am 37 years old and have had eight children, three of whom died of tuberculosis," a woman wrote to Dr Jonathan Leunbach, who published a book of letters from desperate

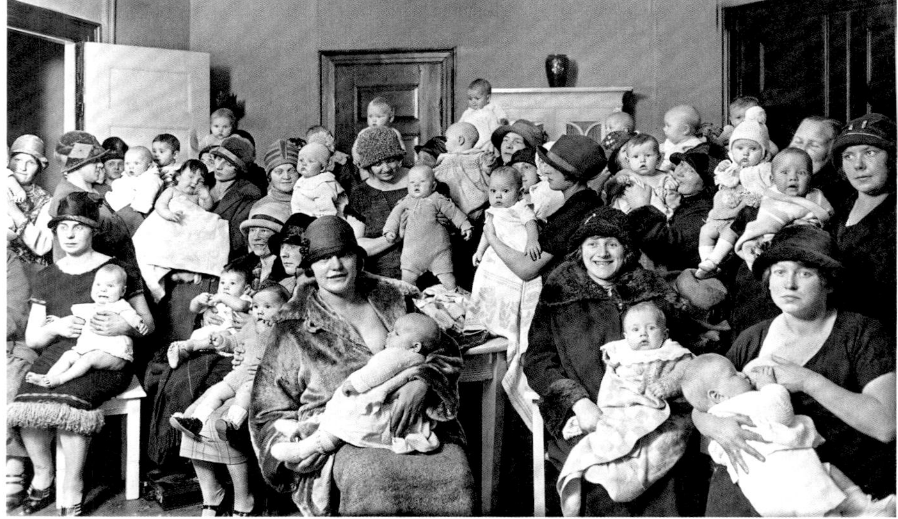

In the 1920s competitions on raising healthy children were held, here at the clinic of Dr Eli Møller in Copenhagen in 1926. The government and private organisations launched campaigns on the role of breastfeeding in improving infants' chances of survival. Working-class women were used to breastfeeding in the company of others – their living conditions left them no option.

It took decades to dismantle the myth that motherhood was a condition women could not avoid. Jonathan Leunbach was one of Denmark's contraception pioneers. His friends and supporters greeted him when he was released from prison, where he had served a sentence for performing illegal abortions.

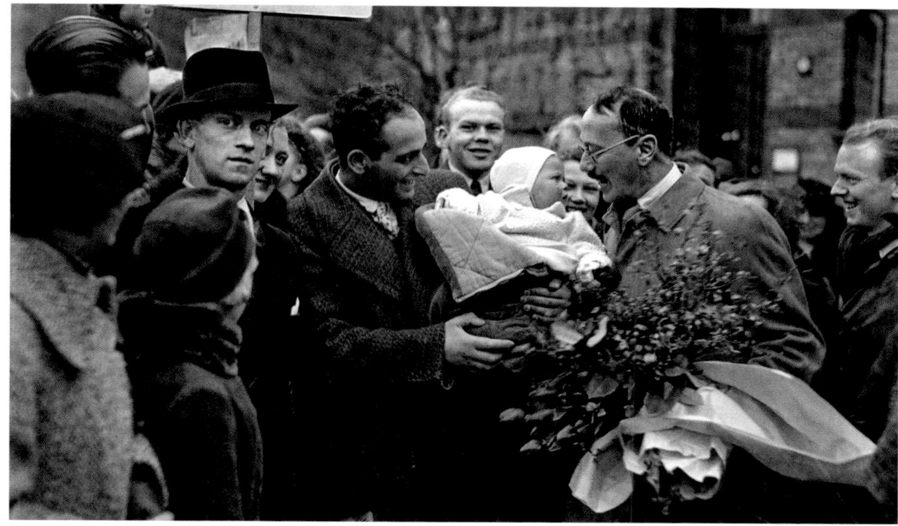

pregnant women and their equally desperate husbands called *Women in Need* in 1932. She continued: "We now have twins in a sanatorium, the 11-year-old has tuberculosis too, and the three-year-old is very weak. You will understand our fear of having more children, for which reason we have been using French letters since we had our youngest child. However we had the misfortune of one breaking." The book is a record of poverty, illness and desperation, as in this case of a mother with seven children aged 18 months to 14 years: "I'm worried it's happened again. Would it help if I flush with soapy water every day? We cannot provide for all the children with my husband's poor weekly wage. I'm only fourteen days overdue, so if I could make it go away with soapy water that wouldn't be a sin, would it?" Yes, it would. "Foeticide", as an abortion was called, was a sin in the eyes of the church and a crime in the eyes of the law and society.[6]

Far too many pregnancies, births, miscarriages and illegal abortions destroyed the health of women, and large numbers of children destroyed family finances and the possibility of raising healthy children. Yet still the political elite, including the leaders of the Danish Women's Society, continued to see contraception as a ticking bomb under the institution of the family. Instead, a mixed group of forward-looking individuals provided information on birth control. Under the slogan "Voluntary Motherhood", during the interwar period the author Thit Jensen became one of Denmark's most active campaigners for the diaphragm as a method of contraception. This made her popular, but also sparked vehement opposition, with one Danish bishop calling her vermin. Members of parliament tried for three consecutive years to get her lifelong author's stipend removed from the annual state budget, but throughout Denmark people flocked to hear her lectures, just as women descended on Jonathan Leunbach's sex clinic for information about contraception. Several decades later Leunbach proudly wrote: "During the course of 25 years I have taught around 40,000 women how to use a diaphragm." Leunbach, however, received most attention for providing more than 300 abortions for women whose pregnancies threatened their health or life. This was deemed illegal, and he was sentenced to three months imprisonment and deprived of his civil rights for five years, including his right to practice medicine.

Training for Motherhood

During the interwar years, the spread of word-of-mouth knowledge about contraception resulted in falling populations throughout Europe. This worried those in power, who were increasingly aware of the clouds of war gathering on the horizon. Where would the soldiers come from if women stopped giving birth? Totalitarian states banned the sale of contraceptives, increased sentences for abortion, and rewarded women with large numbers of children. In Scandinavia leading politicians and officials took a different path, focusing on public health instead. In the early 1930s the infant mortality rate was still around eight percent, tuberculosis and rickets were still widespread, and the average life expectancy was 62 for men and 63 for women.

Inspired by sociologist Alva Myrdal and economist Gunnar Myrdal, both Swedish Social Democrats, Scandinavian countries developed policies to boost public health. Women were at the centre of the Nordic welfare state: rather than having a larger number of children, they were to be trained to raise physically strong, well-behaved children in healthy families. Part of the new plan was the founding of the Danish National Council for Domestic Science in 1935. Two years later the nursing bill was passed, and in 1938 needlework became obligatory in junior school and domestic science in secondary school. Training women as housewives was done in alliance with Danish housewives' associations, which boomed. They had more than 200,000 members, and offered courses in nutritional theory, cheap and healthy cooking, cleaning, budgeting, personal hygiene and the theory of childcare. The idea that mothers had a natural duty to breastfeed and raise their children paved the way for the view that poor and unmarried mothers should also have the *right* to keep their children, and that their children should have the *right* to grow up with their mothers instead of being taken into care, adopted – or aborted. Mothers' Aid, a small Copenhagen philanthropic society, became the recipient of state support via the annual budget in 1939, enabling it to become a national organisation providing advice to married and unmarried women aimed at "removing every obstacle that could make women seek to terminate a pregnancy".[7]

Inspired by the highly controversial case against Leunbach for performing abortions, in 1937 the Danish parliament passed a bill granting women the right to a legal abortion if a pregnancy threatened their health. Very few were actually given permission, with dreadful consequences. The authorities estimated that between 12,000-16,000 women a year had an illegal abortion, and this continued during the 1950s and 1960s. Many children were born to mothers who were neither socially nor economically able to raise them. This peaked after the Nazi occupation, when more than 2,000 children a year – a total of more than 10,000 children from 1945-1950 – were put up for adoption.

The fact that Mothers' Aid was not allowed to teach women who were not already mothers or pregnant about contraception stands as an absurd symbol of the state's refusal to grant women independence and control of their own bodies. Over the years the organisation established contact with almost all unmarried mothers and the poorest married mothers in Denmark. It provided women with free medical examinations during pregnancy, accommodation and care after giving birth, rest cures, and packages of baby clothes, a cot and a pram. The organisation also administered the 'milk aid' introduced by the Pregnancy Hygiene Bill of 1945 entitling pregnant members of a sick-benefit association to half a litre of milk a day during the last six months of pregnancy, and a whole litre of milk during the first six months of the baby's life – if the baby was breastfed. The same bill entitled all pregnant women to three free doctor's visits and seven home visits by a midwife. These political initiatives were a huge success: infant mortality was halved to four percent of births in less than 20 years, and by 1950 life expectancy had increased by six-seven years to 60 for men and 70 for women.

The Golden Age of the Nuclear Family

In the years after World War II the concept of motherhood changed yet again. Whereas in the past advice on caring for and raising children had a largely scientific basis in medicine and hygiene, during the 1950s psychologists held sway. Breastfeeding increased in status even more as a basis of *mental* health. Melanie Klein, one of the leading psychoanalysts of the post-war period, insisted that a child who had problems despite being breastfed would have been even worse if had this not been the case. Nobody demanded she validate the claim.[8]

In his classic work *The Art of Loving* from 1956 the influential psychologist Erich Fromm described ideal parenthood as follows: "Mother is the home we come from, she is nature, soil, the ocean; father does not represent any such natural home. He has little connection with the child in the first years of its life, and his importance to the child in this early period cannot be compared with that of the mother. But while the father does not represent the natural world, he represents the other pole of human existence; the world of thought, of man-made things, of law and order, of discipline, of travel and adventure. Father is the one who teaches the child, who shows him the road into the world."[9]

Equally set views about gender differences were promoted by Aksel Tofte, a psychiatrist at the National Hospital of Denmark, in his book *Sexual Hygiene*: "As in physique, the woman is also less intellectually developed than the man, and is in many ways akin to the child. This is important in her role as a mother, given that she retains a greater understanding of the child, whereas the man, given his advanced development, diverges from the child and is thereby alienated in relationship to it."[10] Drawing on Freud, Tofte explained to his readers that a healthy woman *wants* to be a mother. Wanting anything else he attributed to penis envy: "This complex is at work in the subconscious of endless women. They hate the lot of being born women, envy the other sex and fail to appreciate the true value and mission of women. They try desperately to imitate and behave like men, or even to outdo them. As a result their entire demeanour has the pathological character of a split personality which prevents healthy, female development", as he wrote in his heavy handbook, which had repeated print runs totalling 125,000 copies between 1941 and 1957. What Klein, Fromm and Tofte described as a law of nature for the relationship between mothers, children and fathers, politicians, doctors, health visitors and educators spent the

Danish women were trained to be good mothers. Home visits by nurses were key to halving the infant mortality rate between the 1930s and 1950. Mothers' Aid and compulsory domestic science for girls were part of the same campaign.

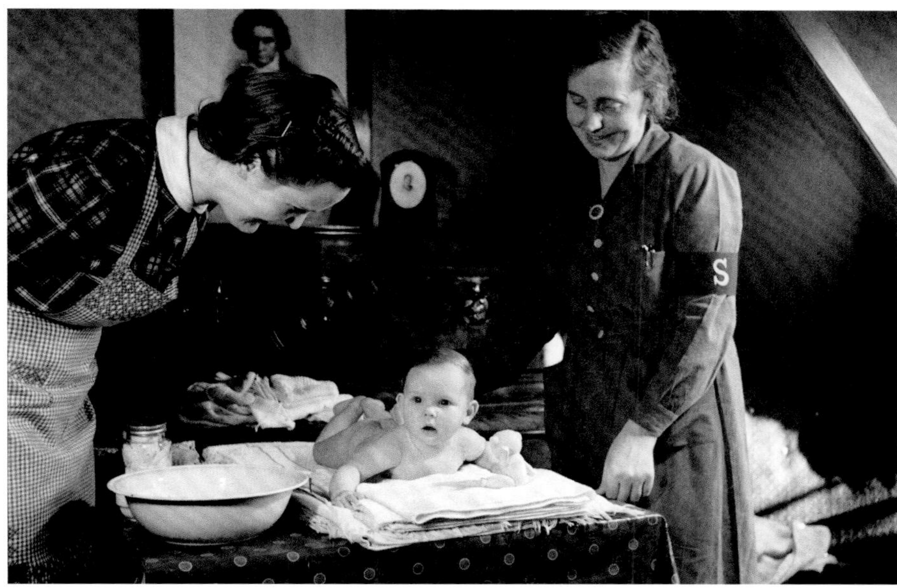

20th century shaping into an ideal for the middle-class family of industrial society, with a male breadwinner working outside the home and a housewife inside it.

In 1960 as many as 860,000 housewives were economically dependent on their husbands, whereas less than 20 percent of married women had paid full-time or part-time work. By this stage in Danish history people rarely had more than two or three children, technical wonders like the washing machine, fridge and vacuum cleaner had made housework easier, and so for urban and suburban housewives it could be difficult to finds ways to kill the time once their children had started school. At the same time, married women were increasingly frustrated that men were the ones earning the money and often deciding unilaterally what it should be spent on. In 1962 the Danish poet and author Tove Ditlevesen, who edited the agony column of the women's magazine *Familiejournal*, summed up her first six years' as an agony aunt in an article on the frontlines being drawn within the average, Danish nuclear family: "Through thousands of letters a grim, marital balance of terror starts to emerge, equal in strength to that between the East and West. The weapons are money on one side, sex on the other ... Most common is that he, with an air of largesse, hands over 500 crowns a month ... It's called 'housekeeping money' ... and can just about cover a half-decent diet. The man does not know that children need clothes. They get them in the end, after arguments, threats, tears and insane scenes. He knows nothing of the hairdresser, tram tickets, sewing thread, resoling, children's birthdays, tea with girlfriends, and a hundred other trifles that people who have an income of their own never have to think about. The consequence is a constant lack of ready money and an everyday life where financial disablement entirely obstructs the woman's horizon and totally blocks her mind."[11] Women were ready for major change.

Revolution on the Home Front

Industrialisation and the economic growth of the 1960s generated a massive increase in the demand for workers. Over the next three decades 800,000 more women joined the tax-paying labour force, whereas the figure for men during the same period only increased by around 100,000. As a result, by the beginning of the 1990s younger and middle-aged women were in paid employment to the same extent as men of the same age, whether they were married or not. This was a revolution. In a single generation the balance of power between men and women changed in the family and society. The family ideal changed from having a male breadwinner at the head of the family to having two breadwinners. Paid employment was a real life prospect for women, and they could now be both educated and economically independent. Parallel to this, the welfare state expanded, and trained women assumed many of the housewife's former duties of caring for children, the sick and the elderly.

In the wake of the explosive demands for personal freedom of the 1960s, women at long last won control over their own bodies: "Your body, your rights", as a slogan of the new women's liberation movement put it. The contraceptive pill, introduced in Denmark in 1965, was a reliable form of birth control controlled by women themselves, and the legalisation of abortion in 1973 gave women the right to decide whether they wanted to go through with an unplanned pregnancy or not. Parallel to these developments, compulsory sex education in schools from 1970 meant that young Danes learned the basics of sex, reproduction and contraception. Illegal abortions were a thing of the past, and the number of new-born babies put up for adoption dwindled to almost zero. It became morally and socially acceptable to be an unmarried, single mother.

This revolution on the home front also gradually changed ideas about 'the good father'. In the 1960s men were still not considered psychologically capable of taking care of small children – their job was to provide economically for them and their mother. Today young Danish fathers increasingly behave as if they were born to change nappies and feed, cuddle and comfort their offspring – and mandatory paternity leave is repeatedly a hotly debated issue on the Danish political agenda.

Motherhood in a New Light

During the women's movement of the 1970s, female artists started to represent motherhood in radically new and different ways. Dea Trier Mørch's linocut series *Into the World* portrayed a hospital birth in natural, physical detail. She zooms in on the woman's lower body, on the baby's head and shoulders pushing their way into the world, on the helping hands of the midwife, and daily life on a maternity ward with breastfeeding women, softly swaddled babies, babies in incubators and on the changing table, and on cleaning staff as well as medical staff.

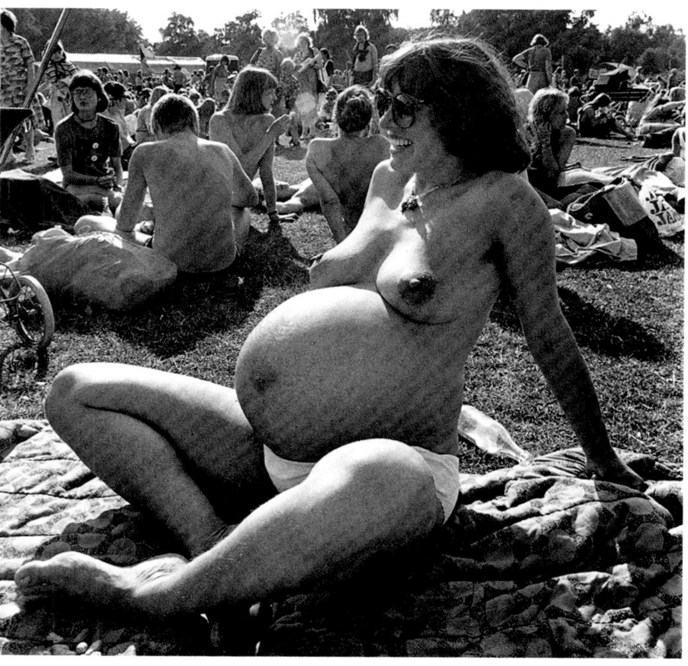

Henrik Saxgren photographed his girlfriend Kirsten Emborg at the Women's Festival in Fælledparken in 1979 a week before their daughter Ivalo was born. Women became proud of their pregnant wombs once motherhood was felt to be voluntary. The picture radiates happiness over bearing life and was used innumerable times in left-wing newspapers and periodicals.

Winter's Child, Trier Mørch's iconic novel on life on the maternity ward of the National Hospital of Denmark, puts equally sensory experiences of the pregnant body and childbirth into words: "The baby's body makes its way through the last soft part of the birth passage, a log gliding over a shore and on out into the sea – something large and firm and dark is thrust out of her body, out between her legs, a dark parcel, a bloody lump."[12] Intimate and powerful, vulnerable and respectful. Both the artwork and novel were received as welcome artistic tributes to the reproductive labour of women. The images were hung on the walls of many Danish homes, and the book became a permanent fixture on the bookshelves of an entire generation.

During the past decade a new wave of authors have dealt with the challenging metamorphosis from life as a woman with a large portion of their identity and self-respect invested in work, to becoming a mother and having to reinvent themselves in the balancing act between meeting the demands of a child, a partner and a job.

The theme of Maja Lucas' 2016 novel *Mother – A Story Written in Blood*[13] deals with the taboo of a mother's inability to fully love her child. The mother is overwhelmed by "the violence of the mundane". She breaks down in the face of the dictatorship of her baby's needs, and both parents are confronted by the gap between the dream of equal parenting and the realities: "No matter how much the decision to have a baby had been shared, she was the one who had all the morning sickness and discomfort. The father helped and supported her, as he still does, but he cannot take the burden of biology from her." With the child at her breast the mother concludes: "His pain was being dispensable. Hers was being indispensable."

Cecilie Lind's *My Child* from 2019[14] is a rambling, long poem where the words run, stumble, and skid across the pages in bursts of love, tenderness, self-loathing, anger at the father and a chronic lack of sleep resulting in lines steeped in exhaustion: "Mid in the smell of cooking I stand as erect as a rose and weep." Grief at the transformation of the body seeps out in verses like: "I drip/ If someone asks me who I am I have to tell them/ I'm the one that drips/ Milk, tears, blood, piss."

Both Lucas and Lind's texts are permeated by shock at the way motherhood dismantles the ideal of gender equality. The same theme permeates Olga Ravn's magnum opus *My Job* from 2020.[15] Ravn suffered from postnatal depression after the birth of her first child. She – and Anna, the narrator of the novel – are healed by writing. Through the poems, diary entries, prose extracts and letters that comprise the book she – Olga/Anna – works through the crisis towards a new sense of self that can embrace an identity as author as well as mother.

Ravn's novel is a literary investigation of and confrontation with the narrow ideals of *the good mother*, something she emphasised in an interview when the book was published: "I've encountered quite a bit of what you could call mind control in my life, but never has it been so invasive as when I fell pregnant. You soon realise that you no longer belong to yourself, but have become public property. Complete strangers come up to you and touch your body, everywhere you go you hear warnings and reprimands. It becomes obvious that parents – and historically primarily mothers – are responsible for producing a labour force and citizens with the vote. It is in the public interest that these future citizens are raised according to a set of values that make it possible to maintain the status quo. For me having responsibility for a child is one of the most politically charged positions there is."[16]

Olga Ravn's statement zooms in on a fundamental paradox of modern motherhood, because despite decades of women's liberation, the ideological and social control of motherhood continues to be ruthless. And despite contemporary ideals of individuality and personal freedom of choice, there is still very little recognition that women can be pregnant, feed, breastfeed and structure their maternity leave and working life in many different ways – and still be good mothers.

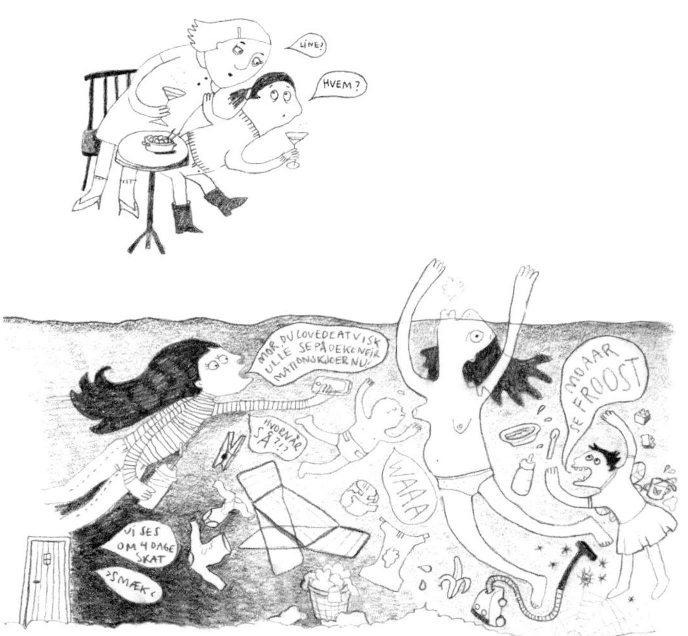

Line Jensen's first graphic short stories from 2017, *Hver dag starter det forfra* (Every Day it Starts All Over Again) present a satirical portrait of life in a family with three children.

1 Carl Nielsen, *Min fynske barndom*, 1927.
2 Anne Løkke, *Døden i barndommen: Spædbørnsdødelighed og moderniserings-processer i Danmark, 1800-1920*. Gyldendal, 1998.
3 Jan William Rasmussen (ed.), *Børnehjemmet af 1870*. Jubilee publication, 1970.
4 Svenn Monrad, *Moderens Bog: Det sunde Barns pleje*, 1916.
5 Ephesians chapter 5, verses 22-23, cited in Pia Fris Laneth: *1915 – da kvinder og tyende blev borgere*, Gyldendal, 2015.
6 Preben Hertoft, *Det er måske en galskab,* 1983.
7 Cited in Pia Fris Laneth, *Moderskab og Mødrehjælp*, Kristeligt Dagblad, 2014.
8 Cited in Elisabeth Badinter, *The Myth of Motherhood: A Historical View of the Maternal Instinct*. Souvenir Press, 1981 pp. 274-75.
9 Erich Fromm, *The Art of Loving*, New York: Harper & Row, 1974, pp. 35-36.
10 Aksel Tofte, *Seksuel hygiejne – håndbog i seksuel oplysning*, 1941 & 1957.
11 Cited in Pia Fris Laneth, *Lillys danmarkshistorie*, Gyldenal, 2006.
12 Dea Trier Mørch, *Winter's Child*, translated by Joan Tate. University of Nebraska Press, London, 1986 (1976), p. 122.
13 Maja Lucas, *Mor – en historie om blodet*, C&K Forlag, 2016.
14 Cecilie Lind, *Mit barn*, Gyldendal, 2019.
15 Olga Ravn, *Mit arbejde*, Gyldendal, 2020.
16 Interview with Olga Ravn by Bror Axel Dehn. *Vagant*, 14/10/2020.

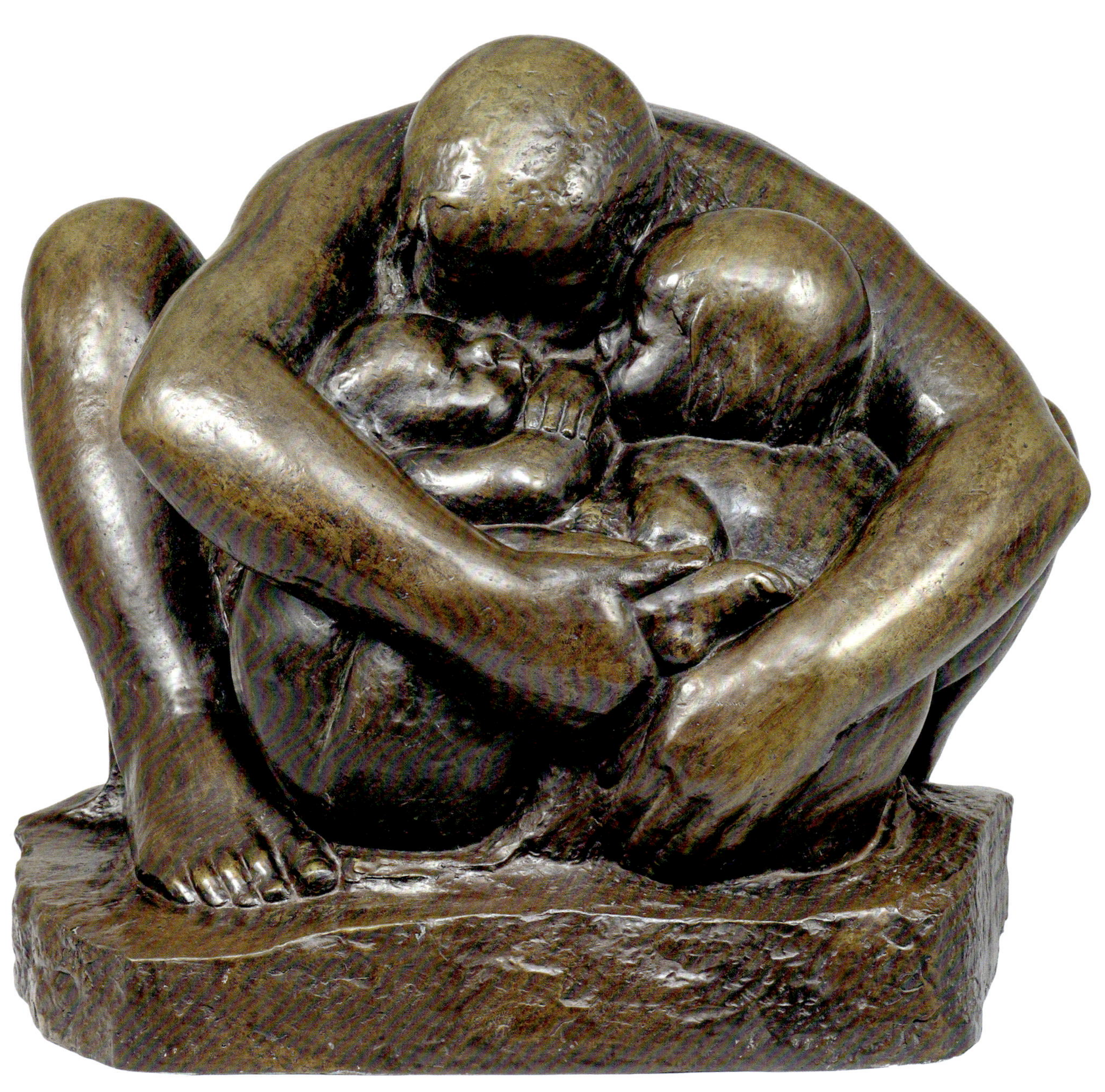

cat. 55
Käthe Kollwitz: *Mutter mit zwei Kindern*, 1932-1936
Mother with Two Children

Right page: cat. 12
Mary Cassatt: *Jenny and Her Sleepy Child*, c. 1891-1892

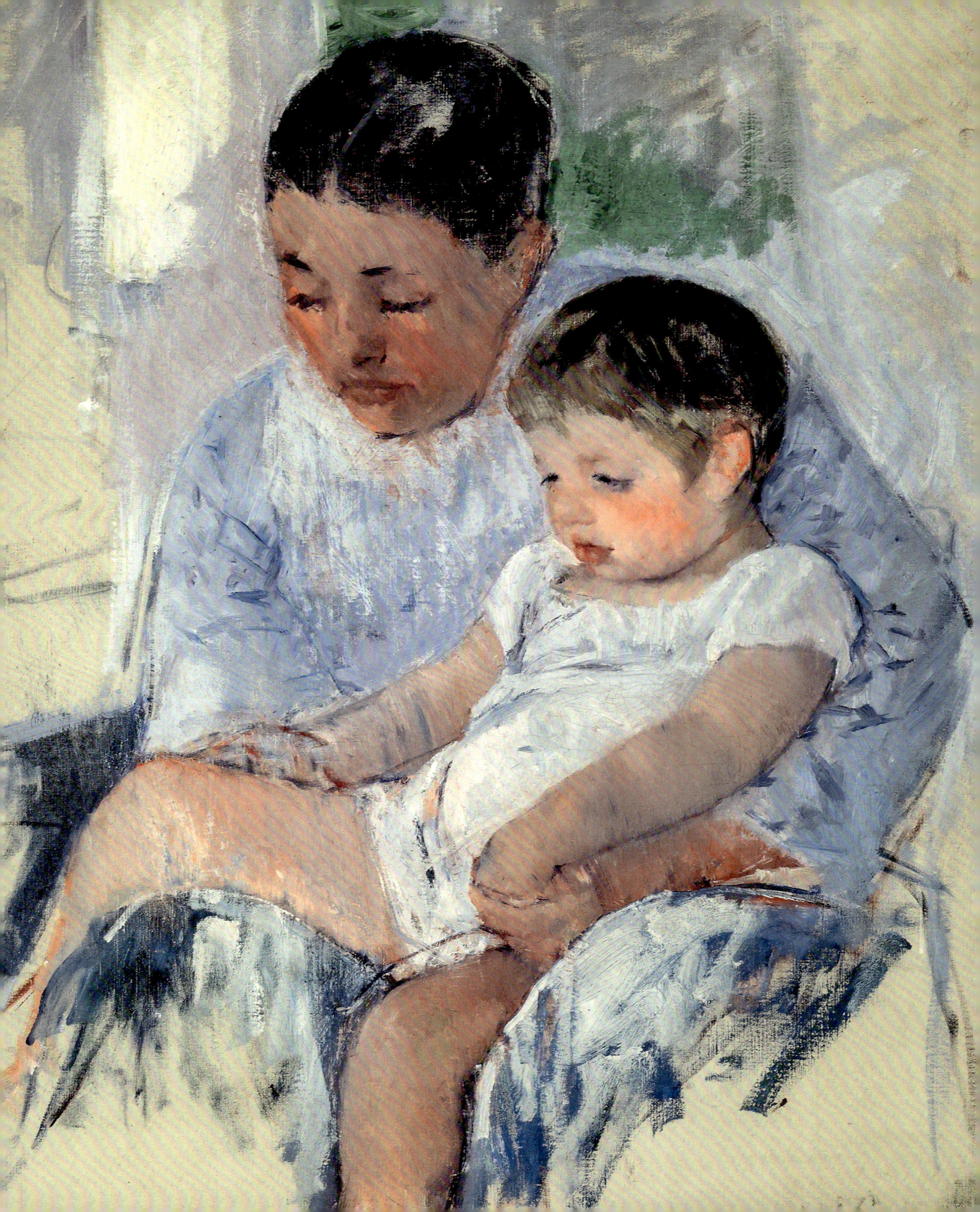

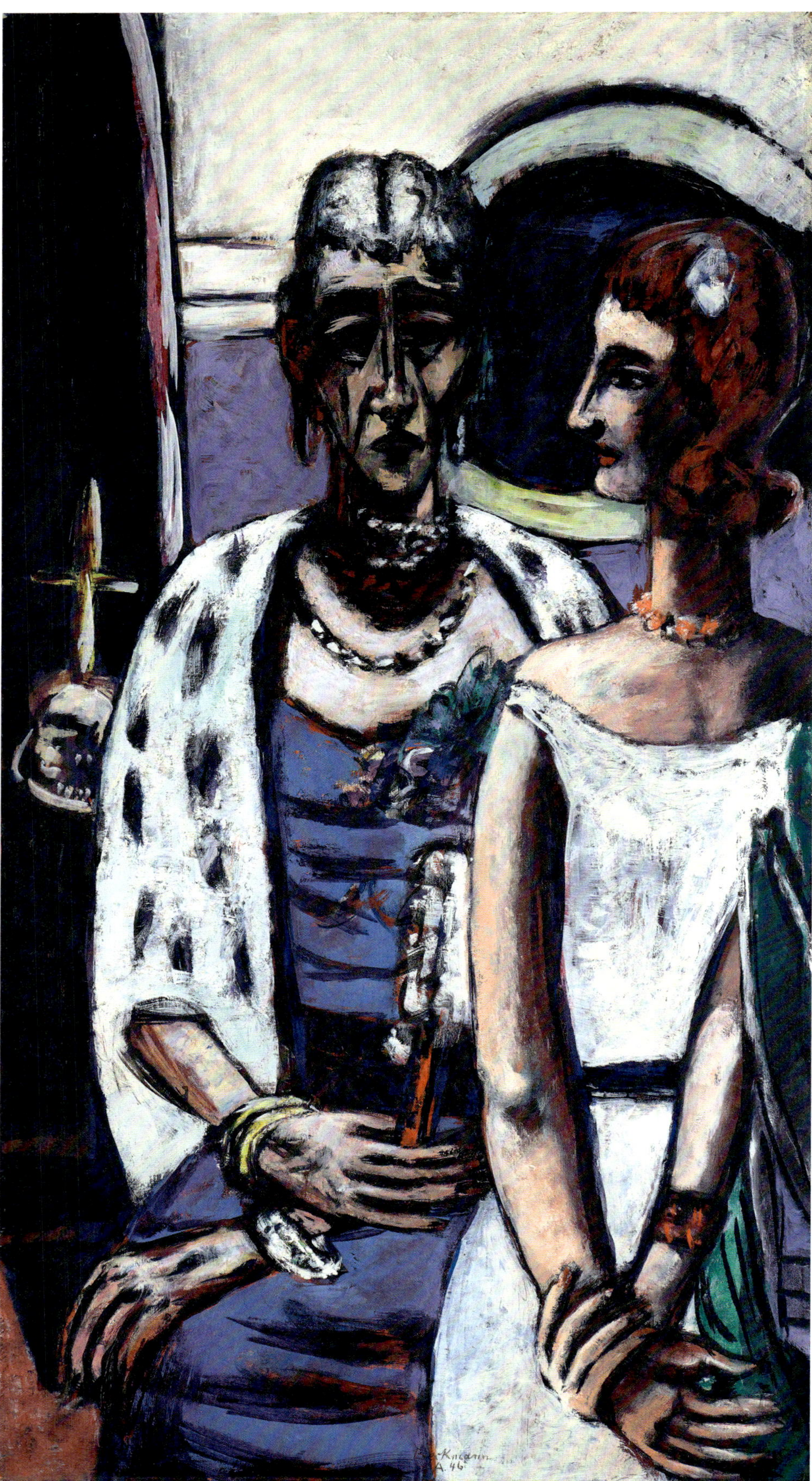

cat. 2
Max Beckmann: *Mutter und Tochter*, 1946
Mother and Daughter

Right page: cat. 61
Jeanne Mammen: *Kindesmörderin*, 1910-1914
Child-Murderess

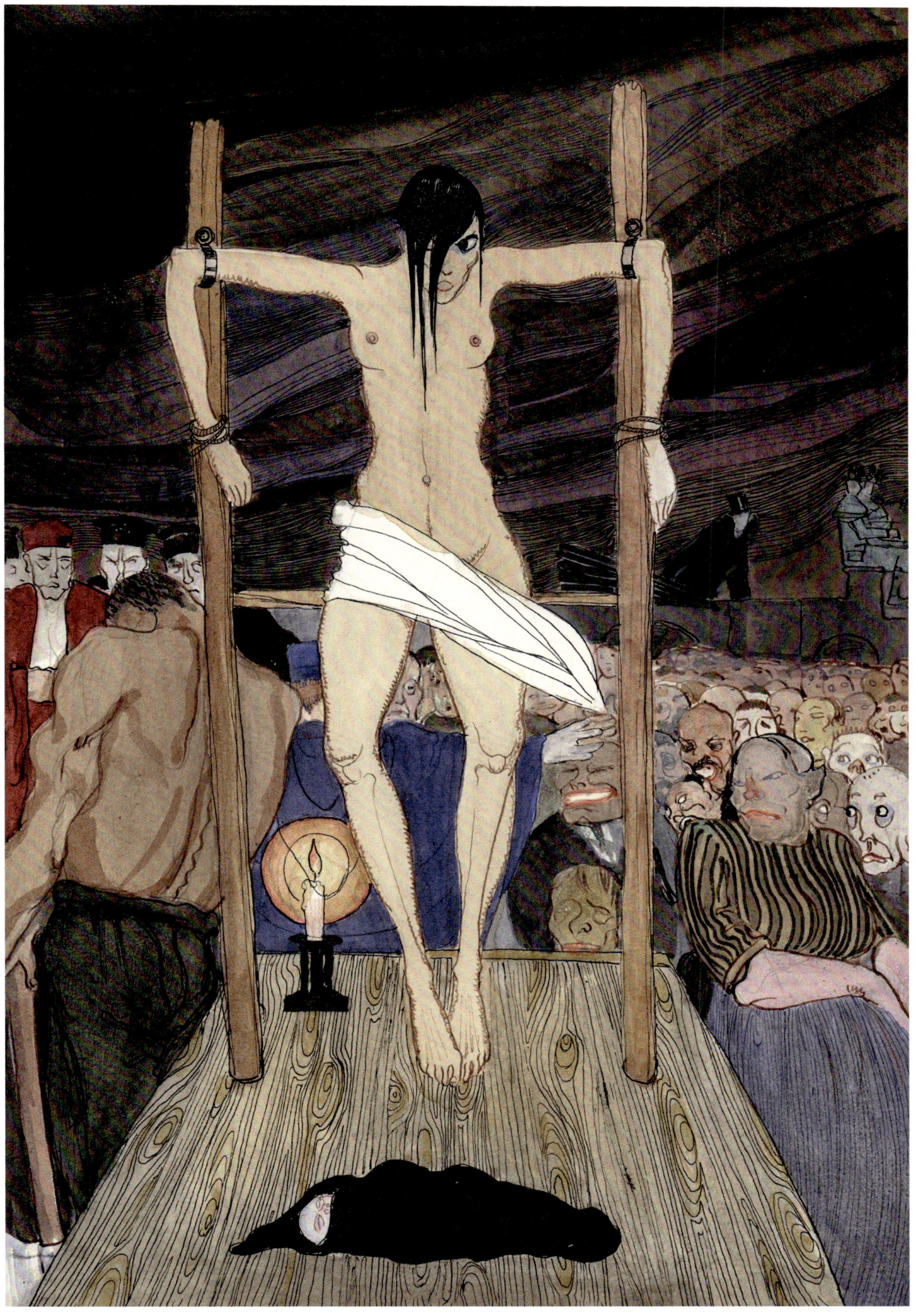

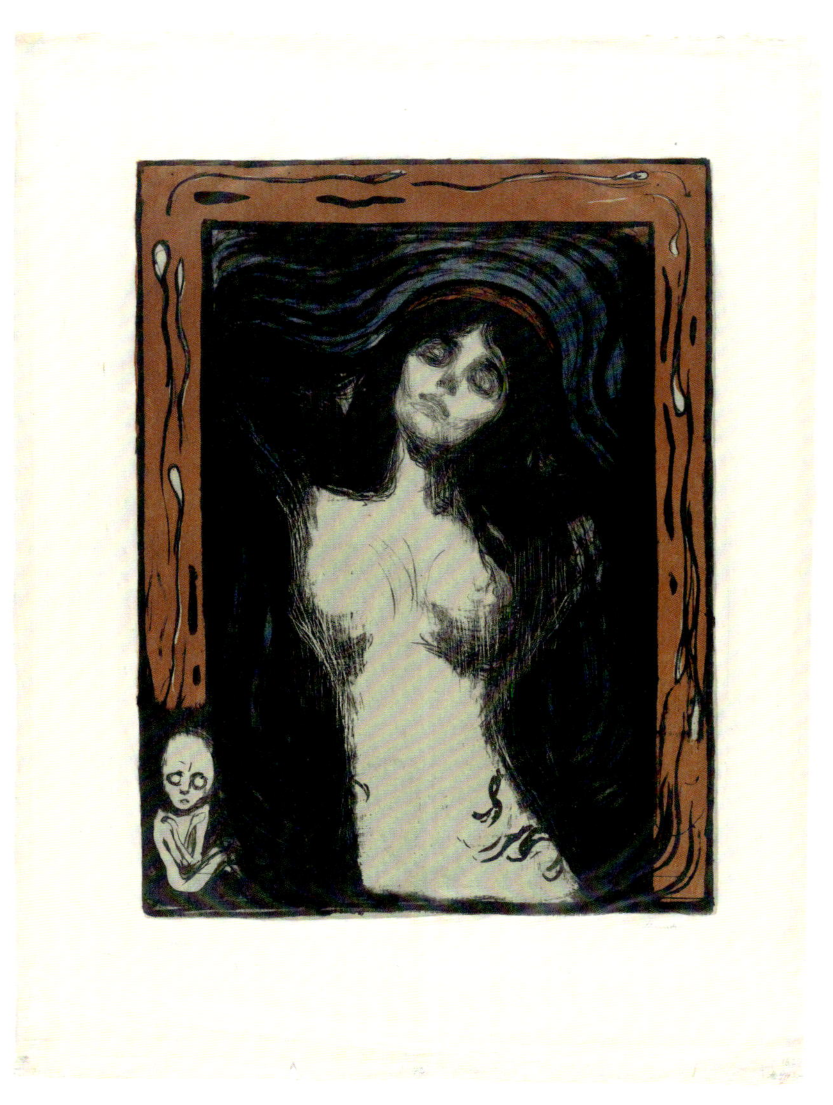

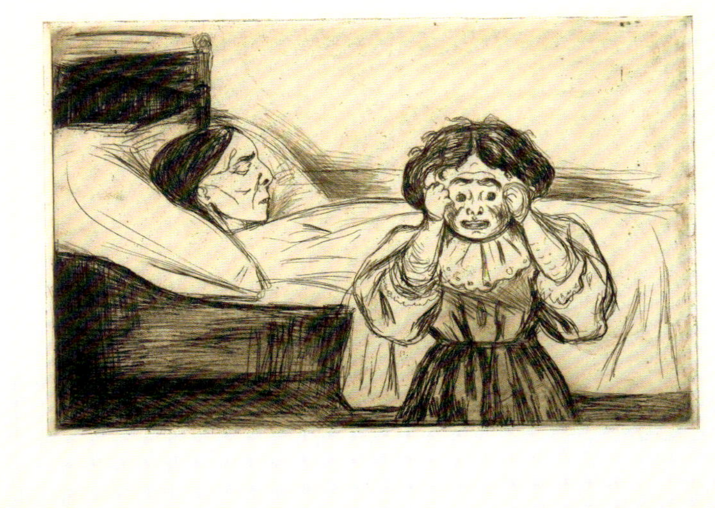

cat. 81
Edvard Munch: *Madonna (Elskende kvinne)*, 1895/1902
Madonna (Loving Woman)

cat. 80
Edvard Munch: *Den døde mor og barnet*, 1901
The Dead Mother and Her Child

Right page: cat. 56
Wilhelm Lachnit: *Schwangeres Proletariermädchen*, 1924/26
Pregnant Working Class Girl

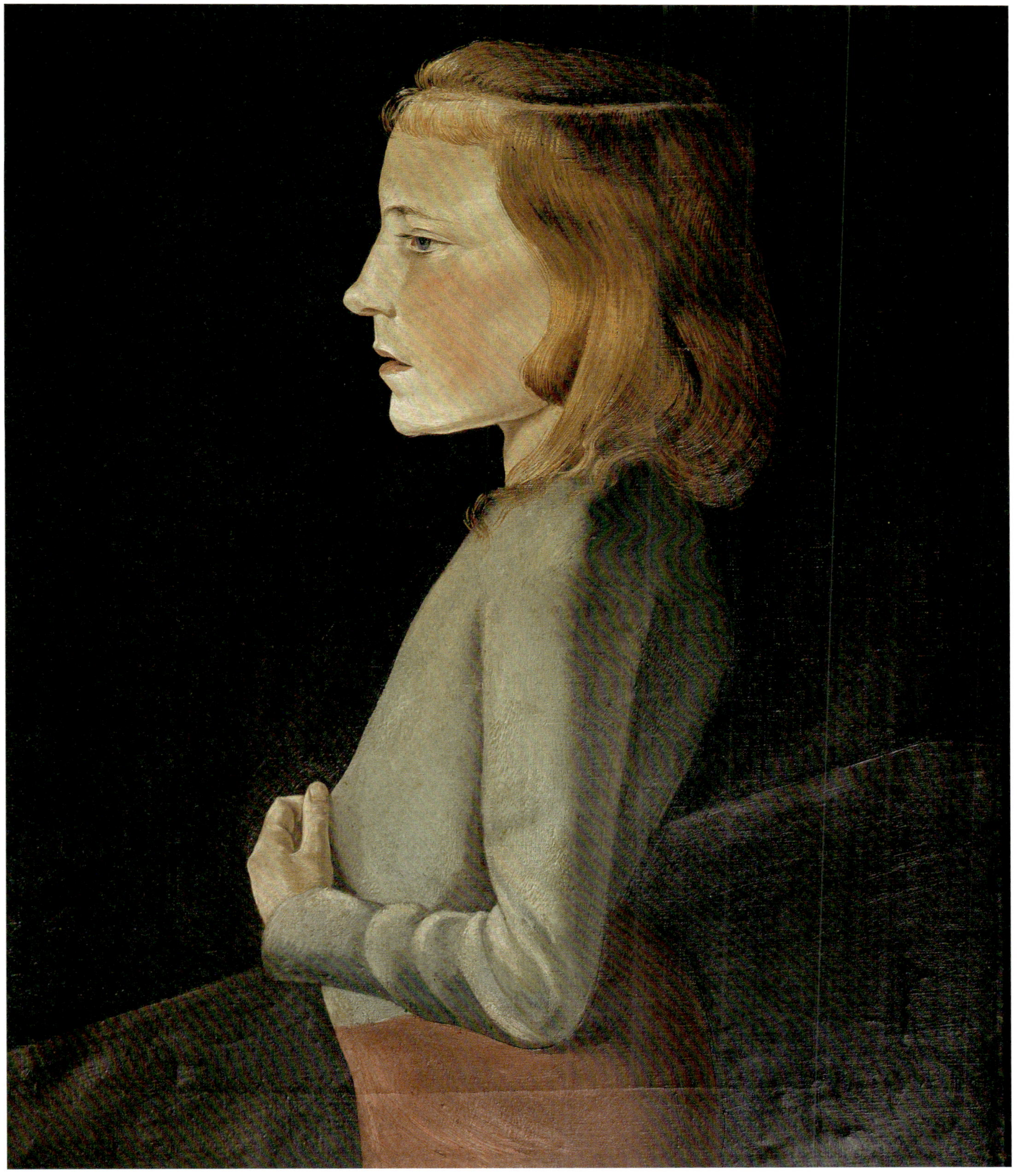

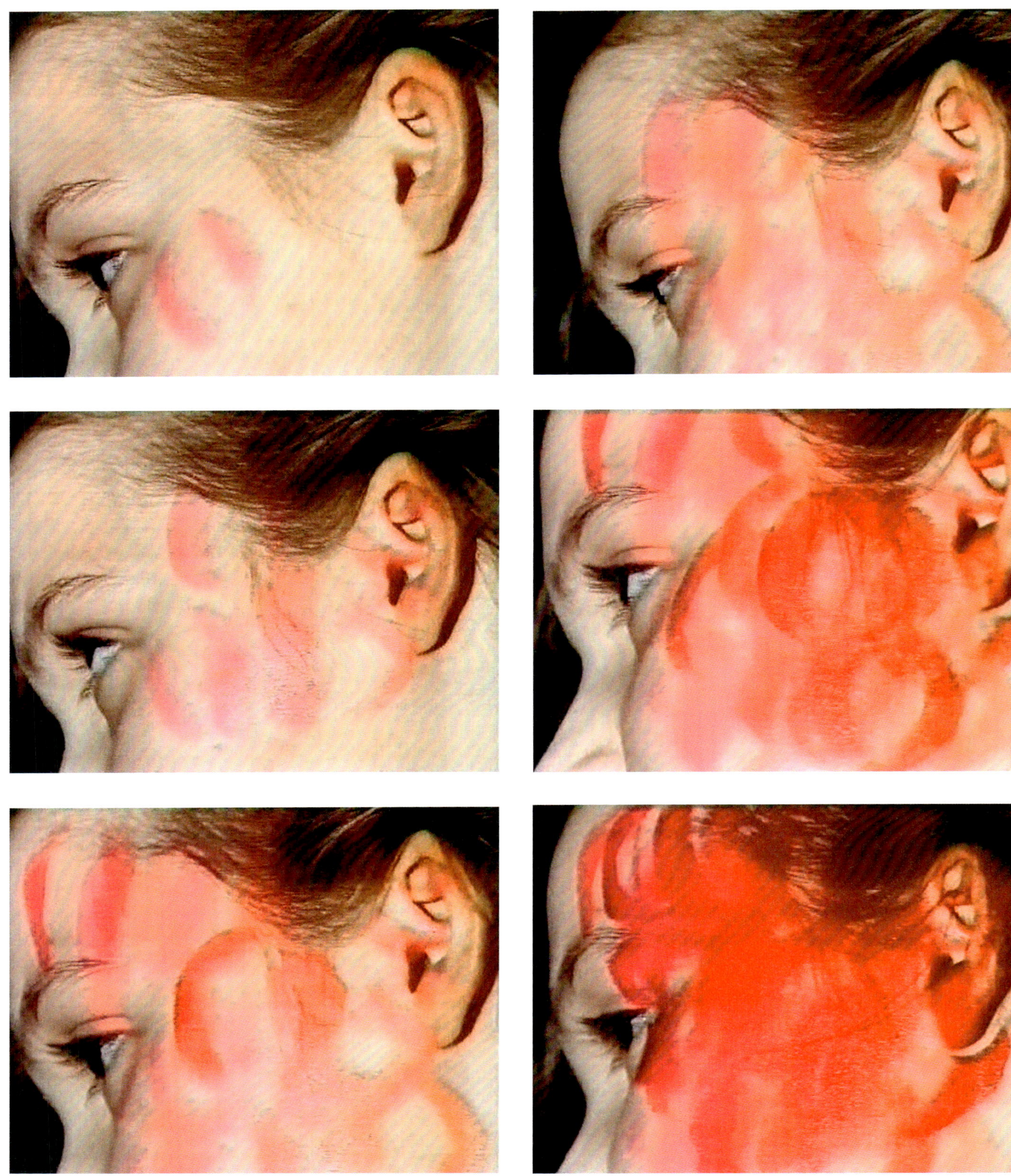

cat. 106
Ulrike Rosenbach: *Mutterliebe*, 1977
Mother's Love

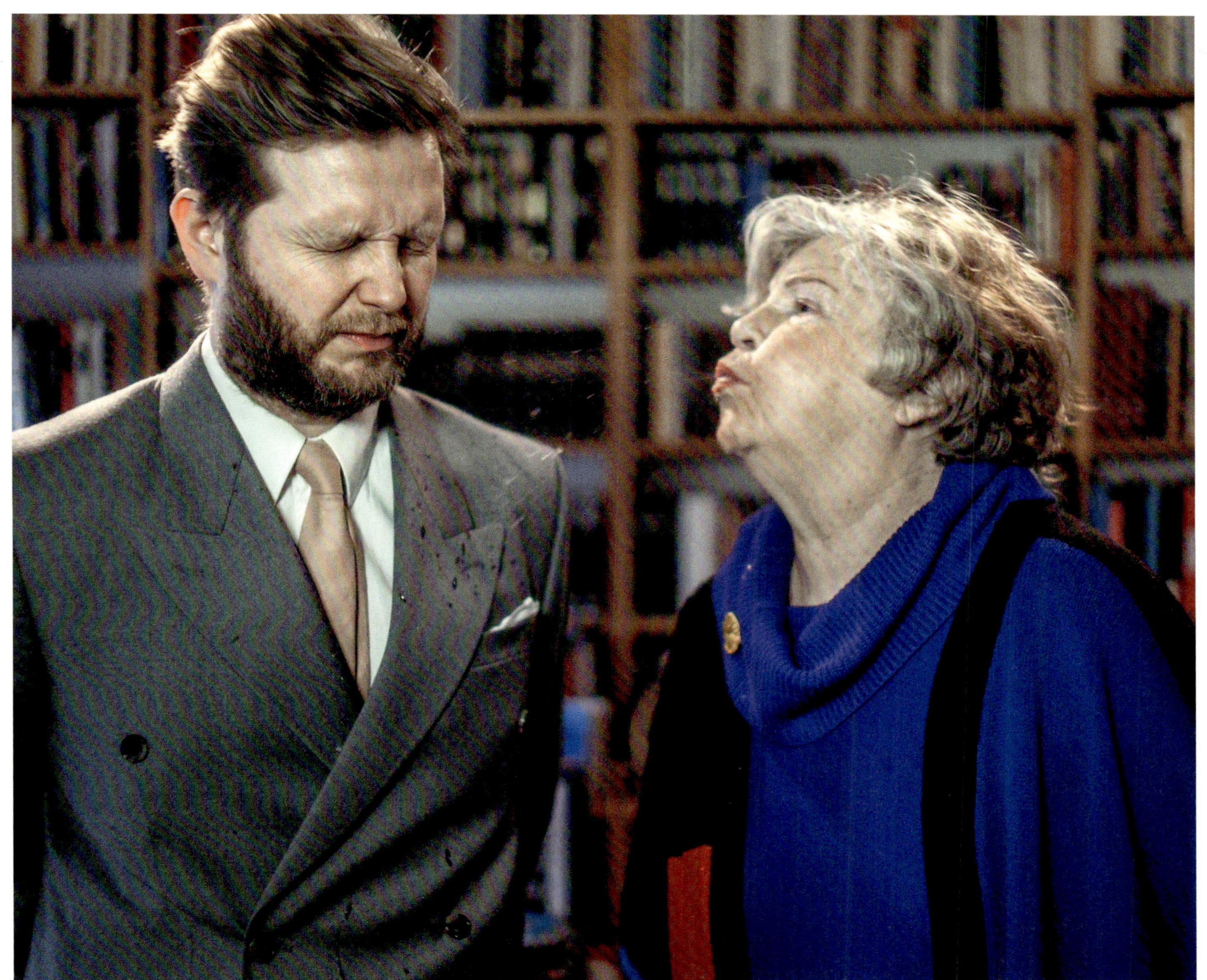

cat. 54
Ragnar Kjartansson: *Me and My Mother*, 2015

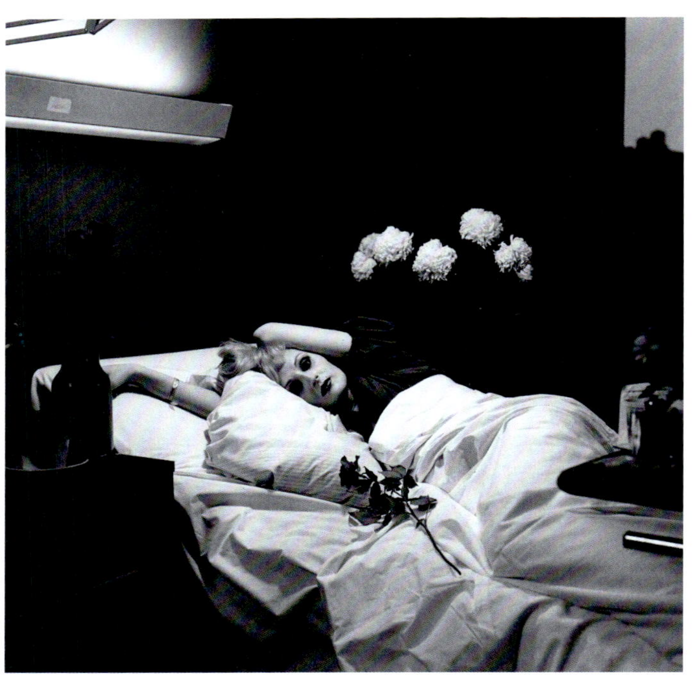

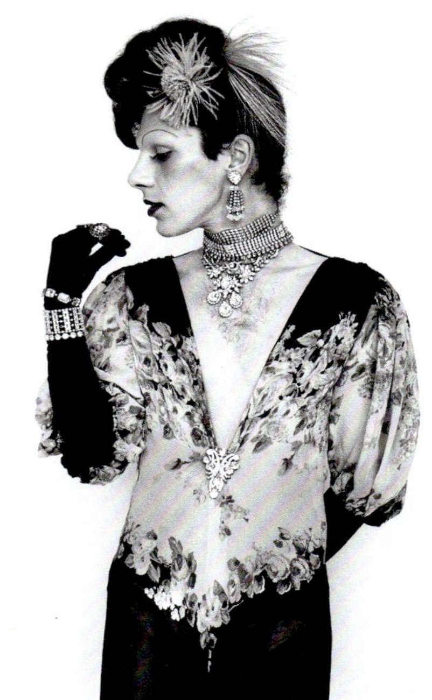

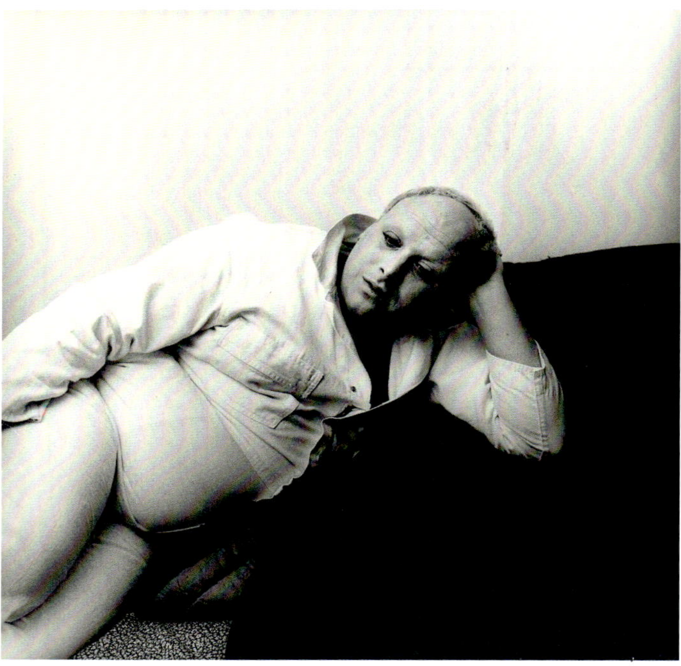

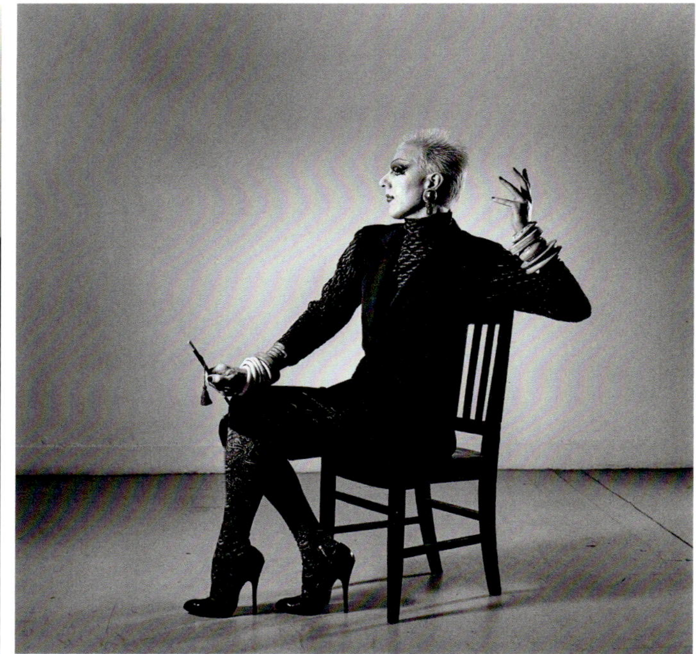

cat. 31
Peter Hujar: *Candy Darling on Her Deathbed*, 1973

cat. 32
Peter Hujar: *Divine*, 1975

cat. 30
Peter Hujar: *John Rothermel (Cockette)*, 1971

cat. 34
Peter Hujar: *Ethyl Eichelberger in a Fashion Pose*, 1981

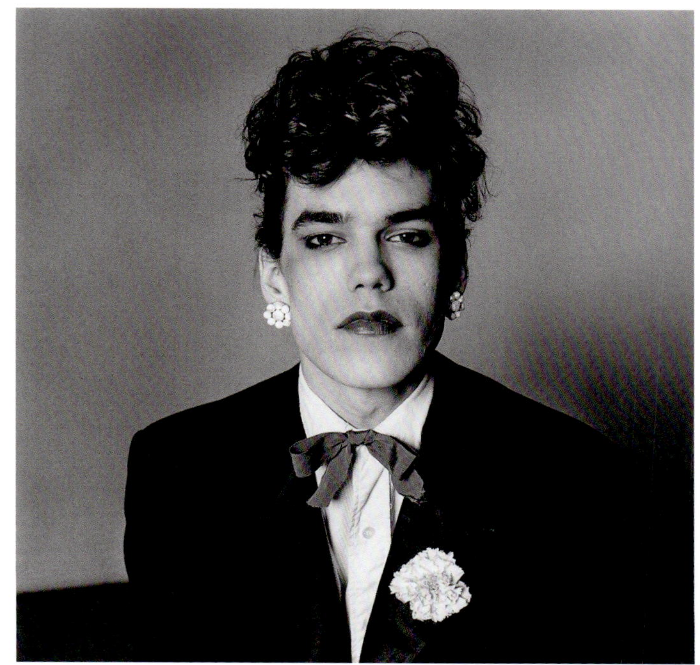

cat. 35
Peter Hujar: *David Brintzenhofe #6*, 1982

cat. 33
Peter Hujar: *Ethyl Eichelberger as Nefertiti (II)*, 1981

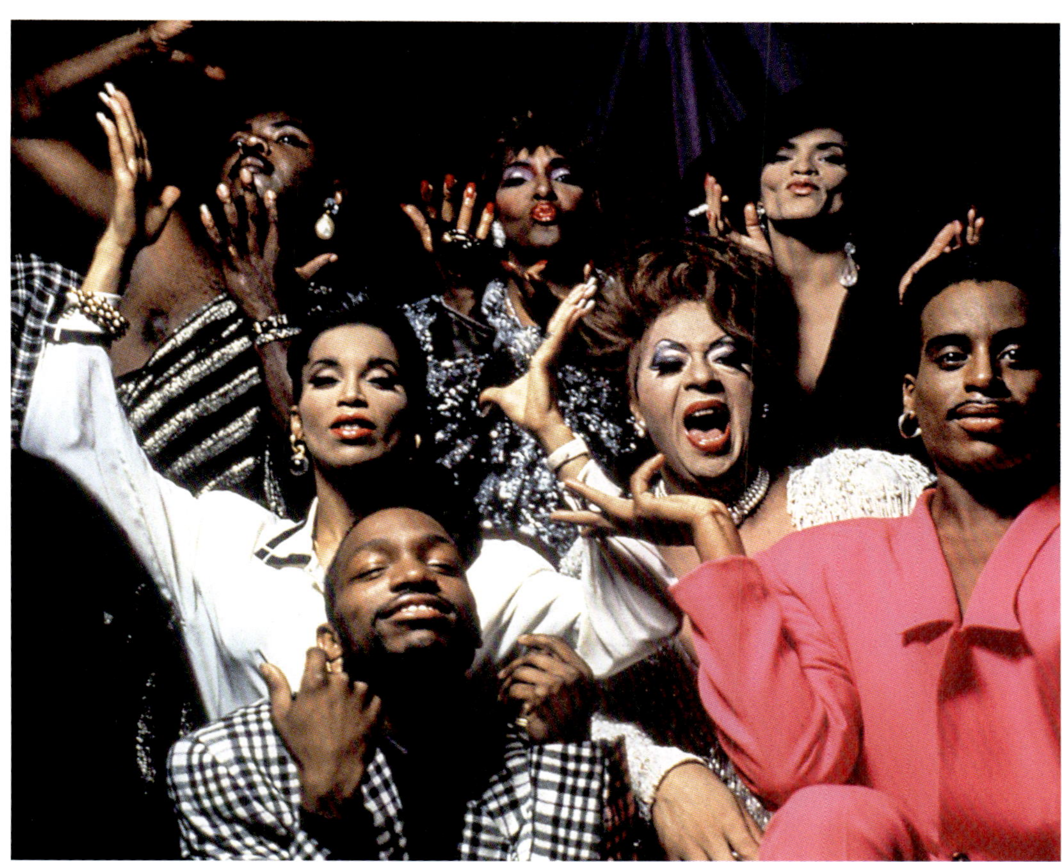

cat. 58
Jennie Livingston:
Paris is Burning, 1990

A History of Fertility

By Adam Bencard

Adam Bencard is Associate Professor of Medical Humanities at Medical Museion in Copenhagen and at the Novo Nordisk Foundation Center for Basic Metabolic Research at the University of Copenhagen. He is curator of the exhibition *Mind the Gut* and is currently working on *The World Is In You*, a project exploring how our bodies, health and diseases are impacted by the world around us.

Children will always be at the heart of our existence as a species. Having children, and surviving childbirth, has fascinated people through the ages. There have been stories of infertility as far back as stories have been recorded. Ancient Egyptian medical texts describe how to tell if a woman is fertile and provide advice for ensuring conception. The medical tradition of ancient Greece likewise contains copious descriptions of infertility problems and the appropriate remedies. The *Hippocratic Corpus*, a collection of medical texts from the classical world that figured prominently in Western medicine even up to the early 19th century, dedicates an entire work to fertility problems. Beyond the medical tradition, infertility and the desire to have children are a recurring cultural theme across cultures. Sarah and Abraham's desperate wish for a child is a cornerstone of Christianity and Judaism. As Rachel, in another Old Testament tale, says, "Give me children, or else I die." Stories of childlessness, miracle births, adoption and similar themes appear in Icelandic sagas, Greek myths and Indian epic poetry. Rare is the mythology that does not have at least one fertility god or goddess.

Likewise, the story of birth care – the endeavour to understand and alleviate the dangers inherent in the complex biology of childbirth – is as long as humanity itself. Just as pregnancy has always been both natural and dangerous at once, so childbirth has been a cause of existential concern, scientific interpretation, and dreams of treatment. The story of midwifery and obstetrics is the story of medical science attempting to comprehend and control childbirth – a critical juncture for the mother, child, and society at large – and how those attempts, spreading like ripples in water, have changed society and how we live. Fertility, pregnancy, and childbirth have been the object of a vast scientific and scholarly effort that has fundamentally changed the limits and expectations of who can have children, and how and when they can have them. The following is a look at fertility and birth care from the perspective of the history of medicine.

Fertility

Remedies and explanations have changed over the centuries. Religion has often played a key role through an impressive array of prayers, pilgrimages and saints. Medical ingenuity has also been great and varied. In the Middle Ages, crushed animal genitals were taken in the hope of boosting fertility. In the 18th century, spas and hydrotherapy were prescribed to calm the nervous system of the childless woman and prevent spasms in the womb. In the early 20th century, adoption was recommended for

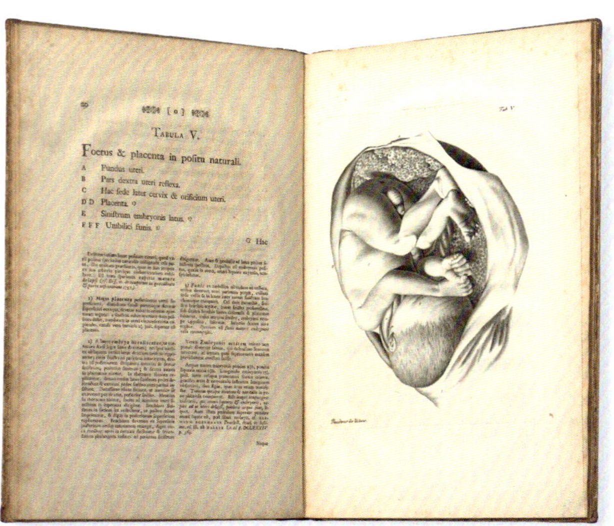

cat. 104
Johann Georg Röderer: *Icones Uteri Humani*, 1759

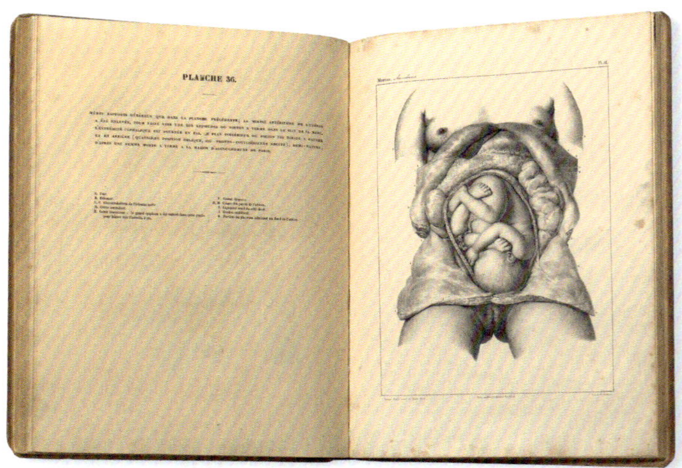

cat. 79
François-Joseph Moreau: *Traité Pratique des Accouchemens*, 1839

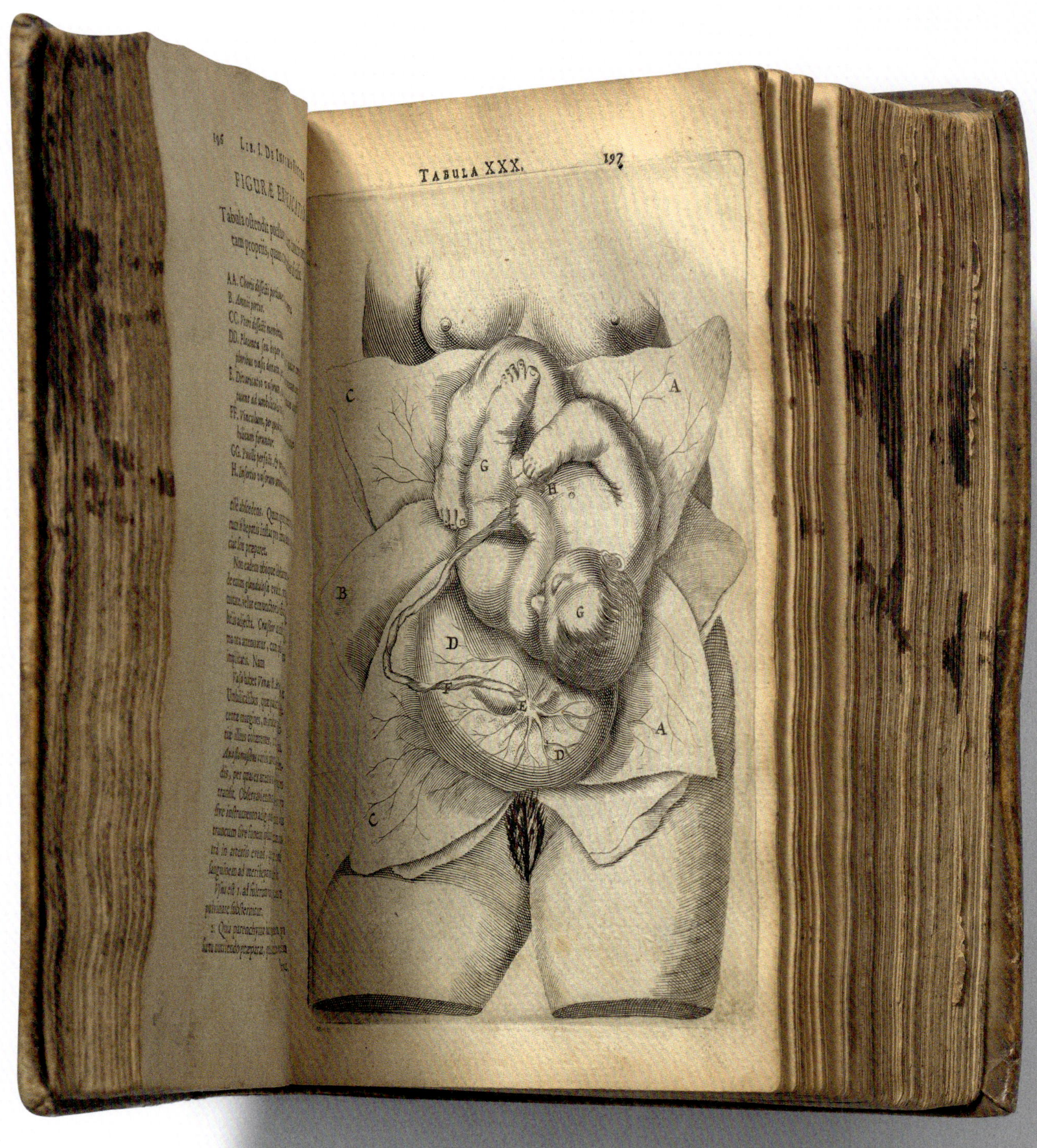

cat. 1
Thomas Bartholin: *Anatomia, ex Caspari Bartholini Parentis Institutionibus, Omniumque Recentiorum & propriis Observationibus, Tertium ad sanguinis Circulationem Reformata*, Leiden, 1671

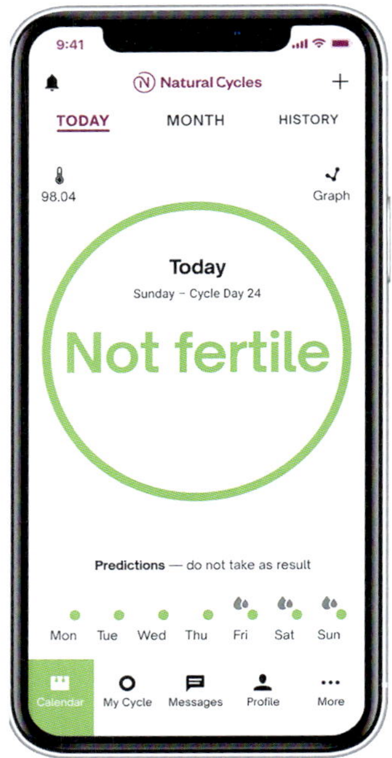

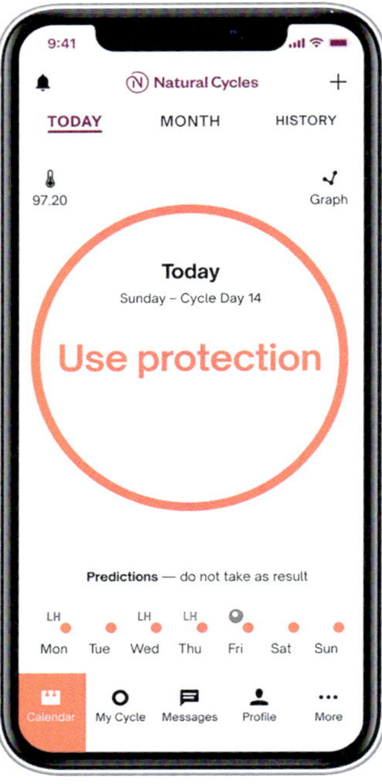

cat. 160
Digital Fertility Awareness App, 2020

psychosomatically unclogging a blocked system. The variations are countless, the problem timeless. Equally timeless and culturally ubiquitous is that the interpretation of infertility, across cultures, has been distorted by gender bias. There has been a disproportionate focus on the infertile woman, not the man. The childless woman has often been seen as less than a woman, less feminine, unseemly, an object of pity and social ostracism, even at times outright morally impaired or otherwise suspect. Nineteenth-century doctors linked childlessness to abortion, venereal disease and sexual promiscuity.

It is important to include this at once both eternal and ever-changing story in the often heated discussions and anxieties about fertility that have marked the last several decades, as it has become increasingly clear that many societies are no longer near the magical fertility rate of 2.1. Once an individual existential crisis, childlessness today encompasses a host of far greater, multilayered issues. Explanations range from social and cultural – access to birth control, changed patterns of education, shifts in the job market, increased pressure to self-actualize, to name a few – to medical and physiological, in the way of a declining sperm count, older first-time mothers, hormonal imbalances, and the like. The tension between the social and the physiological is particularly pronounced in terms of the many technological advances made since the mid-20th century. Even as we seem to be able to do more with the aid of technology, our ways of living are pulling in the opposite direction. The body is able to do less. It is still unclear what impact the invention and pervasiveness of fertility technologies is having on our perceptions of the complex relationship between the body and technology.

Fertility technologies have fundamentally changed our view of pregnancy and childlessness. By the 1930s, it was already possible to measure progesterone levels in urine and, consequently, detect pregnancy much earlier. Home pregnancy kits have been available since the late 1960s. Ultrasound was developed in the 1950s and, by the 1970s, was a commonly used technology in obstetrics and midwifery. Enabling us to visualize the foetus in the womb, these technologies have been hugely important to the understanding and politics of reproduction. Pregnancy has lost the fluid character it once had, where subjective experience ruled. Pregnancy is increasingly an absolute state. You are either pregnant or not. There is no grey area. What today is seen as a linear development from conception to birth used to involve a far more subjective reading of signs, and medical science was not an absolute authority. Technology is helping to define this state of affairs.

The technological development came to a head in the middle of the last century, symbolized by the birth of an English baby, Louise Brown, on 25 July 1978. The first child to be born after being conceived through artificial insemination (in vitro fertilization, or IVF), she was touted as a medical miracle, a victory over nature. IVF and later assisted reproductive technologies put infertility in a new perspective and changed how pregnancy is handled. Today, children born with the assistance of reproductive technologies like IVF and hormone treatments do not make headlines, while the perception of such technologies as pure miracles has also been dented by their variable efficacy and often great personal and economic cost.

No matter how fertility, childlessness, and birth rates are viewed, the entanglement between body, society, and technology is all too apparent. Fertility technologies have crucially affected our sense of what a normal pregnancy is. From birth-control pills and abortions on one side to ultrasound and pregnancy tests in the middle and IVF and hormone treatments on the other, the effects of the scientific unfolding of fertility are ambiguous and multifaceted. There is a noticeable tension between how pregnancy

The ivory models of pregnant women were used to teach male medical students. The models are carved in minute detail and constructed such that the abdomen can be opened to reveal a small foetus. The anatomical ivory figures, besides being an educational tool, were luxury collectors' items.

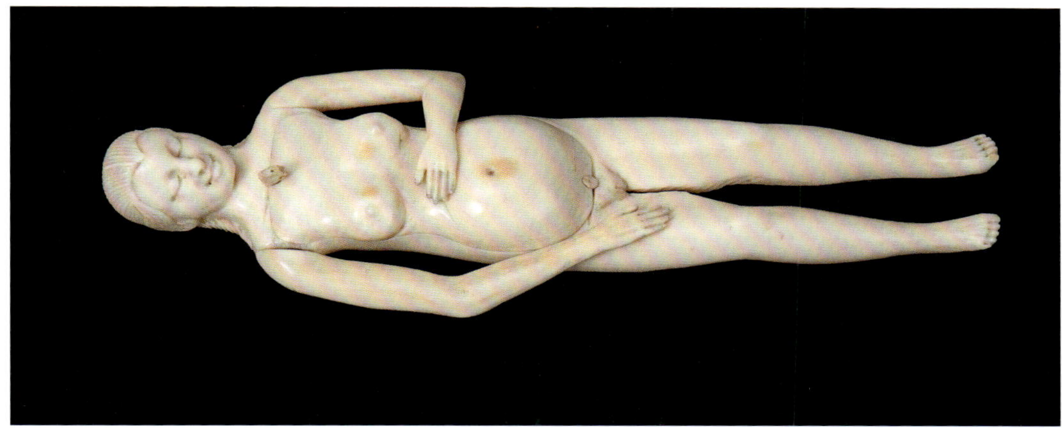

cat. 149
Anatomical teaching model of a pregnant woman, Nuremberg, c. 1700

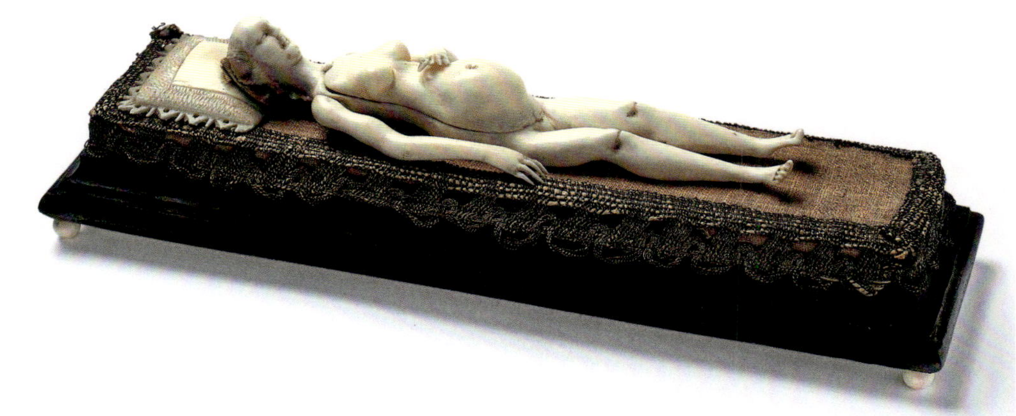

cat. 150
Anatomical teaching model of a pregnant woman, undated

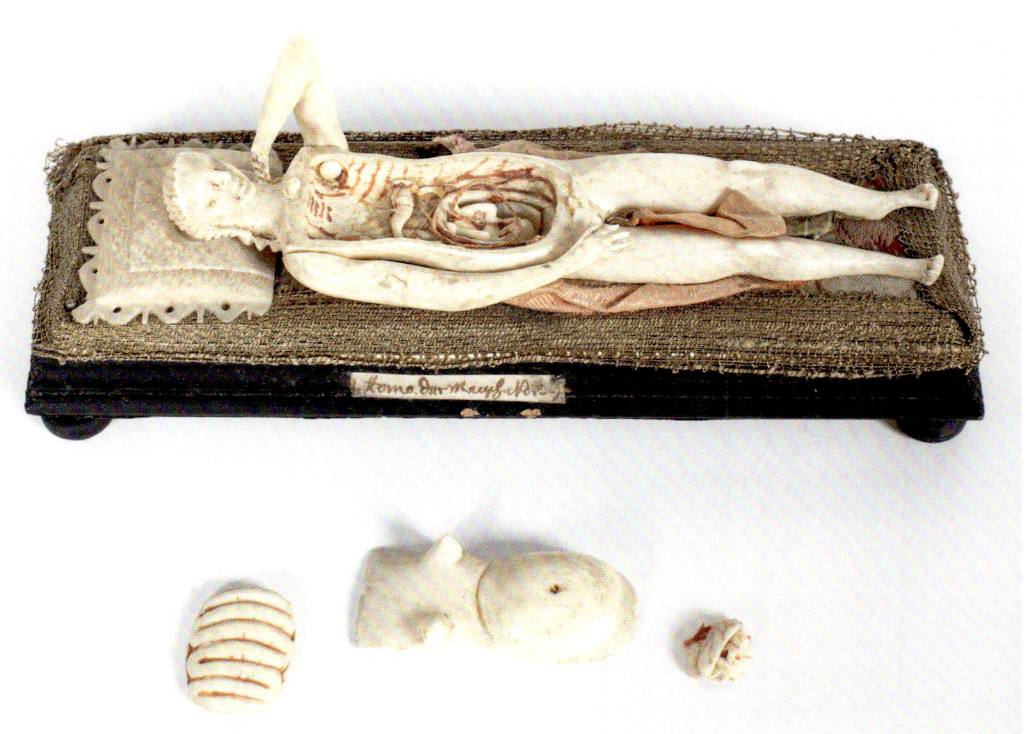

cat. 118
Stephan Zick: Anatomical teaching model of a pregnant woman, Nuremberg, c. 1680

has been unlocked as a technical and scientific problem and the increasing need for such technologies as our physical reproductive ability, for various reasons, appears to be declining.

Dangers of Childbirth

In 2002, Medical Museion in Copenhagen published *A History of Birth Care* by Mogens Osler, chief of surgery and obstetrics at the Department of Gynaecology at Copenhagen's Rigshospitalet from 1969 to 1996 and professor at the Midwifery School in Copenhagen. The book surveys the long and complex history of birth care and the many technical and medical advances – from barber surgeons, superstition, and a high mortality rate for mother and child to ultrasound scans, safe surgery, and death in childbirth as an extremely rare occurrence. All the same, an unresolved tension can be detected in the book's epilogue, as Osler reflects on the history of his field: "Through the ages, birth care has mainly been a matter of preventing death, damage and disease in the mother, the foetus, and the newborn child. In other words, normality has always been desired and sought: a normal pregnancy, a normal birth, a normal child. But today the course of a normal pregnancy and birth is far from equivalent to a natural one. On the contrary, modern obstetrics and its many preventive measures are increasingly widening the gap between the natural and the normal."

In many ways, the long history of birth care hinges on this tension between a normality, whose boundaries are constantly shifting, and a naturalness that is inherently unpredictable and opaque. Much has been gained over the course of this history, but fundamental changes have also been made to the framework around pregnancy and birth.

Childbirth is dangerous. The WHO estimates that 15 percent of all women in labour develop serious complications requiring immediate and effective treatment to prevent chronic problems or death. Being born is even more dangerous. Through most of human history, child mortality rates have been at levels that are hard to fathom from the perspective of a hi-tech society. In 18th-century Denmark, roughly 20-25 percent of newborns died within their first year of life, and one percent of women are estimated to have died in childbirth. This statistic should be seen in light of the fact that most women used to give birth every two and a half years during their fertile years. Of course, these figures are skewed by the enormous differences in living conditions between rich and poor. Things are not much better today. About 2.5 percent of children in Bangladesh die before the age of one. In Denmark, the child mortality rate did not drop below 10 percent until the 20th century. Death has always been an intimate companion, a persistent shadow, and a visitor at childbirth. In *Brought to Bed: Childbearing in America 1750-1950*, the historian Judith Walzer Leavitt quotes from an 1885 letter from a woman describing the course of her third pregnancy: "Between oceans of pain there stretched continents of fear; fear of death and dread of suffering beyond bearing." Childbirth is at once both lethal and life affirming, routine and an existential abyss. That is why birth care has most likely always existed in one form or another; its history is as long as humanity itself. Only the form of the care has changed across historical, cultural, social, and economic divides. For the vast majority of history, the care was social and emotional rather than medical and technical, and was handled by family and women in the community. Long into the 20th century, almost all births in Denmark took place at home. The woman in labour was often assisted by female relatives and friends and perhaps a midwife (and in rare cases, a doctor). The midwife is a recurring figure: historical evidence shows the existence of a midwifery trade very early on. Midwives were women who not only had experience from their own births but regularly assisted at others'. For most of European history, there was no formal education, training programmes, or syllabi for midwives, much less professional licenses or official regulations. Women learned how to assist and support from practical experience and each other.

New Anatomy, New Insight

In the 17th century, the picture slowly begins to change. From the perspective of Western medicine, the history of obstetrics – especially with regard to improved knowledge and options for surgical intervention in difficult births – is inextricably linked to the history of anatomy. The mid-16th century sees the emergence of an anatomical tradition that is concerned with understanding the fabric of the body; *Fabrica* is the title of a pathbreaking 1543 work by Andreas Vesalius (1514-1564). Out of this anatomical movement grew new knowledge and insight into the structures of the body, including pregnancy and the baby *in utero*.

Three wax tablets in the exhibition date to the early 19th century and once belonged to the Royal Danish Academy of Surgery, where they were used for

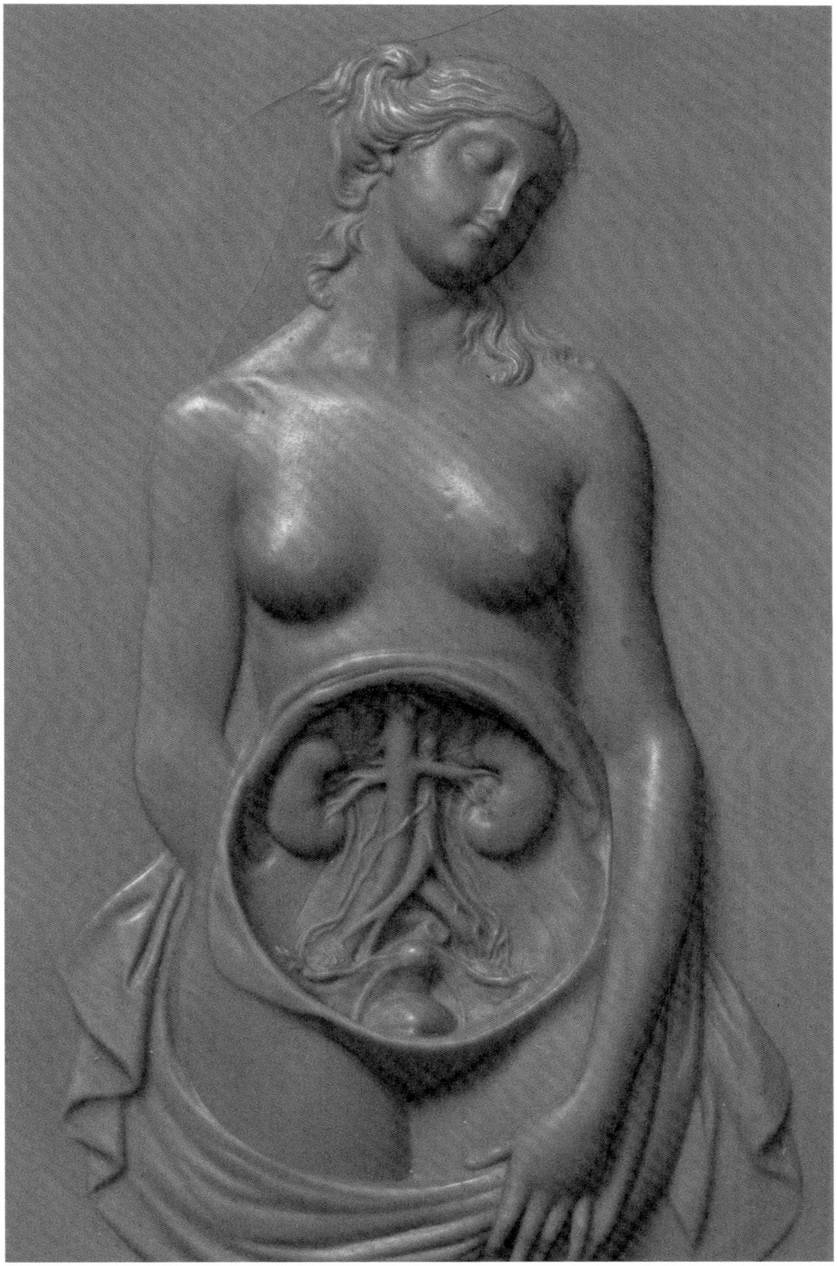

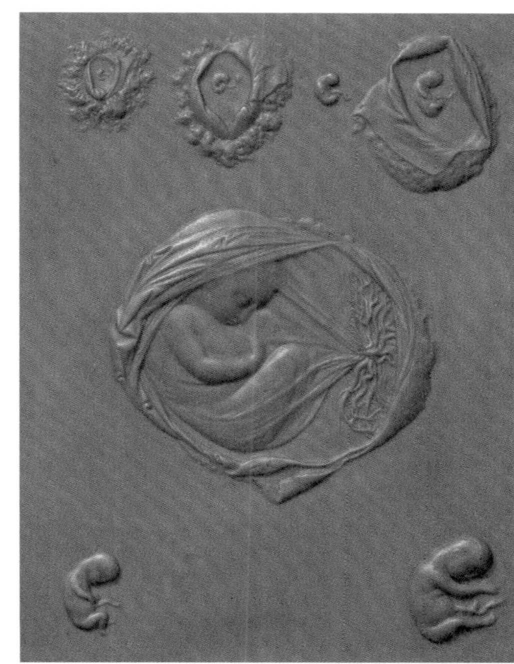

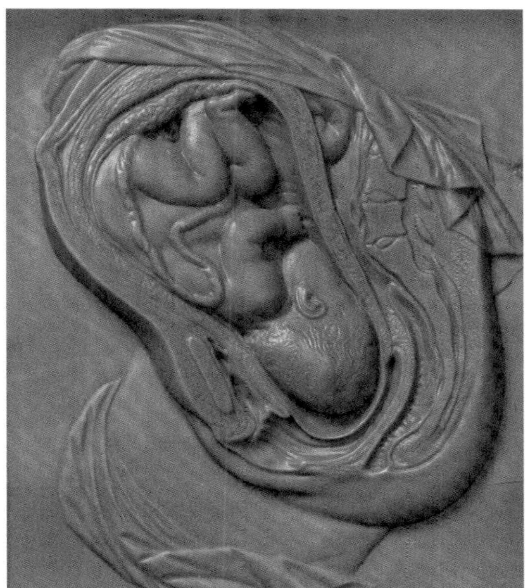

In the 1800s wax tablets were used to teach female anatomy and the development of the foetus. These were further developments of the anatomical mapping of the body that began in the Renaissance.

cat. 153
Wax tablet showing the back of the female abdomen, early 1800s

cat. 151
Wax tablet showing the foetal development in 7 figures, early 1800s

cat. 152
Wax tablet showing a pregnant woman, early 1800s

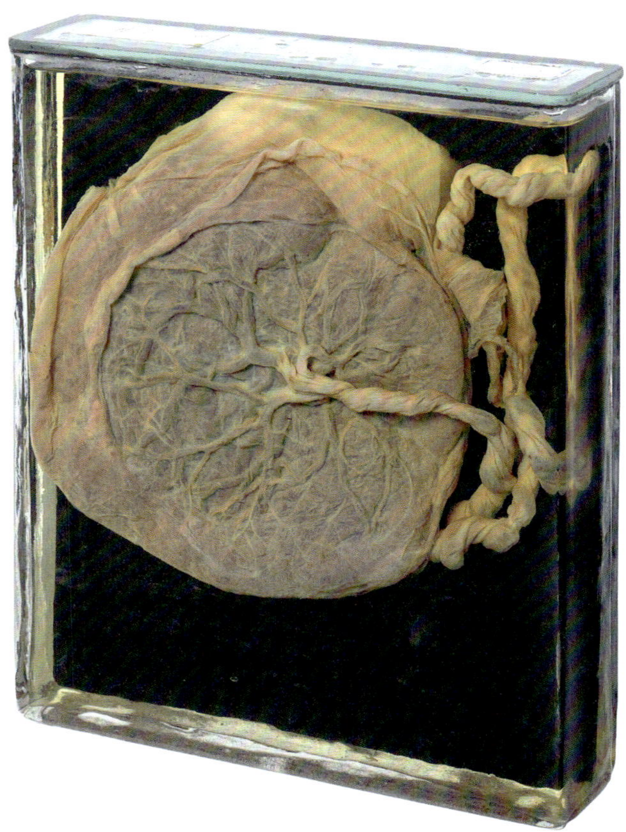

cat. 154
Placenta Circumvallata, c. 1932

instructional purposes. They show, respectively, foetal development in seven stages, a longitudinal section of a pregnant uterus with an approximately nine-month old foetus, and the posterior abdominal wall with kidneys, blood vessels, and more. The tablets represent the incremental collection and substantiation of anatomical knowledge that had begun in the Renaissance. They illustrate how knowledge about the anatomy of both the mother and baby is part of the institutionalization and professionalization that lay the foundation for the emergence of modern medicine in the late 19th century. Knowledge of human anatomy, especially the physiology of birth, gradually improves, transforming birth care and the relationship between the midwife and the doctor. The improvement in medical knowledge is an important element in the general professionalization and institutionalization of the medical science and profession that pick up speed into the 18th century – better knowledge, better education of both doctors and midwives, and new institutions, including philanthropic maternity clinics, which also serve as places of learning. In 1750, The Maternity Foundation opens in Copenhagen, allowing unmarried women to give birth without providing their name or that of the father. This development is linked to the gradual expansion of the nation state and the growing perception that the state has a role to play in the health and illness of the individual citizen.

This period also sees the publication of the first noteworthy textbooks by midwives for midwives. Louise Boursier (1563-1636), a French midwife who trained at the Hôtel Dieu hospital in Paris, wrote the first such textbook in 1609. These books testify to the increase in dissemination, centralization and institutionalization of knowledge that distinguished the early modern period of medical science. But they also embody the divide that would mark birth care even into the late 20th century – the division between the midwife as female and the obstetrician as male.

Male Midwives and Doctors Enter the Arena of Childbirth

The growing anatomical and medical interest in childbirth gradually paved the way for the arrival of males into what had been an exclusively female domain. Where barber surgeons with razors and pliers, in rare cases, could be called to assist in births when the baby was stuck and endangered the life of the mother, a technological advance in the 18th century helped change childbirth forever: forceps. Originally invented in the 17th century, obstetrical forceps did not become widely used until the mid-18th century, when a British male midwife, William Smellie, popularized their use and significance in his book *A Treatise on the Theory and Practice of Midwifery*. The forceps made it possible to pull out babies that had become lodged in the birth canal. This tool represented a technological expansion of the options available during risky births, improving the odds of survival for both the mother and the child. It opened up a new role for the male doctor that went beyond the effort to save either the mother or the child during a birth gone wrong and instead constituted a real opportunity to intervene positively. The forceps represented both a technological advance that saved lives and a gradual overturning of the hierarchy and agency of the male doctor, the obstetrician, and the female midwife.

From the 18th century, as knowledge of anatomy grew, more tools were added to the obstetrician's bag. The mid-19th century saw the arrival of the first effective treatments for pain – first laughing gas and ether, then chloroform, invented by the Scottish obstetrician James Young Simpson in 1847. Simpson immediately began to administer chloroform in his practice, despite the opposition of religious institutions to the use of painkillers during childbirth (as we know, Eve's punishment for eating the apple is pain in childbirth). The critics slowly fell silent, however, and in 1853, when Simpson administered chloroform to Queen Victoria during the birth of her eighth child, the official seal of approval was complete. Likewise, the emergence of antisepsis toward the end of the 19th century led to much improved understanding of septicaemia and to new surgical practices based on cleanliness. Together, anaesthetics and antiseptics fundamentally changed the conditions of surgery. In obstetrics, caesarean sections gradually became routine. Ever since, a host of medical and technical innovations have improved the power of medicine to understand and handle problematic childbirths: antibiotics, blood transfusions, epidural blocks, ultrasound scans, chromosome testing, and much more.

From a soaring bird's-eye view, the history of birth care in the Western world can be described as a gradual medicalization, a process in which something natural (and often dangerous) has been annexed into medical normality. Childbirth has gone from almost exclusively taking place at home to almost exclusively taking place at maternity wards in hospitals, where childbirth is increasingly publicly supervised and part of a public healthcare system. The attendants to the woman in labour have gone from family, friends, and perhaps an uncertified but experienced midwife, to a highly educated, professional midwife who, in difficult or dangerous situations, can call in a (historically almost always male) specialist obstetrician. Childbirth has become a normalized part of a medical system, exemplified by the fact that, although home births are rising rapidly, more than 95 percent of all children are born in a hospital. One set of experiences has gradually been replaced by another.

Separating the Child from the Mother

The story of birth care is also the story of the power inherent in the enormous medical and technological change that childbirth has undergone, pulling our understanding of the body in the direction of the tools developed to treat it. Obstetrical forceps produce a birth situation that requires intervention with forceps more often. Ultrasound scans give the foetus an existence it never had before. Accordingly, the gradual medicalization of childbirth has also produced a large number of less measurable but no less significant consequences. As Barbara Katz Rothman, a sociologist who has extensively studied the history of maternity, puts it, "Diagnostic technologies, from the most routine ultrasound to the most exotic embryo transplant, have in common that they work toward the construction of the fetus as a separate social being. The history of Western obstetrics is the history of technologies of separation. We've separated milk from breasts, mothers from babies, fetuses from pregnancies, sexuality from procreation, pregnancy from motherhood. It is very very hard to conceptually put back together that which medicine has rendered asunder."

The history of birth care is a dual history. It boasts great advances all but guaranteeing the safety of what once was fraught with danger, fear, despair, pain, grief, disablement, and death. But it has also entailed a gradual medicalization process shaping the perceptions, experiences, and attitudes of all the parties involved: the pregnant woman, the family, the doctor, the midwife, the medical system, and, ultimately, the whole society in which we live.

This duality leaves us with the tension articulated by Mogens Osler. The boundary between the normal and the natural, between too little and too much control and intervention, remains an issue. All the medical advances have left everyone – the pregnant woman, her surroundings, the attendants at birth, and the medical system at large – with a number of choices for which no formula exists. Perhaps the current concern with the ambiguity of motherhood, as embodied in the *Mother!* exhibition, is a reaction to that duality.

cat. 4
Louise Bourgeois: *The Reticent Child*, 2003

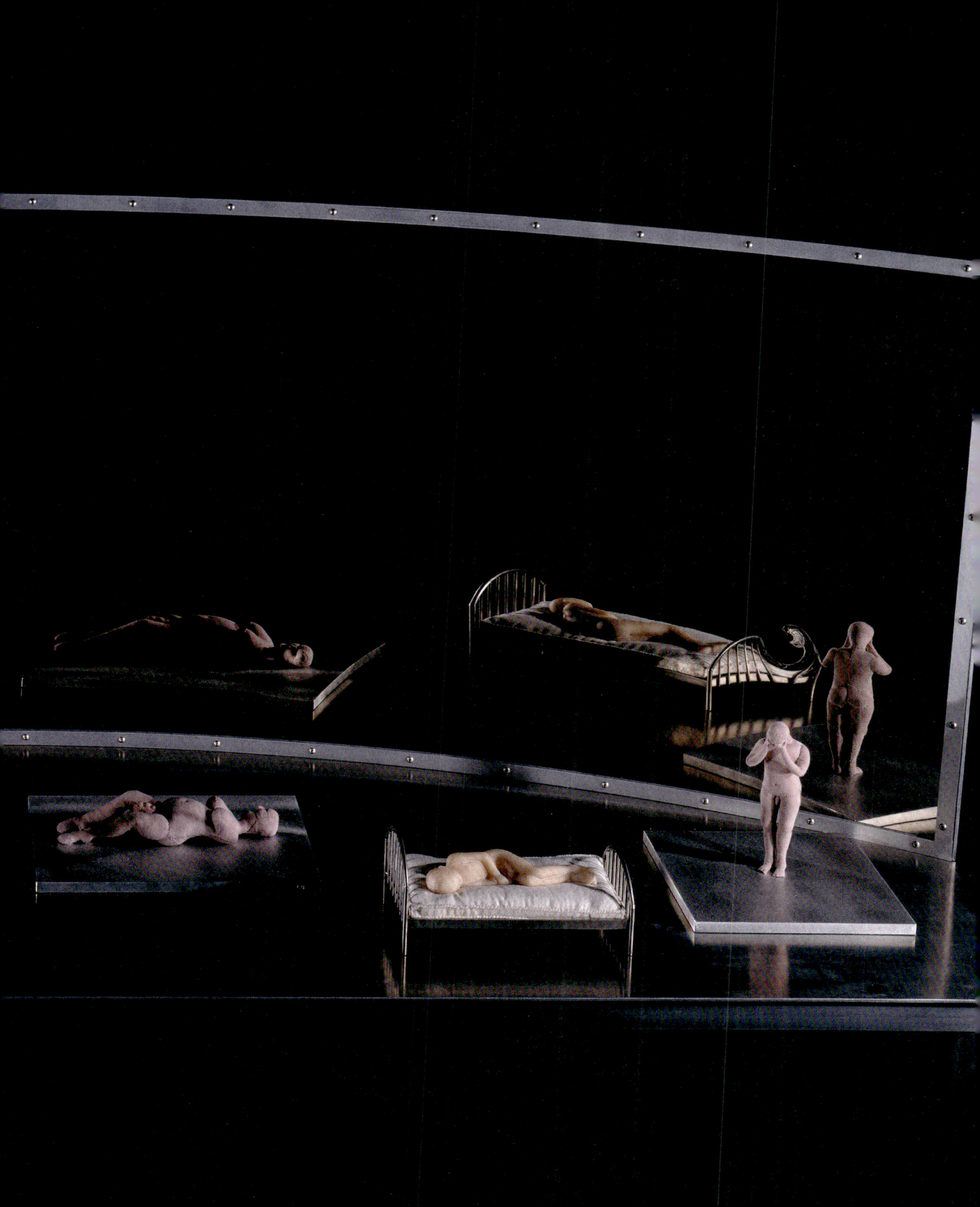

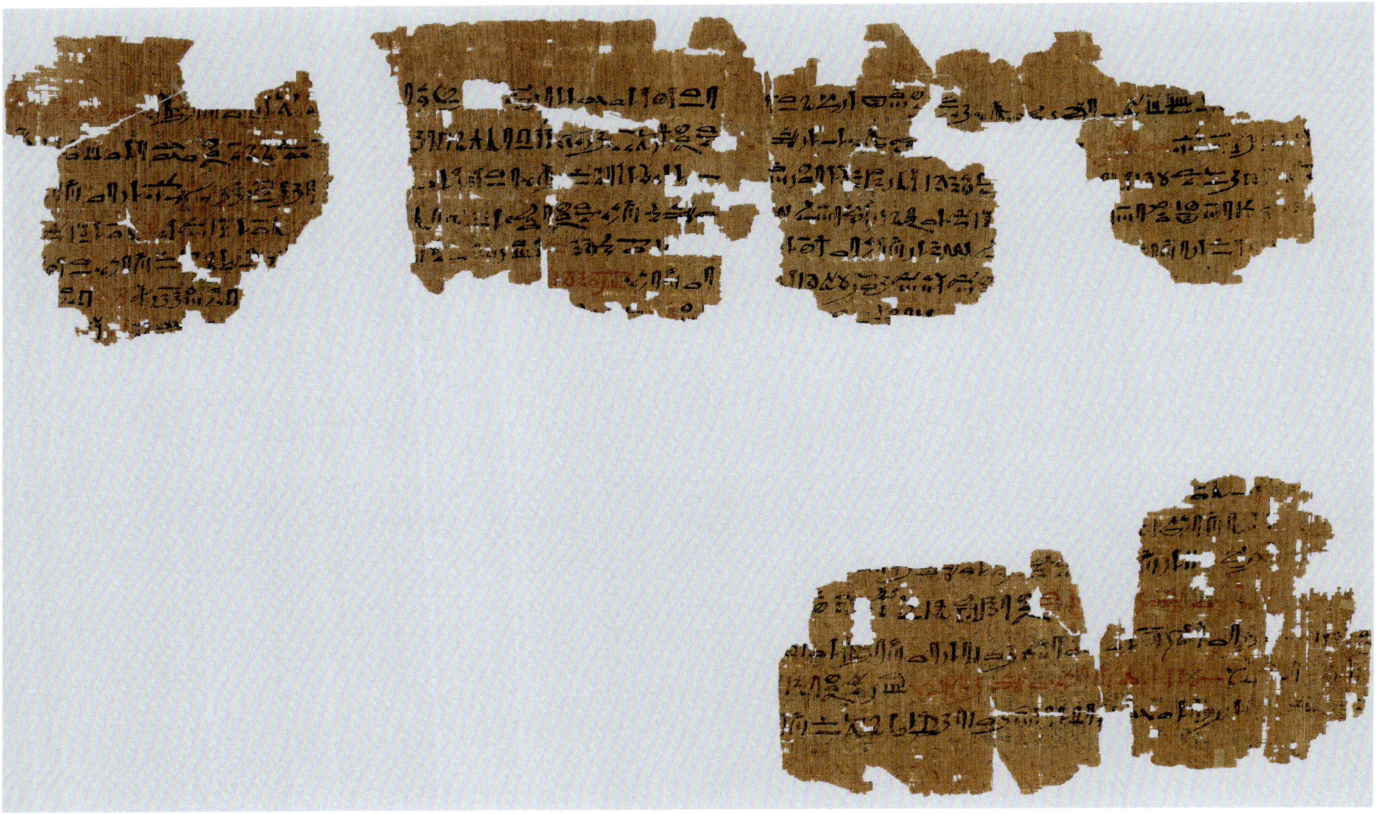

One of the earliest written documents about fertility, pregnancy and birth is this papyrus, which describes forecasts about pregnancy in Ancient Egypt.

cat. 120
Papyrus Carlsberg 8, c. 1300 BC

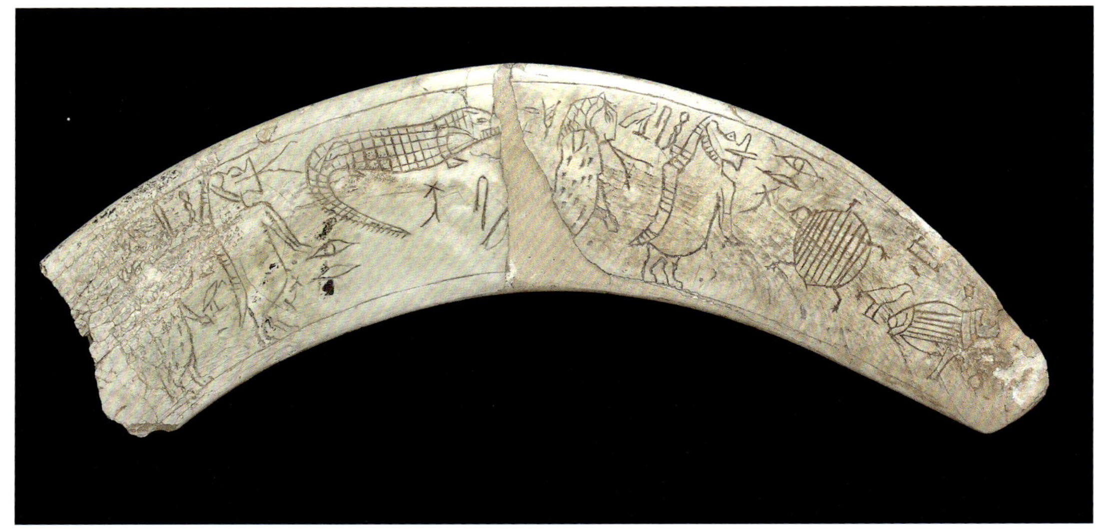

This magic staff or knife of hippopotamus tooth would have served as protection for children and child-bearing women, with the legend: "Cut the head off those enemies who enter the chamber of Nebet-Sekhti-Re's children."

cat. 119
Magic staff or knife, Egypt, 2060-1785 BC

Figures of naked, standing women (see also following spread), presumably depicting the Mother Goddess, were used as votive offerings or grave goods for the dead.

cat. 134
Idol from the Cyclades, Amorgos, Greece, 2700-2300 BC

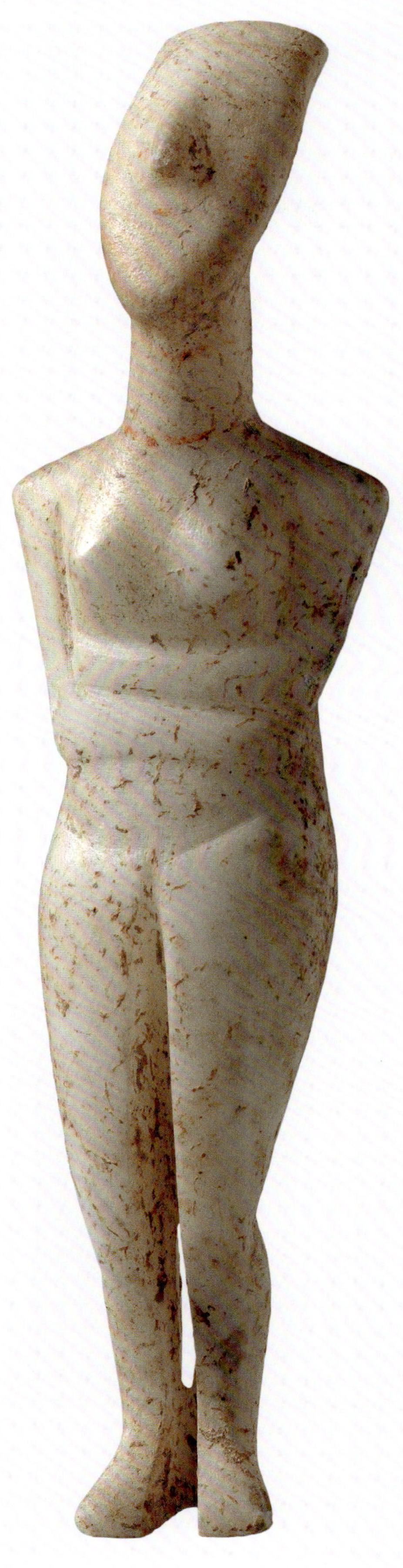

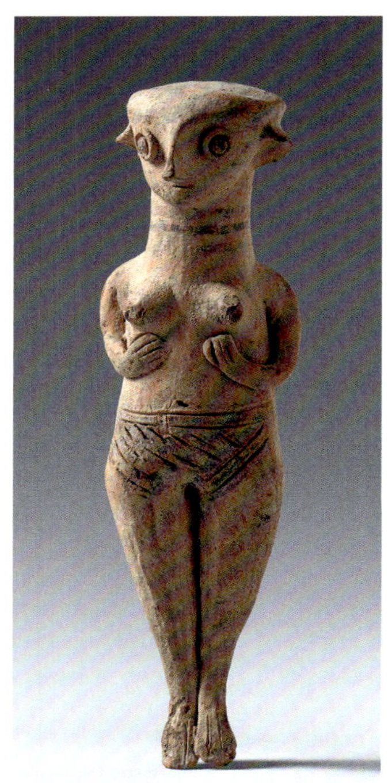

cat. 131
Mother Goddess, Cyprus,
1450-1200 BC

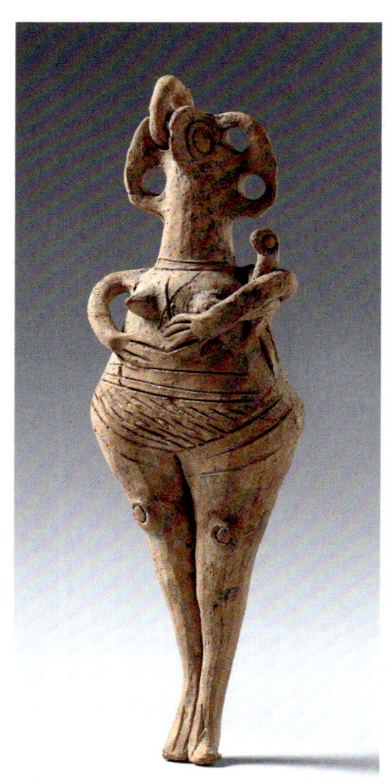

cat. 130
Standing female nude, holding
a child on her left arm,
Cyprus, 1450-1200 BC

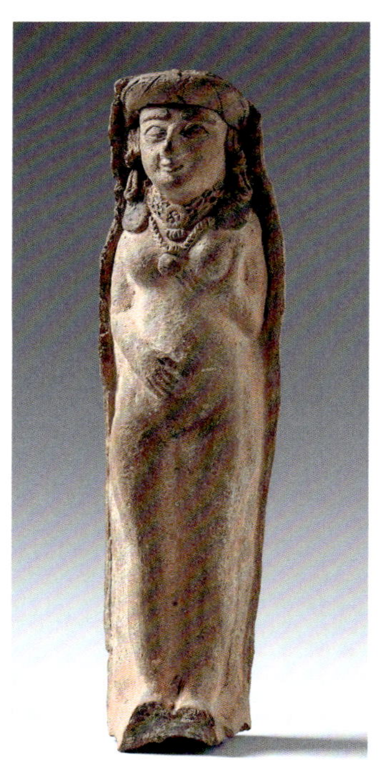

cat. 133
Cypriot terracotta figurine
(Aphrodite), Cyprus, 600-500 BC

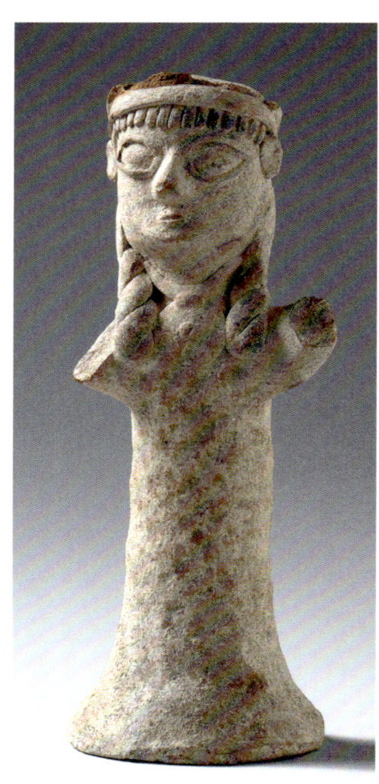

cat. 132
Cypriot terracotta figurine
(Aphrodite), Cyprus, 600-500 BC

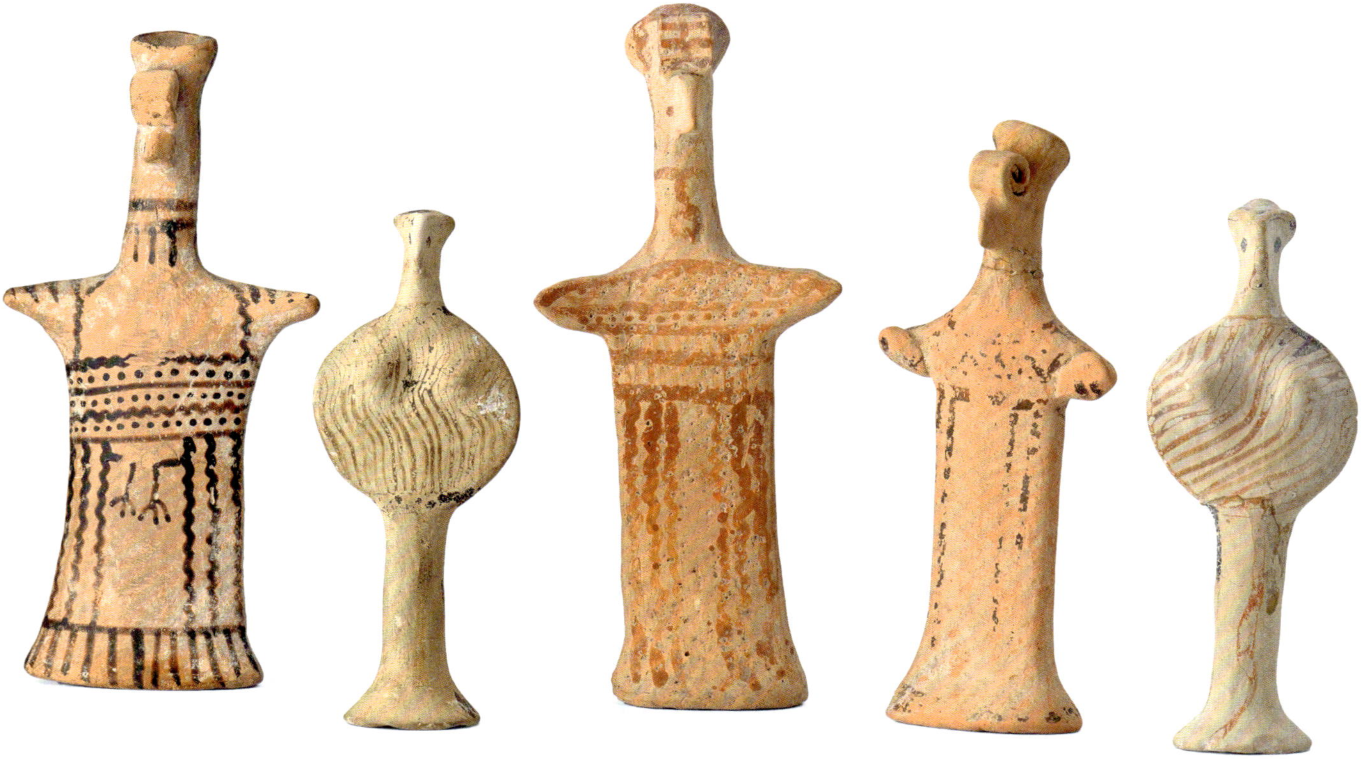

cat. 135-139
Mycenaean idols, c. 1000 BC

cat. 23
Alberto Giacometti: *Femme-cuillère*, 1926/1927
Spoon-Woman

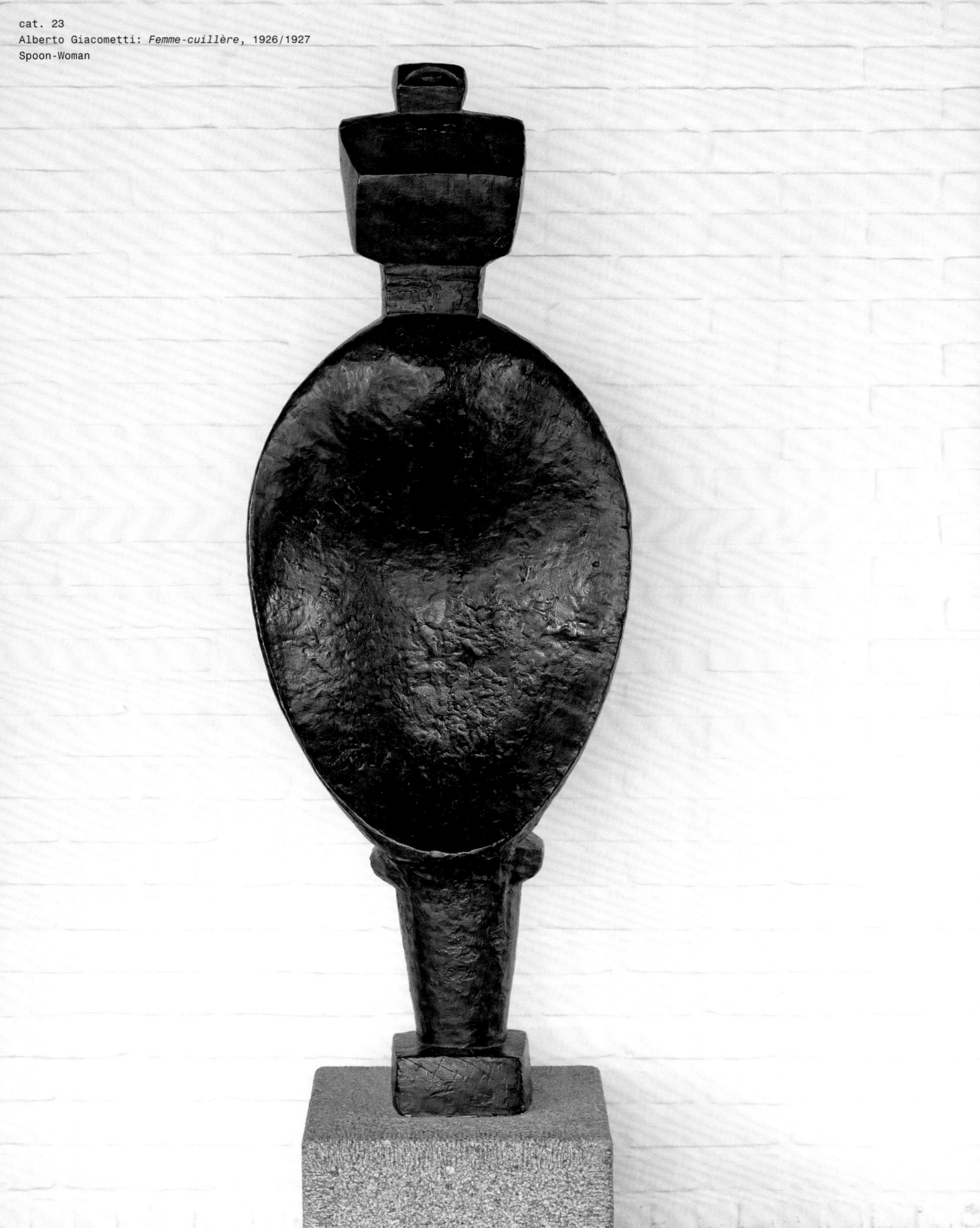

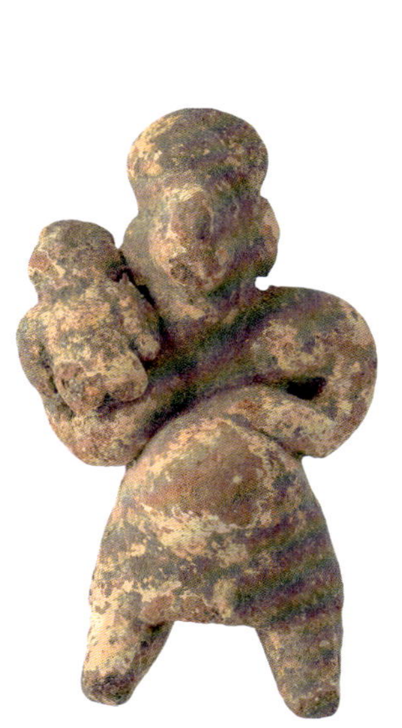

cat. 127
Pre-Columbian ceramic figurine, Mexico, 200 BC-200 AD

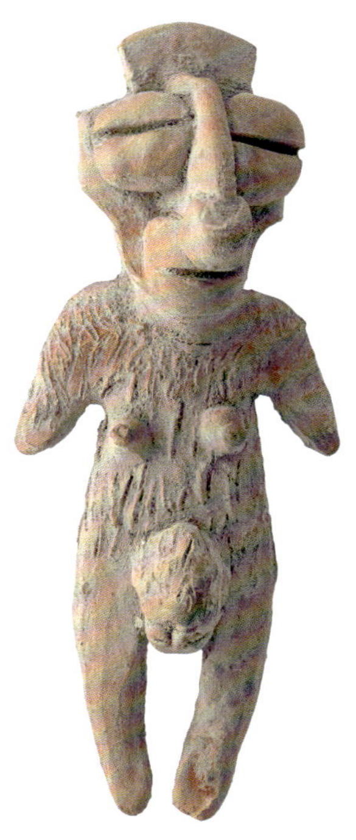

cat. 129
Pre-Columbian ceramic figurine, Ecuador, undated

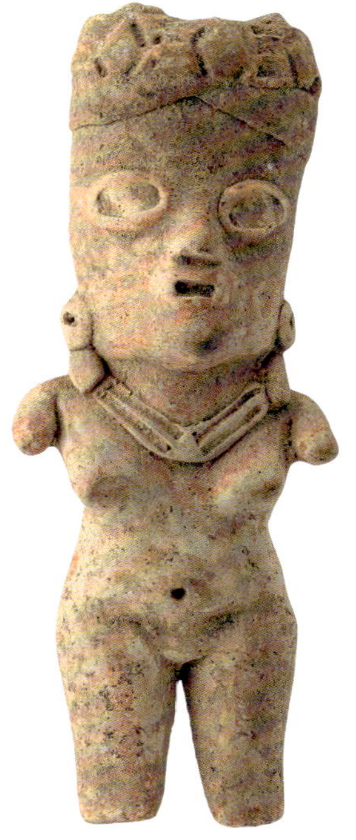

cat. 125
Pre-Columbian ceramic figurine, Mexico, 1200-500 BC

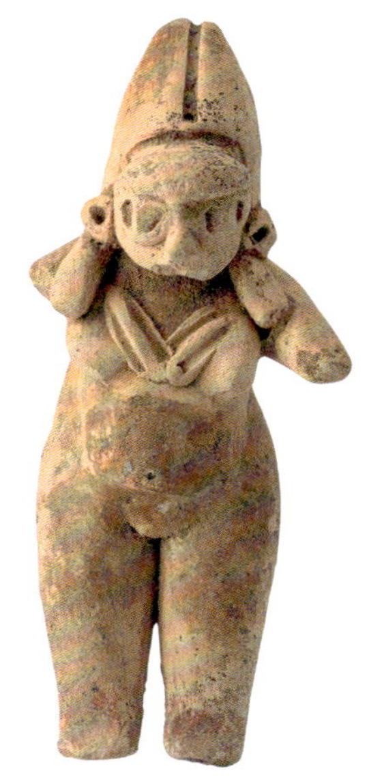

cat. 128
Pre-Columbian ceramic figurine, Mexico, undated

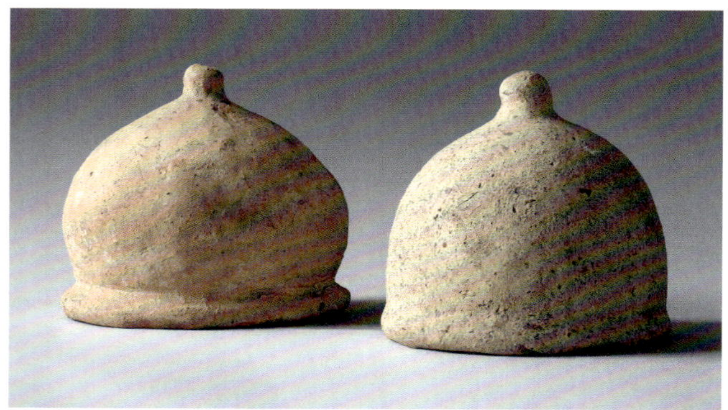

Votive figures in the form of a womb or breasts in clay were common as offerings to the gods with the aim of ensuring the fertility of the family or as thanks for a new-born child.

cat. 144
Votive sculpture, female breasts, Italy, 400-100 BC

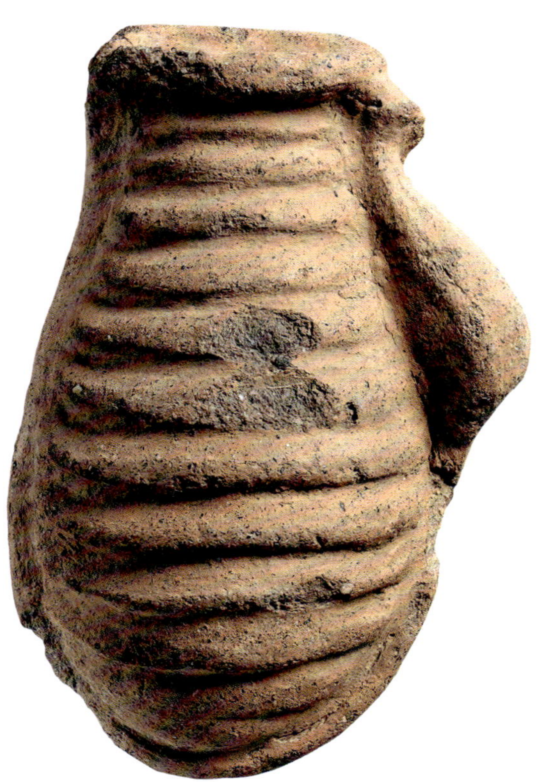

cat. 142
Terracotta sculpture of a womb, Italy, 400-100 BC

cat. 27
Svend Wiig Hansen: *Siddende kvinde*, 1964
Seated Woman

At the bottom: cat. 64
Ana Mendieta: *Untitled: Silueta Series*, 1978

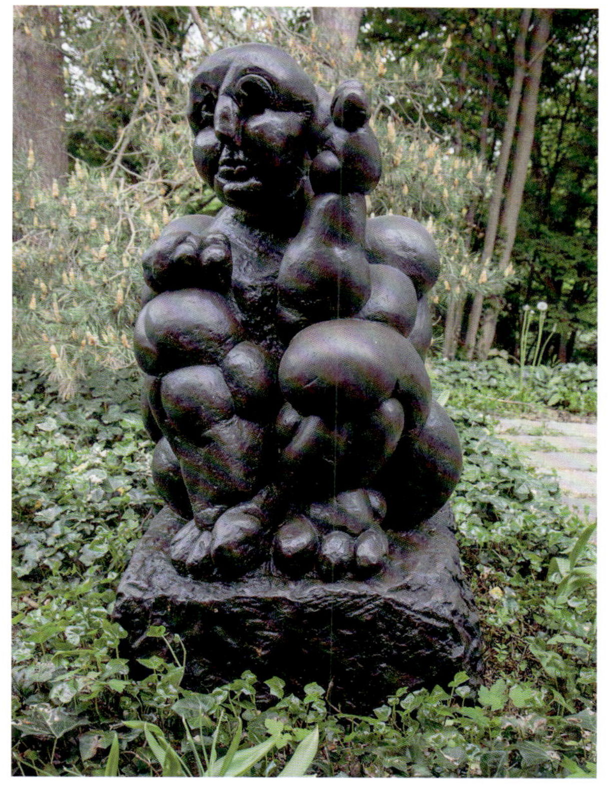

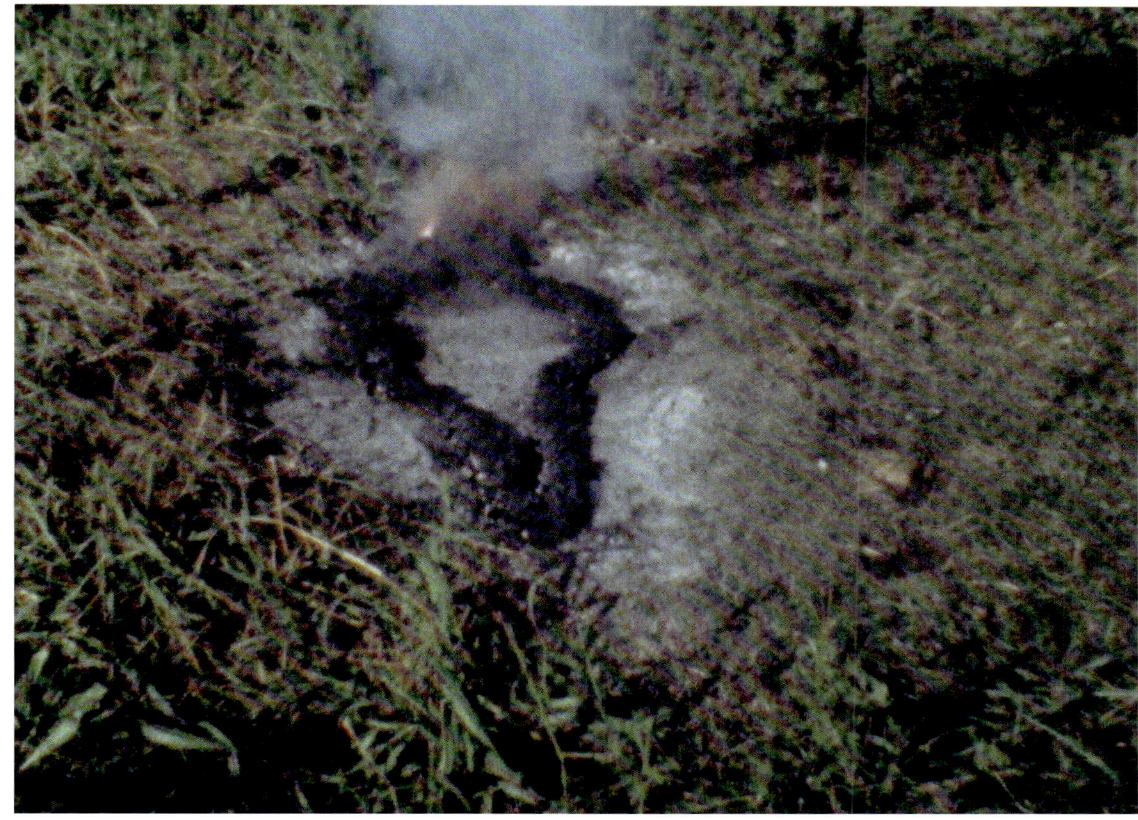

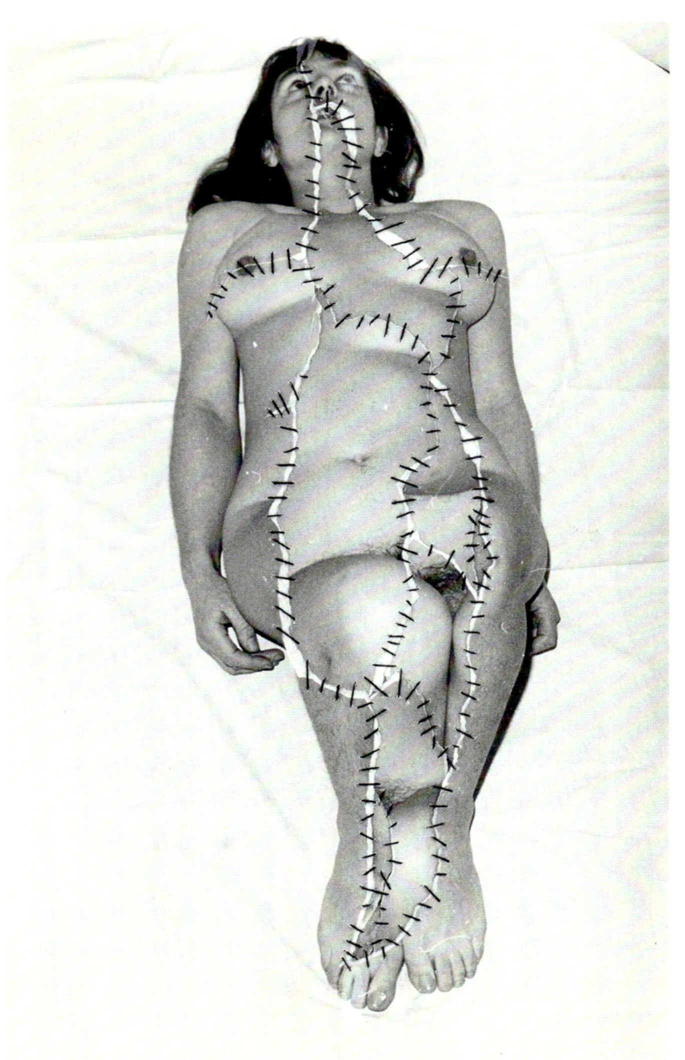

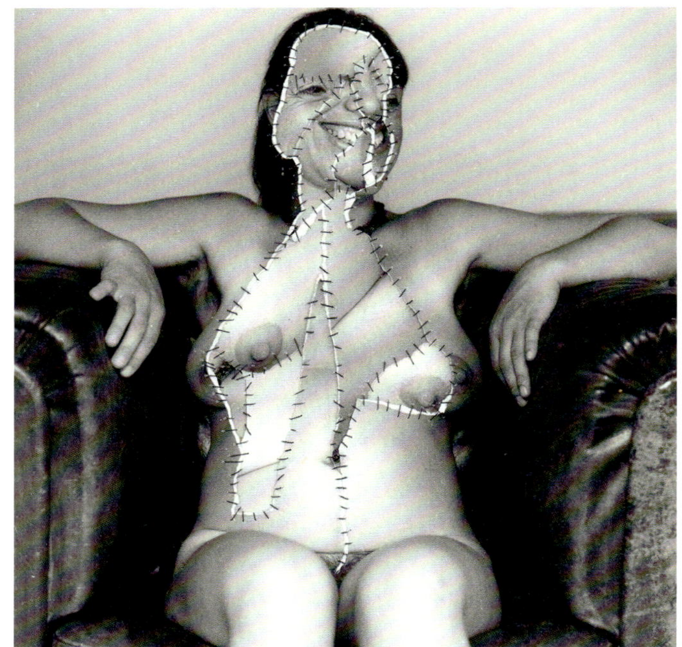

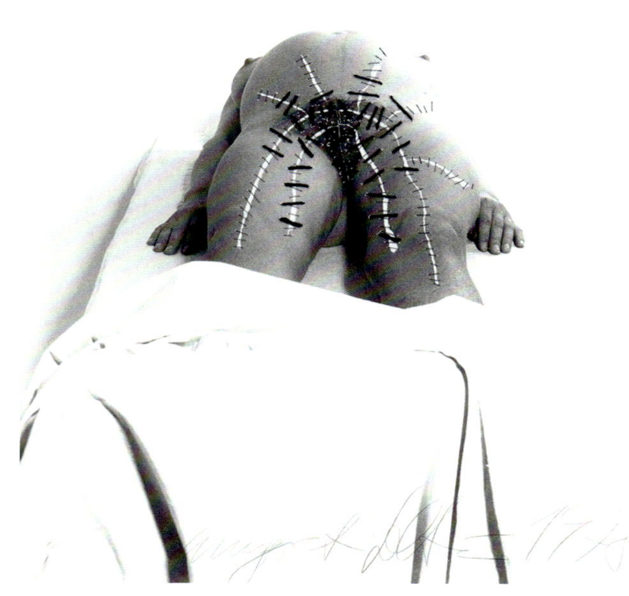

cat. 111
Annegret Soltau: *Schwanger*, 1978
Pregnant

cat. 112
Annegret Soltau: *Schwanger I*, 1978
Pregnant I

cat. 113
Annegret Soltau: *Auf dem Geburtstisch, schwanger I*, 1978
On the Birthing Table, Pregnant I

Right page: cat. 16
Otto Dix: *Die Schwangere*, 1931
The Pregnant Woman

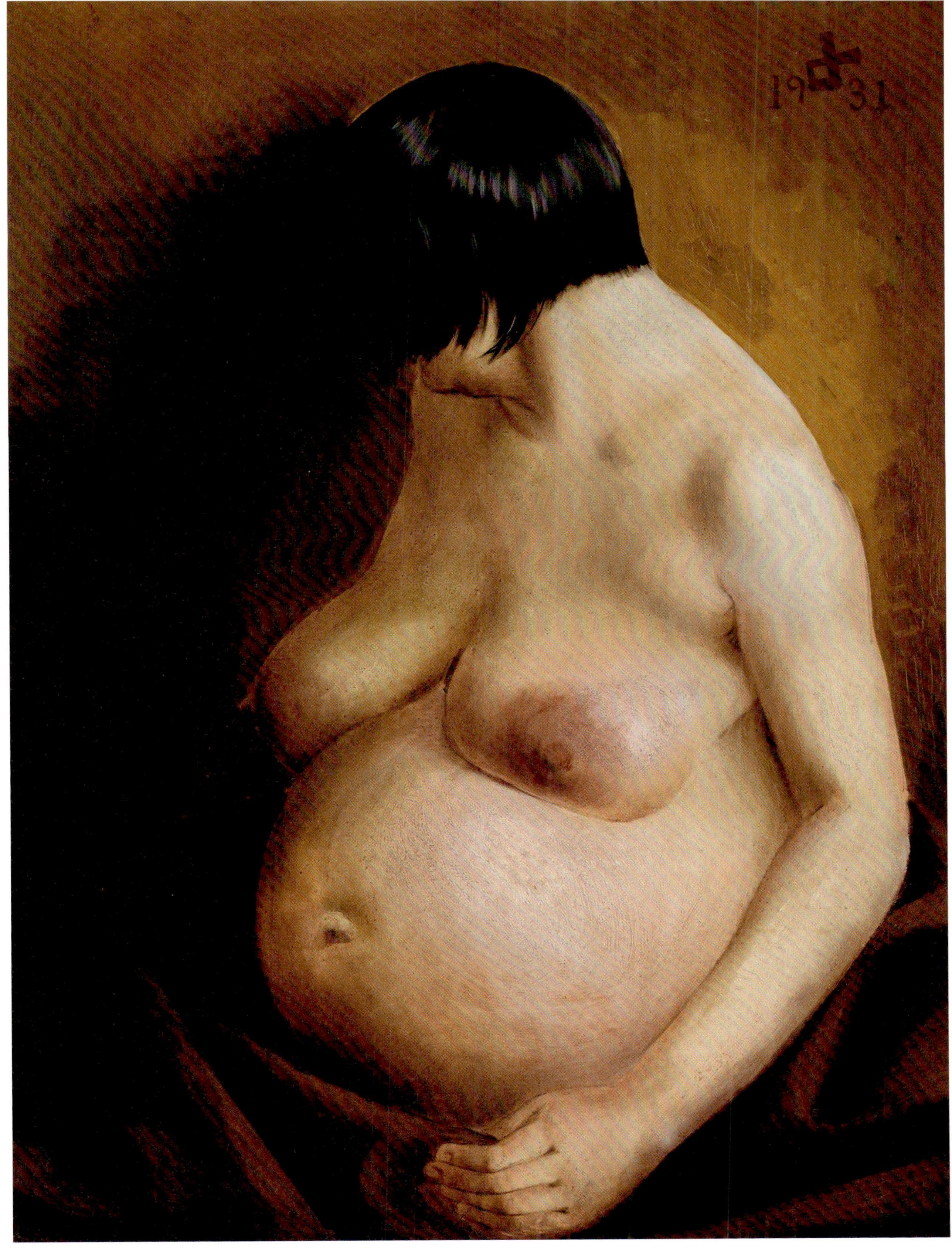

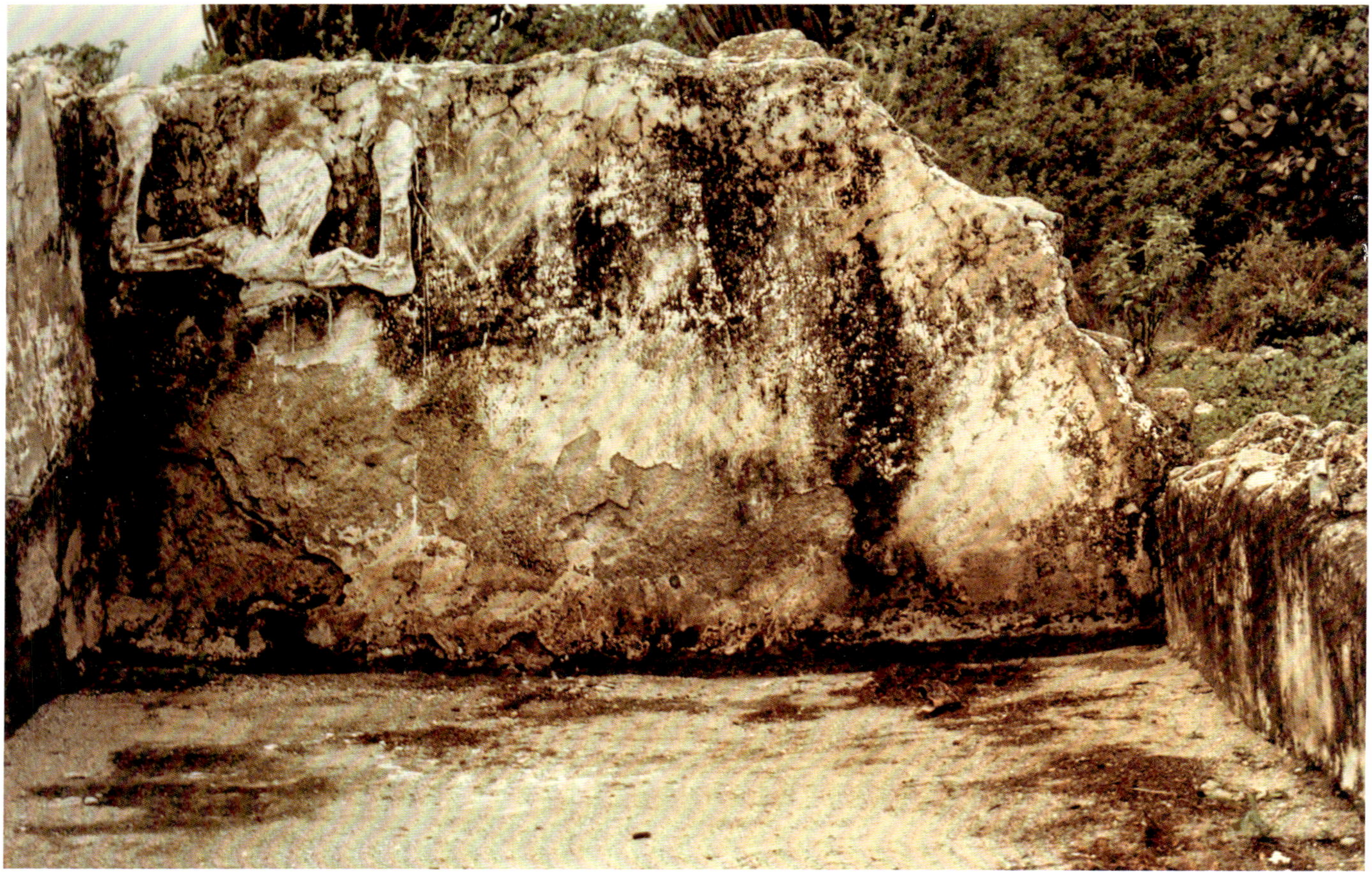

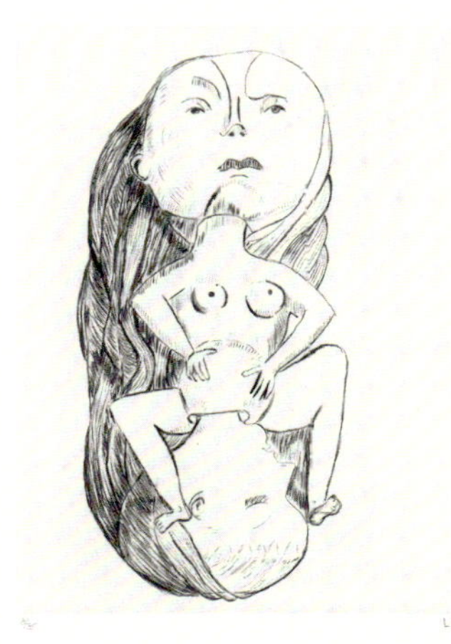

cat. 63
Ana Mendieta: *Silhueta del Laberinto, Yágul, Mexico*, 1976

cat. 3
Louise Bourgeois: *Birth*, 1995

Right page: cat. 107
Niki de Saint-Phalle: *L'Accouchement rose*, 1964
The Pink Delivery

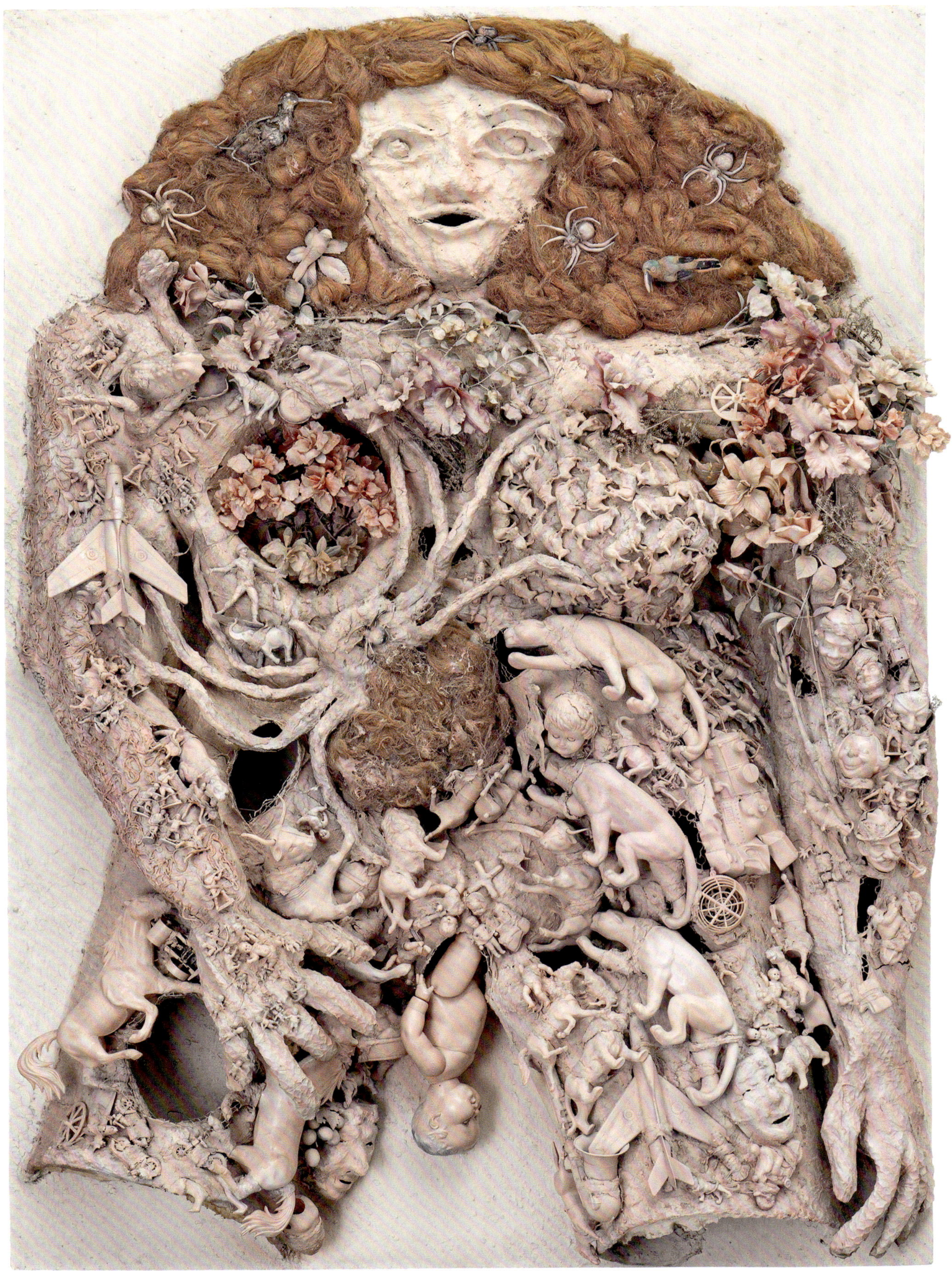

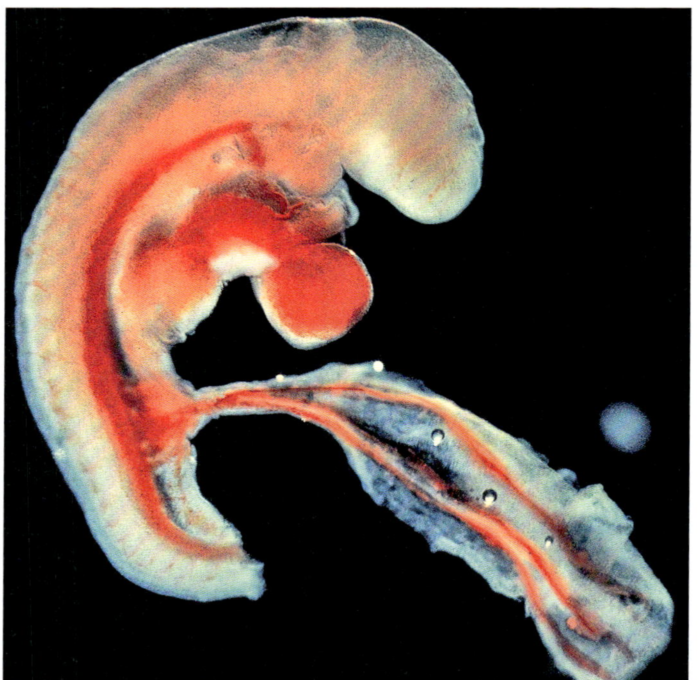

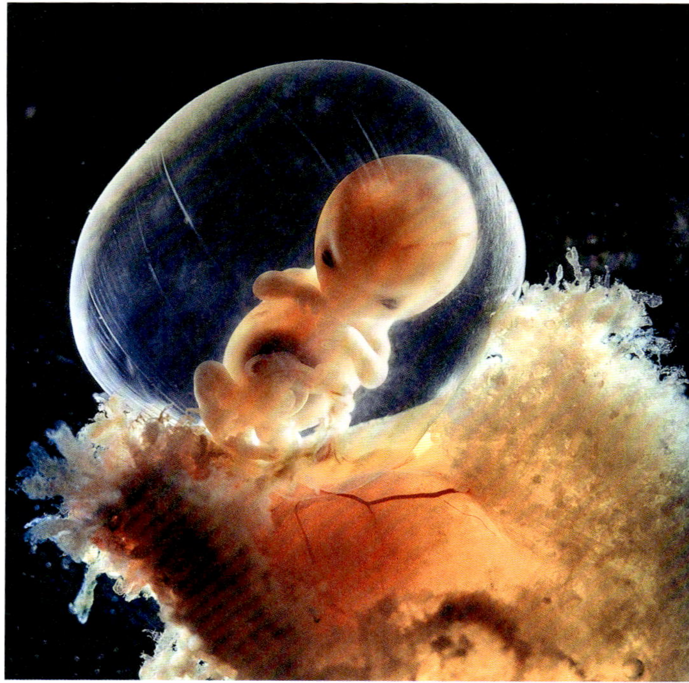

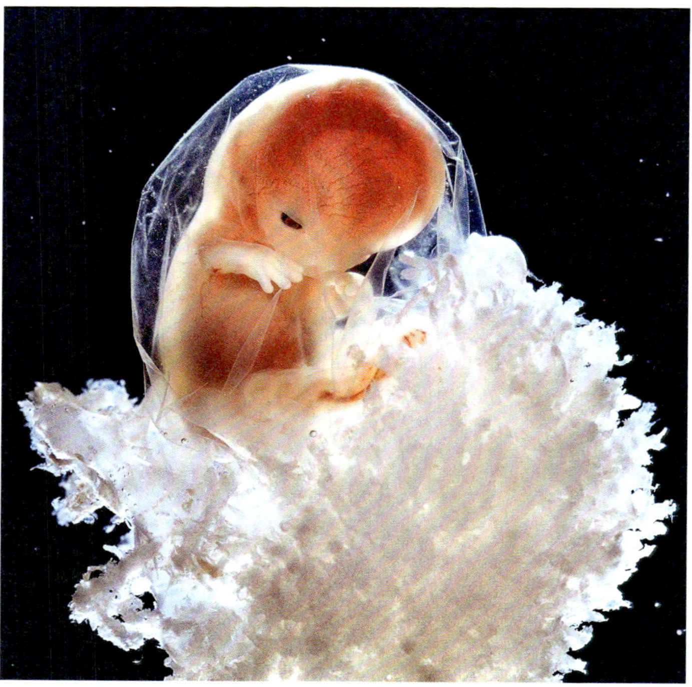

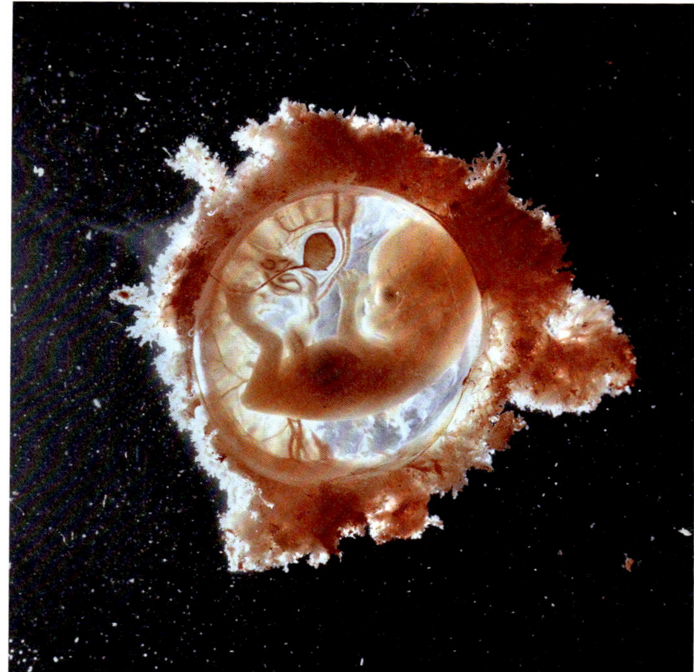

cat. 88
Lennart Nilsson: Embryo, 4 weeks, 1965
From the series "A Child Is Born", 1965-2009

cat. 91
Lennart Nilsson: Foetus, 10 weeks, 1965
From the series "A Child Is Born", 1965-2009

cat. 90
Lennart Nilsson: Embryo, 8 weeks, 1965
From the series "A Child Is Born", 1965-2009

cat. 92
Lennart Nilsson: *The Space Odyssey*, foetus, 13 weeks, 1965
From the series "A Child Is Born", 1965-2009

Right page: cat. 114
Alina Szapocznikow: *Buste étincelant I*, 1967
Glowing Bust I

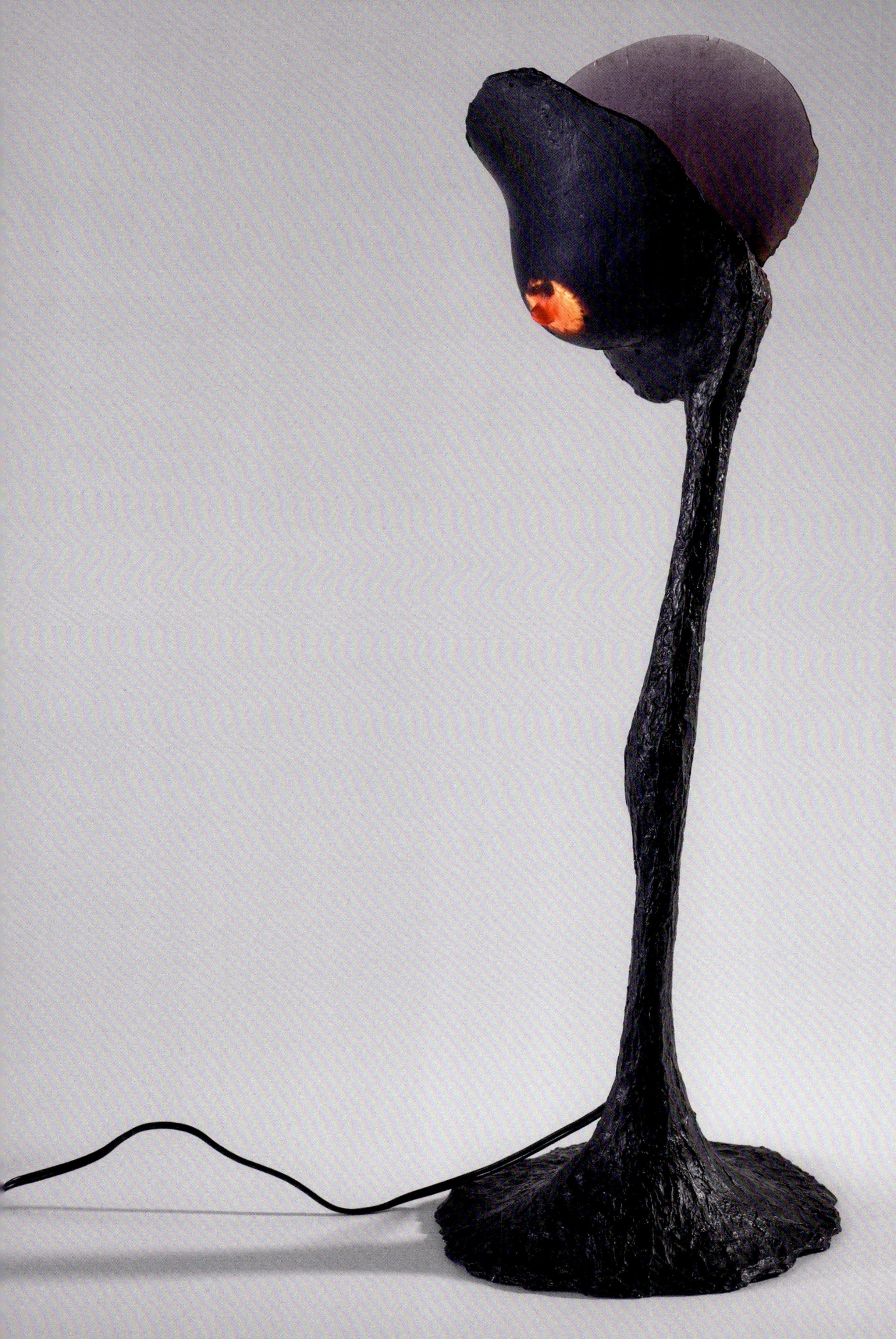

List of Works

Thomas Bartholin (1616-1680)
1 *Anatomia, ex Caspari Bartholini Parentis Institutionibus, Omniumque Recentiorum & propriis Observationibus, Tertium ad sanguinis Circulationem Reformata, Leiden*, 1671
Book with illustrations, 19 × 13.5 cm
Medical Museion, University of Copenhagen

Max Beckmann (1884-1950)
2 *Mutter und Tochter*, 1946
Mother and Daughter
Oil on canvas, 150 × 80.5 cm
Art Gallery of New South Wales
Art Gallery of New South Wales Foundation, purchase 1987

Louise Bourgeois (1911-2010)
3 *Birth*, 1995
Drypoint and aquatint on paper, 48 × 24 cm
Louisiana Museum of Modern Art

4 *The Reticent Child*, 2003
Installation, mixed media, 183 × 284.5 × 91.5 cm
Collection The Easton Foundation

Dieric Bouts (ca. 1415-1475)
5 Virgin and Child, after 1454
Oil on panel, 42.5 × 27.5 cm
SMK, National Gallery of Denmark

Candice Breitz (1972-)
6 *MOTHER*, 2005
Video installation with 6 screens, colour and audio, 13:15 min.
Louisiana Museum of Modern Art. Acquired with support from The New Carlsberg Foundation and Museumsfonden af 7. december 1966

Elina Brotherus (1972-)
7 *My Dog Is Cuter Than Your Ugly Baby*, 2013
Pigment ink print on paper, 80 × 53 cm
Louisiana Museum of Modern Art
Acquired with funding from The Augustinus Foundation

Sophie Calle (1953-)
8 *The Giraffe*, 2012
Digital photograph, text, wooden frames, 205 × 110 cm and 50 × 50 cm
Courtesy of the artist & Perrotin

9 *Obituary*, 2012
Colour photograph, text, wooden frames, 170 × 100 cm and 50 × 50 cm
Courtesy of the artist & Perrotin

10 *Dead in a Good Mood, 2013*
Colour photograph, text, wooden frames, 50.5 × 50.5 cm and 76.5 × 50.5 cm
Courtesy of the artist & Perrotin

11 *Today My Mother Died*, 2013
Colour photograph, text, wooden frames, 76.5 × 50.5 cm and 50.5 × 50.5 cm
Courtesy of the artist & Perrotin

Mary Cassatt (1844-1926)
12 *Jenny and Her Sleepy Child*, c. 1891-1892
Oil on canvas, 71 × 58.5 cm
Terra Foundation for American Art, Daniel J Terra Collection

Ane Crabtree (1965-)
13 Costume of the handmaids, from the TV series based on the novel by Margaret Atwood, "The Handmaid's Tale" of 1985, 2016
Various materials and dimensions
Courtesy of MGM Television

Rineke Dijkstra (1959-)
14 *Julie, Den Haag, Netherlands, February 29 1994*, 1994
Photograph, inkjet print, 145 × 122 cm
Collection Rineke Dijkstra

Walt Disney (1901-1966)
15 *Snow White and the Seven Dwarfs*, 1937
Film clip, colour and audio
Walt Disney Studios

Otto Dix (1891-1969)
16 *Die Schwangere*, 1931
The Pregnant Woman
Egg tempera and oil on linen mounted on plywood, 83 × 62 cm
Worcester Art Museum, Worcester, MA
Stoddard Aquisition Fund

17 *Mutter und Kind (Stillende Mutter)*, 1932
Mother and Child (Nursing Mother)
Charcoal and opaque white pigment on paper, 70.5 × 61 cm
Kunsthalle Mannheim

Nathalie Djurberg (1978-)
& Hans Berg (1978-)
18 *Once Removed on My Mother's Side*, 2008
Clay animation, single channel video, colour and audio, 5:20 min.
Courtesy of Lisson Gallery

Tracey Emin (1963-)
19 *Feeling Pregnant II*, 1999-2002
Children's shoes in showcase and framed texts, 6 parts, showcase: 50 × 57 × 17 cm; framed texts, each 35 × 26.5 cm
Private collection

20 *I do not Expect*, 2002
Appliqué blanket, 264 × 185 cm
Art Gallery of New South Wales. Gift of Geoff Ainsworth AM 2018, donated through the Australian Government's Cultural Gifts Program

VALIE EXPORT (1940-)
21 *Ohne Titel*, 1976
Untitled
Photograph, black-and-white, 60 × 43.5 cm
Courtesy of VALIE EXPORT

Lucian Freud (1922-2011)
22 *The Painter's Mother, Resting I*, 1976
Oil on canvas, 105 × 105 cm
Private collection, on loan to Irish Museum of Modern Art

Alberto Giacometti (1901-1966)
23 *Femme-cuillère*, 1926/1927
Spoon-Woman
Bronze, 145 × 51 × 23 cm
Louisiana Museum of Modern Art

Jean-Paul Goude (1940-)
In collaboration with Antonio Lopez
24 The Grace Jones Show: Constructivist maternity costume, New York, 1979
Installation, mixed media, 300 × 182 cm
Courtesy of the artist

Jacob Ludwig Karl Grimm (1785-1863) &
Wilhelm Carl Grimm (1786-1859)
25 *Grimm's Fairy Tales,* Copenhagen 1941
Book, Danish translation by Carl Ewald, illustrated by Anton Hansen
Private collection

Petrit Halilaj (1986-)
26 *It is the first time dear that you have a human shape (diptych 1 – earring)*, 2012
Iron, brick dust of the ruins from the artist's family house, each earring 40 × 150 × 400 cm
Private collection

Svend Wiig Hansen (1922-1997)
27 *Siddende kvinde*, 1964
Seated Woman
Bronze, 125 × 69 × 75 cm
Louisiana Museum of Modern Art
Long-term loan: Museumsfonden af 7. december 1966

Henry Heerup (1907-1993)
28 *Vanløse-madonna*, 1934
Madonna of Vanløse
Oil on burlap, 171.5 × 115 cm
Kunsten Museum of Modern Art Aalborg

Alfred Hitchcock (1899-1980)
29 *Psycho*, 1960
Film clip, black-and-white and audio
Courtesy of Universal Studios Licensing LLC

Peter Hujar (1934-1987)
30 *John Rothermel (Cockette)*, 1971
Vintage gelatin silver print, 51 × 40.5 cm
Courtesy of The Peter Hujar Archive and Pace Gallery, New York

31 *Candy Darling on Her Deathbed*, 1973
Photography, pigmented ink print, 40.5 × 51 cm
Courtesy of The Peter Hujar Archive and Pace Gallery, New York

32 *Divine*, 1975
Vintage gelatin silver print, 51 × 40.5 cm
Courtesy of The Peter Hujar Archive and Pace Gallery, New York

33 *Ethyl Eichelberger as Nefertiti (II)*, 1981
Vintage gelatin silver print, 51 × 40.5 cm
Courtesy of The Peter Hujar Archive and Pace Gallery, New York

34 *Ethyl Eichelberger in a Fashion Pose*, 1981
Photography, pigmented ink print, 51 × 40.5 cm
Courtesy of The Peter Hujar Archive and Pace Gallery, New York

35 *David Brintzenhofe #6*, 1982
Vintage gelatin silver print, 51 × 40.5 cm
Courtesy of The Peter Hujar Archive and Pace Gallery, New York

Miyako Ishiuchi (1947-)
36 *Mother's #14*, 2001/2004
Gelatin silver print, 107.5 × 73.5 cm
Courtesy of the artist and Fergus McCaffrey, New York and Tokyo

37 *Mother's #29*, 2002/2004
Gelatin silver print, 104.5 × 73.5 cm
Courtesy of the artist and Fergus McCaffrey, New York and Tokyo

38 *Mother's #37*, 2001/2006
Colour photograph, 19 × 28.5 cm
Courtesy of the artist and Fergus McCaffrey, New York and Tokyo

39 *Mother's #38*, 2002
Colour photograph, 28.5 × 19 cm
Courtesy of the artist and Fergus McCaffrey, New York and Tokyo

40 *Mother's #42*, 2001/2002
Gelatin silver print, 19 × 27 cm
Courtesy of the artist and Fergus McCaffrey, New York and Tokyo

41 *Mother's 25 Mar #46*, 2000
Gelatin silver print, 108 × 74 cm
Courtesy of the artist and Fergus McCaffrey, New York and Tokyo

42 *Mother's #54*, 2002
Colour photograph, 28.5 × 19 cm
Courtesy of the artist and Fergus McCaffrey, New York and Tokyo

43 *Mother's #57*, 2004/2005
Colour photograph, 19 × 28.5 cm
Courtesy of the artist and Fergus McCaffrey, New York and Tokyo

44 *Mother's #65*, 2001/2002
Gelatin silver print, 19 × 27 cm
Courtesy of the artist and Fergus McCaffrey, New York and Tokyo

45 *Mother's 25 Mar 1916 #66*, 2000
Gelatin silver print, 108 × 74 cm
Courtesy of the artist and Fergus McCaffrey, New York and Tokyo

Chantal Joffe (1969-)
46 *Self-portrait Combing Esme's Hair*, 2009
Oil on canvas, 41 × 51 cm
Collection of the artist.
Courtesy of Victoria Miro, London and Venice

47 *Self-portrait with Esme at Bedtime*, 2018
Oil on canvas, 41 × 51 cm
Collection of the artist.
Courtesy of Victoria Miro, London and Venice

48 *Me and Esme in the Garden*, 2020
Oil on canvas, 80 × 60 cm
Courtesy of Victoria Miro, London and Venice

Kirsten Justesen (1943-)
49 *Omstændigheder*, 1969
Circumstances
Glass fibre reinforced epoxy, 4 parts, each 58.5 × 44 × 26 cm
SMK, National Gallery of Denmark

Peter Keler (1898-1982)
50 *Bauhaus-Wiege*, 1922 (copy: 1996, Henning Seilkopf)
Bauhaus cradle
Wood, lacquer and rope weave on a frame, 92 × 92 × 98 cm
Bauhaus Dessau Foundation, Germany

Mary Kelly (1941-)
51 *Post-Partum Document: Introduction*, 1973
Mixed media, 4 parts, each 25.5 × 20.5 cm
Hammer Museum, Los Angeles
Gift of Eileen Harris Norton

52 *Post-Partum Document: Documentation IV*, 1976
Mixed media, 11 parts, each 35.5 × 28 cm
Kunsthaus Zürich. Vereinigung Zürcher Kunstfreunde, Gruppe Junge Kunst, 1981

53 *Antepartum*, 1973
8mm film loop transferred to DVD, black-and-white, no audio, 1:30 min.
Courtesy of the artist and Mitchell-Innes & Nash, New York

Ragnar Kjartansson (1976-)
54 *Me and My Mother*, 2015
Single channel video, colour and audio, loop 20:25 min.
Louisiana Museum of Modern Art
Acquired with funding from Museumsfonden af 7. december 1966

Käthe Kollwitz (1867-1945)
55 *Mutter mit zwei Kindern*, 1932-1936
Mother with Two Children
Bronze, 77 × 79 × 84 cm
Private collection

Wilhelm Lachnit (1899-1962)
56 *Schwangeres Proletariermädchen*, 1924/26
Pregnant Working Class Girl
Oil on canvas, 60 × 50 cm
Lindenau-Museum, Altenburg

Julie Laurberg (1856-1925) & **Franziska Gad** (1873-1921)
57 *Women's March on the occasion of the Constitution of 1915*, 1915
Documentary, 35 mm, black-and-white, no audio
The Danish Film Institute

Jennie Livingston (1962-)
58 *Paris is Burning*, 1990
Film clip, colour and audio
Courtesy of Jennie Livingston

Tala Madani (1981-)
59 *The Womb*, 2019
Animation, single channel video, colour, no audio, 3:26 min.
Courtesy of the artist and Pilar Corrias, London

René Magritte (1898-1967)
60 *The Spirit of Geometry*, c. 1936
Gouache on paper, 37.5 × 29 cm
Tate. Presented by the Hon. Ivor Montagu 1966

Jeanne Mammen (1890-1976)
61 *Kindesmörderin*, 1910-1914
Child-Murderess
Watercolour, pencil and ink on paper, 31 × 21 cm
Stadtmuseum Berlin, Jeanne Mammen Foundation

Paul McCarthy (1945-)
62 *Mother Dad*, 1987
Charcoal on paper, 72.5 × 57 cm
Louisiana Museum of Modern Art

Ana Mendieta (1948-1985)
63 *Silhueta del Laberinto, Yágul, Mexico*, 1976
Silhouette of Labyrinth, Yágul, Mexico
Colour photograph, vintage print, 16.5 × 24 cm
Louisiana Museum of Modern Art
Acquired with funding from Museumsfonden af 7. december 1966

64 *Untitled: Silueta Series*, 1978
Super 8mm film transferred to HD file, colour, no audio, 3:14 min
Louisiana Museum of Modern Art
Acquired with the support from Galerie Lelong, New York

Joni Mitchell (1943-)
65 *Little Green*, 1966
FFrom the album "Blue", released 1971
Song, 3:51 min.
Sony/ATV Music Publishing

Paula Modersohn-Becker (1876-1907)
66 *Kind an der Brust, Halbakt*, 1906
Mother Nursing Her Baby, Nude
Oil on cardboard, 74.5 × 52 cm
Von der Heydt-Museum Wuppertal

67 *Stillende Mutter*, 1902
Nursing Mother
Oil on cardboard, 72 × 48 cm
Kunstpalast, Düsseldorf
Acquired with the support of Kulturstiftung der Länder, Bundesregierung and Land Nordrhein-Westfalen

Tracey Moffatt (1960-)
68 *Scarred for Life II: Homemade Hand Knit 1958*, 1999
Offset print on paper, 80 × 60 cm
Louisiana Museum of Modern Art

69 *Scarred for Life II: Pantyhose Arrest 1973*, 1999
Offset print on paper, 80 × 60 cm
Louisiana Museum of Modern Art

70 *Scarred for Life II: Mother's Reply 1976*, 1999
Offset print on paper, 80 × 60 cm
Louisiana Museum of Modern Art

71 *Scarred for Life II: Piss Bags 1978*, 1999
Offset print on paper, 80 × 60 cm
Louisiana Museum of Modern Art

72 *Scarred for Life II: Scissors Cut 1980*, 1999
Offset print on paper, 80 × 60 cm
Louisiana Museum of Modern Art

73 *Scarred for Life II: Suicide Threat 1982*, 1999
Offset print on paper, 80 × 60 cm
Louisiana Museum of Modern Art

Henry Moore (1898-1986)
74 *Mother and Child*, 1932
White alabaster, 33.5 × 15.5 × 17.5 cm
Leeds Museums

75 *Mother and Child, 1956*
Bronze, 17 × 7.5 × 6 cm
The Henry Moore Foundation, gift of Irina Moore 1977

76 *Standing Mother and Child*, 1975
Bronze, 20.5 × 7 × 3.5 cm
The Henry Moore Foundation, acquired 1987

77 *Maquette for "Mother and Child: Upright"*, 1977
Bronze, 19 × 10.5 × 6 cm
The Henry Moore Foundation, acquired 1992

78 *Seated Mother and Child: Thin*, 1980
Bronze, 23.5 × 11 × 12.5 cm
The Henry Moore Foundation, acquired 1986

François-Joseph Moreau (1789-1862)
79 *Traité Pratique des Accouchemens*, 1839
Book with illustrations by Emile Beau, 44 × 33 cm
Medical Museion, University of Copenhagen

Edvard Munch (1863-1944)
80 *Den døde mor og barnet*, 1901
The Dead Mother and Her Child
Etching, aquatint on paper, 44 × 60 cm
Kunsthalle Mannheim

81 *Madonna (Elskende kvinne)*, 1895/1902
Madonna (Loving Woman)
Colour lithograph on paper, 83.5 × 62 cm
Hamburger Kunsthalle, Kupferstichkabinett

Dea Trier Mørch (1941-2001)
82 *Barnet spadserer hen til sin mor*, 1976
Baby Walks up to Its Mother
Linocut on paper, 42.5 × 30 cm
Private collection

83 *Hovedet er født*, 1976
The Head Is Born
Linocut on paper, 42.5 × 30 cm
Private collection

84 *Skuldrene fødes*, 1976
The Shoulders Are Born
Linocut on paper, 42.5 × 30 cm
Private collection

Alice Neel (1900-1984)
85 *Ginny and Elizabeth*, 1975
Oil on canvas, 106.5 × 76 cm
Courtesy of The Estate of Alice Neel and David Zwirner

Maggie Nelson (1973-)
86 *The Argonauts*, 2015
Book, excerpts

Kai Nielsen (1882-1924)
87 *Venus med æblet*, 1918-20
Venus with the Apple
Artificial sandstone, h. 130.5 cm
Kunsten Museum of Modern Art Aalborg

Lennart Nilsson (1922-2017)
88 Embryo, 4 weeks, 1965
From the series "A Child Is Born", 1965-2009
Photograph, Cibachrome, 61 × 51 cm
Hasselblad Foundation Collection

89 Embryo, 6 weeks, 1964
From the series "A Child Is Born", 1965-2009
Photograph, Cibachrome, 61 × 51cm
Hasselblad Foundation Collection

90 Embryo, 8 uger, 1965
From the series "A Child Is Born", 1965-2009
Fotografi, Cibachrome, 61 × 51 cm
Hasselblad Foundation

91 Embryo, 8 weeks, 1965
From the series "A Child Is Born", 1965-2009
Photograph, Cibachrome, 61 × 51 cm
Hasselblad Foundation Collection

92 *The Space Odyssey*, foetus, 13 weeks, 1965
From the series "A Child Is Born", 1965-2009
Photograph, Cibachrome, 52 × 50 cm
Hasselblad Foundation Collection

93 *Sucking Its Thumb*, foetus, 20 weeks, 1974
From the series "A Child Is Born", 1965-2009
Photograph, Cibachrome, 61 × 51 cm
Hasselblad Foundation Collection

Isamu Noguchi (1904-1988)
94 Radio Nurse, 1937
Bakelite, brownish black, 21 × 17 × 16 cm
The Design Museum, Munich

Yoko Ono (1933-)
95 *My Mommy Is Beautiful*, 2004 / 2021
Installation with audience participation
Courtesy of Yoko Ono

Catherine Opie (1961-)
96 *Selfportrait / Nursing*, 2004
C-print, 101.5 × 81.5 cm
Courtesy of Regen Projects, Los Angeles and Lehmann Maupin, New York, Hong Kong and Seoul

Meret Oppenheim (1913-1985)
97 *Votivbild* (Würgeengel), 1931
Votive Picture (Strangling Angel)
Indian ink and watercolour on paper, 34 × 17.5 cm
Private collection, long-term loan to Museo d'arte della Svizzera italiana, Lugano

Frida Orupabo (1986-)
98 *Love at First Site*, 2020
Paper collage mounted on aluminium, 116 × 120 cm
Courtesy of the artist and Galerie Nordenhake Stockholm, Berlin and Mexico City

Pablo Picasso (1881-1973)
99 *Maternité*, 1971
Motherhood
Oil on canvas, 162 × 130 cm
Musée national Picasso, Paris

Sano di Pietro (1406-1481)
100 *Madonna and Child, Worshipped by Angels and Saints*, c. 1450-1455
Tempera on wood, 60.5 × 43 cm
Lindenau-Museum, Altenburg

Mason Poole (1981-)
101 *Beyoncé posing with her newborn twins Sir Carter and Rumi*, 2017
Colour photograph, 225 × 150 cm
Courtesy of Parkwood Entertainment

Marcel Proust (1871-1922)
102 *À la recherche du temps perdu*, 1913-1927
In Search of Lost Time
Book, excerpts from vol. I, "Swann's Way"
Danish translation by Else Henneberg Pedersen
Published by Multivers, 2002-2014

Laure Prouvost (1978-)
103 *MOOOTHERR*, 2021
Installation, mixed media, variable dimensions
Studio Laure Prouvost

Johann Georg Röderer (1726-1763)
104 *Icones Uteri Humani*, 1759
Book with illustrations, 45 × 28 cm
Medical Museion, University of Copenhagen

Ulrike Rosenbach (1943-)
105 *Glauben Sie nicht, dass ich eine Amazone bin*, 1975
Don't Believe I'm an Amazon
Video, black-and-white and audio, 10:31 min.
Louisiana Museum of Modern Art

106 *Mutterliebe*, 1977
Mother's Love
Video, colour and audio, 4:58 min.
Louisiana Museum of Modern Art

Niki de Saint-Phalle (1930-2002)
107 *L'Accouchement rose*, 1964
The Pink Delivery
Relief, mixed media, 219 × 152 × 40 cm
Moderna Museet, Stockholm
Donation from the artist 1964

Egon Schiele (1890-1918)
108 *Tote Mutter I,* 1910
Dead Mother I
Oil and pencil on wood,
32 × 25.7 cm
Leopold Museum, Vienna

Manjari Sharma (1979-)
& **Irina Rozovsky** (1981-)
109 *To See Your Face*,
2016-2017
Colour photographs,
122 prints, each 43 × 29.5 cm
Manjari Sharma and Irina
Rozovsky

Cindy Sherman (1954-)
110 Untitled #216, 1989
Colour photograph,
221 × 142.5 cm
Astrup Fearnley Collection,
Oslo, Norway

Annegret Soltau (1946-)
111 *Schwanger*, 1978
Pregnant
Photo collage, gelatin
silver print with thread
overstitched, 24 × 15 cm
Courtesy of Richard Saltoun
Gallery, London

112 *Schwanger I*, 1978
Pregnant I
Photo collage, gelatin
silver print with thread
overstitched, 25 × 24 cm
Courtesy of Richard Saltoun
Gallery, London

113 *Auf dem Geburtstisch,*
schwanger I, 1978
On the Birthing Table,
Pregnant I
Photo collage, gelatin
silver print with thread
overstitched, 60.5 × 50.5 cm
Courtesy of Richard Saltoun
Gallery, London

Alina Szapocznikow (1926-1973)
114 *Buste étincelant I*, 1967
Glowing Bust I
Mixed media, 58 × 21 × 20 cm
Loevenbruck Collection, Paris
Courtesy of The Estate of
Alina Szapocznikow, Galerie
Loevenbruck and Hauser & Wirth

Osamu Takahashi (1985-)
In collaboration with Taikan
Hoshino, Masaharu Kurosu,
Kyoko Kita and Madoka Yoshio
115 *Father's Nursing*
Assistant, 2019
Prototype, ABS resin,
acrylic resin, 26 × 32 × 10 cm
DENTSU / Ginger Design
Studio / Apex

Kaari Upson (1972-)
116 *Mother's Legs*, 2018-19
Installation, mixed media, 26
pieces, 153.5 × 21.5 cm and
231 × 18 cm
Collection of the artist

Suzanne Valadon (1865-1938)
117 *The Abandoned Doll*, 1921
Oil on canvas, 129.5 × 81.5 cm
National Museum of Women
in the Arts.Gift of Wallace
and Wilhelmina Holladay

Stephan Zick (1639-1715)
118 Anatomical teaching
model of a pregnant woman,
Nuremberg, c. 1680
Ivory, wood and fabric,
l. 12 cm
Olbricht Collection

Culture-Historical Objects

119 Magic staff or knife, Egypt, 2060-1785 BC
Tooth of hippopotamus, c. 27 cm
The National Museum, Copenhagen

120 Papyrus Carlsberg 8, c. 1300 BC
Papyrus, 72 × 36 cm
The Papyrus Carlsberg Collection, University of Copenhagen

121 Statuette of the goddess Isis with Horus child, unknown finding place, 1080-700 BC
Bronze, 21.5 × 6 × 8.5 cm
Ny Carlsberg Glyptotek, Copenhagen

122 Statuette of the goddess Isis with Horus child, possibly Egypt, 950-700 BC
Quartzite, 21.5 × 5 cm
Ny Carlsberg Glyptotek, Copenhagen

123 Statuette of the goddess Isis with Horus child, possibly Egypt, 650-500 BC
Greywacke, 32 × 8 × 17 cm
Ny Carlsberg Glyptotek, Copenhagen

124 Isis with Harpocrates?, Egypt, 3rd cent.
Terracotta, h. 17 cm
Ny Carlsberg Glyptotek, København

125 Pre-Columbian ceramic figurine, Mexico, 1200-500 BC
Yellowish clay with residue of red decoration, 14 × 5.5 × 2.5 cm
Louisiana Museum of Modern Art
Donation: Niels Wessel Bagge Art Foundation

126 Pre-Columbian ceramic figurine, Mexico, 1200-500 BC
Clay with residue of red, yellow and white decoration, 10 × 5.5 × 2 cm
Louisiana Museum of Modern Art
Donation: Niels Wessel Bagge Art Foundation

127 Pre-Columbian ceramic figurine, Mexico, 200 BC-200 AD
Red clay, yellow slipping, partly worn off, partly miscoloured, residue of red decoration, 8.5 × 5 × 3 cm
Louisiana Museum of Modern Art
Donation: Niels Wessel Bagge Art Foundation

128 Pre-Columbian ceramic figurine, Mexico, undated
Yellowish clay with residue of red decoration, 10.5 × 4.5 × 3 cm
Louisiana Museum of Modern Art
Donation: Niels Wessel Bagge Art Foundation

129 Pre-Columbian ceramic figurine, Ecuador, undated
Reddish clay with greyish slipping, 13 × 5 × 3.5 cm
Louisiana Museum of Modern Art
Donation: Niels Wessel Bagge Art Foundation

130 Standing female nude, holding a child on her right arm, Cyprus, 1450-1200 BC
Brown clay, h. 21 cm
The National Museum, Copenhagen

131 Mother Goddess, Cyprus, 1450-1200 BC
Terracotta, h. 20.5 cm
The National Museum, Copenhagen

132 Cypriot terracotta figurine (Aphrodite), Cyprus, 600-500 BC
Terracotta, h. 22.5 cm
The National Museum, Copenhagen

133 Cypriot terracotta figurine (Aphrodite), Cyprus, 600-500 BC
Reddish brown clay, h. 22.5 cm
The National Museum, Copenhagen

134 Idol from the Cyclades, Amorgos, Greece, 2700-2300 BC
White marble, h. 21 cm
The National Museum, Copenhagen

135 Mycenaean idol, c. 1000 BC
Terracotta, 16.5 × 7 × 3.5 cm
Louisiana Museum of Modern Art

136 Mycenaean idol, c. 1000 BC
Terracotta, 12 × 4.5 × 3 cm
Louisiana Museum of Modern Art

137 Mycenaean idol, c. 1000 BC
Terracotta, 15.5 × 7.5 × 3 cm
Louisiana Museum of Modern Art

138 Mycenaean idol, c. 1000 BC
Terracotta, 14.5 × 6.5 × 2.5 cm
Louisiana Museum of Modern Art

139 Mycenaean idol, c. 1000 BC
Terracotta, 12.5 × 5 × 3 cm
Louisiana Museum of Modern Art

140 Enthroned woman with infants, Italy, 3rd cent. BC
Terracotta, 76 × 44 × 39.5 cm
Ny Carlsberg Glyptotek, Copenhagen

141 Terracotta sculpture of a womb, Italy, 400-100 BC
Reddish brown clay with glimmer, 18.5 × 13 cm
The National Museum, Copenhagen

142
Terracotta sculpture of a womb, Italy, 400-100 BC
Light brown clay with glimmer and black particles, 15.5 × 10 cm
The National Museum, Copenhagen

143 Terracotta sculpture of a womb, Italy, 400-100 BC
Brown clay with particles, 14 × 7 cm
The National Museum, Copenhagen

144 Votive sculpture, female breasts, Italy, 400-100 BC
Light brown clay with residue of white surface layer, two sculptures, h. 7.5 and 8 cm
The National Museum, Copenhagen

145 Mother of God Hodegetria, Greece, 1450-1550
Tempera on wood, 34 × 27.5 × 2.5 cm
Ny Carlsberg Glyptotek, Copenhagen

146 Mother of God from Kykkos, Greece, 1800-1850
Tempera on wood, 23.5 × 18.5 × 2 cm
Ny Carlsberg Glyptotek, Copenhagen

147 Mother of God Feodorovskaya, Russia, 1800-1850
Tempera on wood, 31 × 26.5 × 1.5 cm
Ny Carlsberg Glyptotek, Copenhagen

148 Mary with child in a halo, 1470s
Paint on wood, 143 × 47 × 22 cm
Museum Sønderjylland, Sønderborg Castle

149 Anatomical teaching model of a pregnant woman, Nuremberg, c. 1700
Ivory, wood and fabric, l. 15.5 cm
Sammlung Olbricht

150 Anatomical teaching model of a pregnant woman, undated
Ivory, l. 17 cm
Deutsches Medizinhistorisches Museum, Ingolstadt

151 Wax tablet showing the foetal development in 7 figures, early 1800s
Wax moulage in wooden frame, 25 × 19 × 1.5 cm
From the Royal Surgical Academy
Medical Museion, University of Copenhagen

152 Wax tablet showing a pregnant woman, early 1800s
Wax moulage in wooden frame, 20.5 × 18 × 2.5 cm
From the Royal Surgical Academy
Medical Museion, University of Copenhagen

153 Wax tablet showing the back of the female abdomen, early 1800s
Wax moulage in wooden frame, 27 × 18.5 × 2.5 cm
From the Royal Surgical Academy
Medical Museion, University of Copenhagen

154 Placenta Circumvallata, c. 1932
Placenta with umbilical cord, preserved in a sealed glass vessel, 27 × 22 × 6 cm
From The Saxtorphian Collection
Medical Museion, University of Copenhagen

155 The Danish Constitution of 1915, 1915
Book, c. 55 × 36 × 2 cm, box of seal, diam. c. 10 cm
The Danish National Archives

156 *Mutterkreuz*, 1941
Mother's Cross of Honour
Two crosses: silver with blue enamel and blue-and-white ribbon, inclusive of document

157 *Kvinde kend din krop*, 1975
Woman, Know Your Body
Book, published by Tiderne Skifter

158 The early human development from the fertilized oocyte (day 1) to the blastocyst stage ready for implantation in the uterus (day 5), 2008
Film clip
Rigshospitalet, Fertilization Clinic, Copenhagen

159 Fertilization using ICSI (intracytoplasmic sperm injection), 2013
Film clip
Rigshospitalet, Fertilization Clinic, Copenhagen

160 Digital Fertility Awareness App, 2020
App for contraception and pregnancy planning
Natural Cycles Nordic A/B

MOTHER! Origin of Life

Edited by Lærke Rydal Jørgensen, Marie Laurberg and Kirsten Degel
Graphic Design: Marie d'Origny Lübecker
Photo Editors: Sidse Buck and Kim Hansen
Translations: Glen Garner (foreword, Marie Laurberg, Adam Bencard), Jane Rowley (Pia Fris Laneth)
Proofreading: James Manley
Marie Laurberg's article has been peer-reviewed
Cover, front: Dieric Bouts: *Virgin and Child*, after 1454. Oil on panel, 42.5 × 27.5 cm. SMK National Gallery of Denmark
Cover, back: Mason Poole: Beyoncé posing with her newborn twins Sir Carter and Rumi, 2017
Colour photograph, 225 × 150 cm. Courtesy of Parkwood Entertainment
Inside of cover, front: Pablo Picasso: *Maternité*, 1971. Motherhood. Oil on canvas, 162 × 130 cm. Musée national Picasso, Paris
Photo: RMN-Grand Palais Musée national Picasso, Paris / Adrien Didierjean
Inside of cover, back: Paul McCarthy: *Mother Dad*, 1987. Charcoal on paper, 72.5 × 57 cm. Louisiana Museum of Modern Art

Repro & printing: Narayana Press
ISBN: 978-87-93659-38-4
Printed in Denmark 2021
www.louisiana.dk

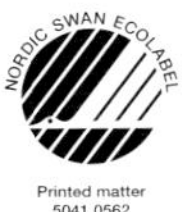

The catalogue is published on the occasion of the exhibition
MOTHER! Origin of Life
The exhibition is organized by Louisiana Museum of Modern Art in collaboration with Kunsthalle Mannheim
Louisiana Museum of Modern Art, Humlebæk, Denmark
28 January – 29 August 2021
Kunsthalle Mannheim, Germany
1 October 2021 – 6 February 2022
This catalogue was going to print when the COVID-19 pandemic halted all activities and the Louisiana was shut down

Curators: Marie Laurberg and Kirsten Degel
Curatorial Assistant: Nanna Stjernholm Jepsen
Curatorial Coordinator/Registrar: Eva Lund
Exhibition Architect: Anne Schnettler
Graphic Design: Marie d'Origny Lübecker
Conservator/Exhibition Producer: Ulrik Staal Strange Dinesen

The exhibition is supported by:

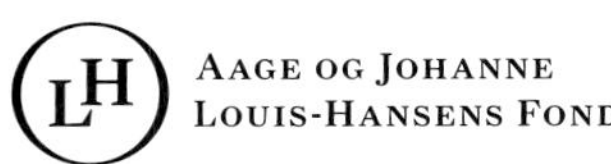

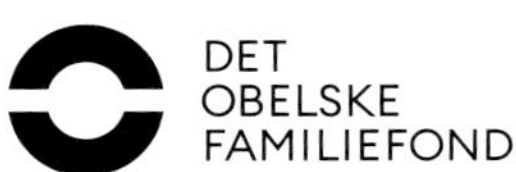

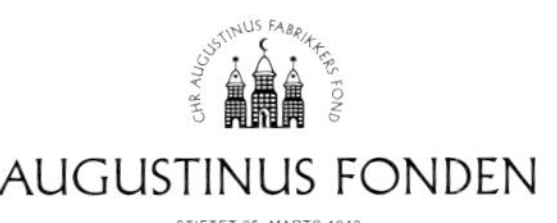

Photos: Cover: SMK, National Gallery of Denmark; p. 1: Courtesy The Estate of Alice Neel and David Zwirner; p. 2: Ny Carlsberg Glyptotek; p. 4: Tate Images; p. 9: Courtesy Lisson Gallery; p. 10: Courtesy the artist and Galerie Nordenhake Stockholm / Berlin / Mexico City; p. 11: Niels Fabæk; p. 13: SMK, National Gallery of Denmark; p. 16: Lee Stalsworth, Fine Art through Photography, LLC; p. 17 top: Courtesy Regen Projects, Los Angeles; p. 17 bottom: Courtesy The Estate of Alice Neel and David Zwirner; p. 18 left: Ritzau Scanpix / Holger Damgaard; p. 18 right: Fotografisk Atelier. DKB; p. 19: Manfred Thumberger; p. 20: Claire Dorn; p. 22: Courtesy the artist and Fergus McCaffrey, New York and Tokyo; p. 23: Anders Sune Berg; p. 24: Courtesy the artist and ChertLüdde, Berlin; p. 26 top: Ritzau Scanpix / Alamy; p. 26 bottom: Ritzau Scanpix / Alamy; p. 27: Diana Panuccio; p. 28: p. 31: Anders Sune Berg; MASI; p. 38: Ny Carlsberg Glyptotek; p. 39: Ole Haupt / Ny Carlsberg Glyptotek; p. 40: Ny Carlsberg Glyptotek; p. 41: Museum Sønderjylland, Sønderborg Castle; p. 42: Lindenau-Museum, Altenburg; p. 44: Kunsthalle Mannheim / Cem Yücetas; p. 46: Henry Moore Foundation; p. 47: Bridgeman Images; p. 48: Niels Fabæk; p. 49 left: Kunstpalast – ARTOTHEK; p. 49 right: Von der Heydt-Museum Wuppertal; p. 53 middle: Ritzau Scanpix; p. 56: Courtesy the artist and Fergus McCaffrey, New York and Tokyo; p. 57: Bridgeman Images; p. 58 top: Courtesy of the artist and Mitchell-Innes & Nash, New York; p. 59: Kunsthaus Zürich; p. 60 top-61: Courtesy Victoria Miro / Benjamin Westoby; p. 64: Stephen White. Courtesy White Cube; p. 82 top: Courtesy Ane Crabtree / MGM; p. 82nm: Courtesy Die Neue Sammlung – The Design Museum; p. 82 bottom right: Esther Hoyer; p. 85: Ritzau Scanpix / Tor Birk Trads; p. 86: Ritzau Scanpix / Holger Damgaard; p. 87: Ritzau Scanpix / Tage Christensen; p. 89: The Royal Library; p. 90: Henrik Saxgren; p. 92: C. Goldberg and P. Fuis; p. 93: Terra Foundation for American Art, Chicago; p. 94: Jenni Carter; p. 95: Stadtmuseum Berlin; p. 96 top: Kunsthalle Hamburg / Christoph Irrgang; p. 96 bottom: Kunsthalle Mannheim; p. 100: Courtesy Pace Gallery, New York and Fraenkel Gallery, San Francisco; p. 101 top: Courtesy Pace Gallery, New York and Fraenkel Gallery, San Francisco; p. 101 bottom: Ritzau Scanpix / Mary Evans Picture Library; p. 104: Natural Cycles; p. 105 top: Deutsches Medizinhistorisches Museum, Ingolstadt; p. 105 middle: Olbricht Collection; p. 105 bottom: Jaron Chubb / Olbricht Collection; p. 110-11: Christopher Burke; p. 112 bottom: The National Museum, Copenhagen / John Lee; p. 113-114 top: The National Museum, Copenhagen / John Lee; p. 118: Courtesy of Richard Saltoun Gallery, London; p. 119: Steve Briggs; p. 122: Science Photo Library / Lennart Nilsson; p. 123: Thomas Barratt; back cover: Mason Poole

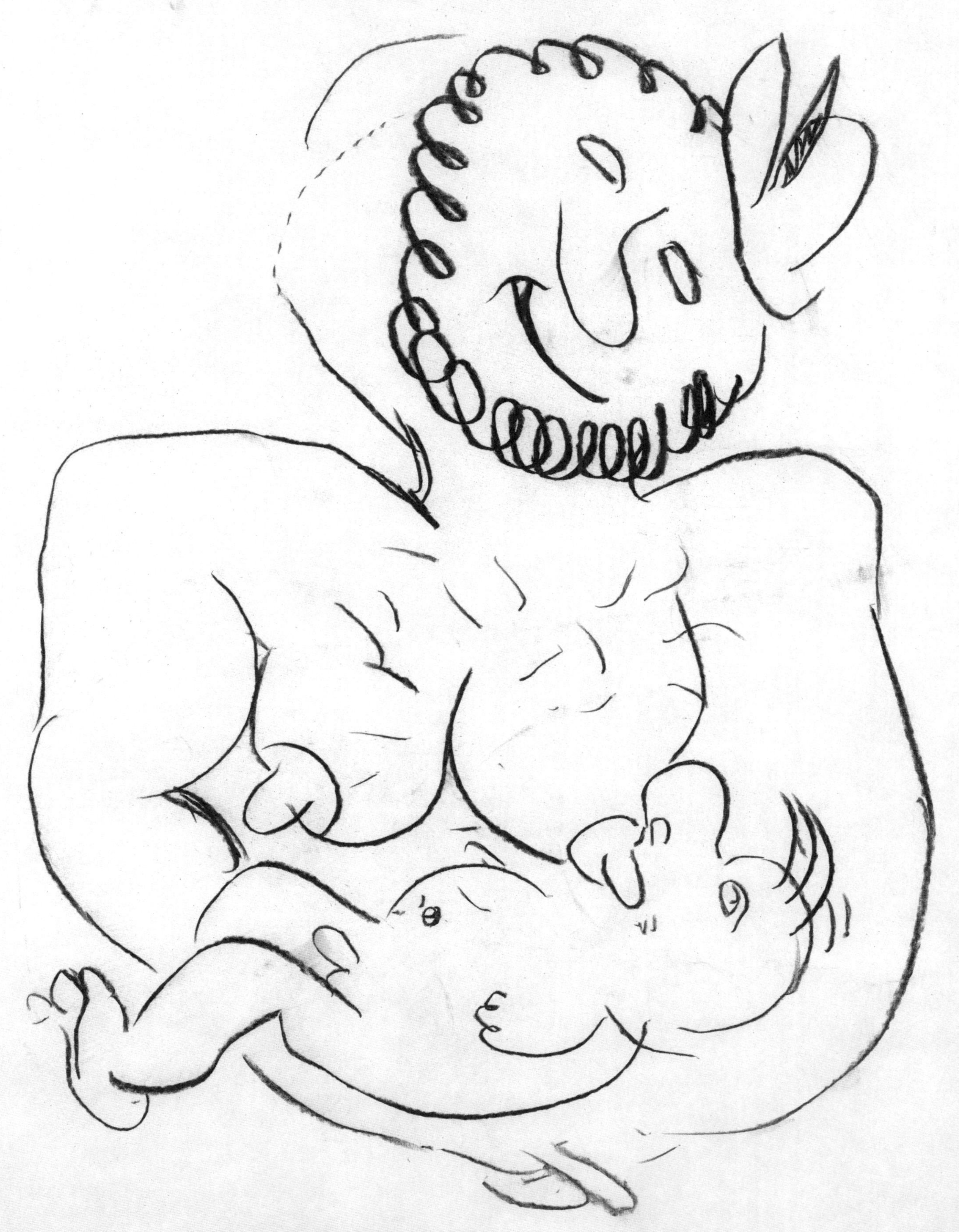